HERITAGE
AND
RENEWAL

The Report
of
The Archbishops' Commission
on
Cathedrals

HERITAGE
AND
RENEWAL

The Report
of
The Archbishops' Commission
on
Cathedrals

CHURCH HOUSE PUBLISHING
Church House, Great Smith Street, London SW1P 3NZ

ISBN 0 7151 3760 3

Published 1994 by Church House Publishing

Printed in England by Rapier Press Ltd.

Contents

Foreword by the Archbishops

Everyone will surely agree that our 42 cathedrals are among the glories of the Church of England in their daily offering of worship and praise to God. But cathedrals are also human institutions which have developed over the centuries and which, from time to time, need to be reviewed and given fresh direction so that they can continue their inspiring involvement in the mission of the whole Church.

Within the last few years deans and provosts have themselves recognised the need for such a review, and we were persuaded that an Archbishops' Commission would be an appropriate means of examining the present role of cathedrals and making proposals for their future development. We were very pleased that Lady Howe agreed to chair the Commission, and the resulting Report shows the thoroughness and detail with which she and her colleagues have undertaken their task.

The Report rightly emphasises the spiritual and mission aspects of a cathedral's role but it also clearly sets out the arguments for good governance and effective administration. Not only does it contain detailed information on such matters as tourism and finance; it draws attention to the importance, too, of encouraging all those people, both ordained and lay, paid and voluntary, who serve in the cathedrals of our nation.

We are most grateful to Lady Howe, to her fellow members of the Commission, and to the many people who have helped them in their wide-ranging work. We urge all those who have an interest in the continuing role of cathedrals to study the Report, and we hope that very careful thought will be given to its recommendations throughout the Church.

+ GEORGE CANTUAR   + JOHN EBOR

Meeting of the Commission on 28 June 1994

Preface by the Chairman

I count it a great privilege to have been invited by the Archbishops of Canterbury and York to chair their Commission to 'examine the future role in Church and nation of the Cathedrals of the Church of England ...'. Such a wide-ranging task, which the Commission members decided very early on should between us include visiting all 42 Anglican cathedrals, had not been undertaken since a similar Commission was appointed by the Church Assembly in 1924. So we felt it right to gain practical first-hand experience of all aspects of cathedrals' life and work.

We have of course been greatly helped by the evidence submitted by individuals, public bodies and other organisations, all of whom are named in Appendix 3. But the experience of our cathedral visits, even for those members familiar with their own cathedral, made us all realise both the invaluable work by cathedrals which is carried out day by day and also the diversity of those 42 cathedrals. As well as the warm welcome given to us by each cathedral, two things particularly stand out in my mind from those most enjoyable as well as informative and inspiring weekends: first, the uniquely high quality of cathedral music as integral to worship, and second, the immensely impressive service willingly given in so many ways by a host of volunteers, including the substantial contribution of cathedral Friends.

Our Report does not seek to lay down a rigid blueprint for cathedrals. It could not, nor would we wish it to do so. The very variety of individual cathedrals and the circumstances which face each of them would preclude this.

What we do attempt is a contemporary restatement of the role and purpose of cathedrals. We seek to articulate a series of principles which can help cathedrals in facing up to the many, often conflicting, objectives and demands, financial and otherwise, which confront them. And we propose a set of governance and other organisational arrangements which should provide a common framework within which longer-term planning can take place, difficult choices can be made, and greater accountability can be achieved. In particular, we strongly recommend that cathedrals share the knowledge of the many good practices which we have seen and heard (some examples are set out in Appendix 6).

Acknowledgements to all those who have supported us in various ways are given in Appendix 1. In addition, I am most grateful to all my fellow members who have contributed so much time and effort to the work and meetings of the Commission (the details are given in Appendix 2). I would particularly like to mention Raymond Furnell and Peter Burnham who, as members of the Sub-Group, added their own expertise which was greatly appreciated; Edward Norman, who has exercised his fine drafting skills on our behalf; Philip Mawer, who has given so much valuable help and guidance to our work; and John Newton, whose detailed analysis of all the evidence was especially useful in our deliberations. Our thanks are also due to our Secretary, Nigel Waring, who, ably assisted in turn by Trish Hetherington and Sandy Meggs, arranged our cathedral visits and organised our business with the greatest care and efficiency. Finally, I am indebted to my Personal Assistant, Pauline Lamb, for all her support during the period of the Commission's work.

After completing our Report, we offer it now to the Archbishops in the hope that it will be helpful to both Church and nation in the coming years.

The Lady Howe of Aberavon

1

Introduction

1. We were appointed in the summer of 1992 by the Archbishops of Canterbury and York 'to examine the future role in Church and nation of the Cathedrals of the Church of England and to make recommendations as to how best that role could be fulfilled, including proposals for their government and support'. Such an enquiry could hardly be described as premature, beginning almost 30 years after the 1963 Cathedrals Measure which set the current legal framework of the cathedrals, and some 65 years after the report of an earlier comprehensive review of the nature and purpose of cathedrals by a Commission appointed by the Church Assembly.

2. The past development of cathedral churches has delivered a richly textured but, by today's standards, rather incoherent pattern of institutions. Some foundations are governed by deans and chapters, others by provosts and councils; deans are appointed by the Crown and most provosts by diocesan bishops. Within these categories, however, there are considerable variations, numerous anomalies, and great differences of structure, age and scale. No sooner has the observer noted one feature which must seem common to them all than an exception, and then another, is found.

3. A desire for greater coherence would not alone justify a review of cathedrals. Behind issues of governance and organisation there lies a much more fundamental question – what are cathedrals for? Some of the answers to that question are, perhaps, timeless. But others are contemporary and each generation needs to provide its own answers in order fully to value these precious aspects of its inheritance.

4. If these were the general context of our review, a more immediate stimulus was provided by events in specific cathedrals, and by the advent of public funding towards the maintenance of cathedral fabric. The outcry over the attempted sale of the *Mappa Mundi* by the Dean and Chapter of Hereford was both a timely reminder of the public interest in cathedrals, and a reflection of cathedrals' urgent financial need in order to maintain their fabric. The publicity attending the differences within the chapter at Lincoln Cathedral, and that surrounding the then Bishop of

Salisbury's visitation charge to his cathedral were further factors. Meanwhile, following an approach by the Archbishops to the government in the summer of 1990, the State had begun a substantial programme of financial assistance towards the cost of fabric maintenance and repair. New questions about how the cathedrals could maintain their independence of management within a proper framework of accountability were being raised. Failure to answer them could undermine continued public confidence and support.

5.   To their great credit, the cathedrals themselves saw the need to act. The deans and provosts, meeting in the autumn of 1990, set up a working party under the Dean of Bristol charged with producing a confidential report for their conference to be held in Exeter in 1991. After some refinements of the report the meeting resolved to invite the Association of English Cathedrals (which had been set up in 1990 to represent the governing bodies of cathedrals solely in matters to do with public funding) to consult with the Archbishops and Secretary-General of the General Synod with a view to the setting up of a commission 'to examine the working of the English Cathedrals', and 'if necessary propose such legislative changes as may be required for their continuing to contribute to the ministry and mission of the Church in the twenty-first century'.

6.   This proposal was approved by all but one of the cathedrals represented, with one abstention: a considerable achievement of consensus from 42 independent corporations. A process of mutual consultation then began. It became clear that there was a widely-expressed conviction that the terms of reference of the Association of English Cathedrals should be broadened, and the Association therefore formed a working party to propose the establishment of an 'Archbishops' Commission'. These are ad hoc bodies, ecclesiastical counterparts of Royal Commissions in parliamentary government, which have had a valued record of furthering debate and action in Church affairs. And so, in July 1992, we met for the first time, under the chairmanship of Lady Howe.

2

The Role of Cathedrals

Introduction

1. This is not the first age in which people have valued the monumental splendour of cathedrals without being entirely certain what they are for. Reformers of the past sometimes exaggerated the dusty decay and the liturgical inconsequence into which they had fallen – in, for example, the early decades of the nineteenth century. Against their observation of neglect, however, must be set the then continuous stream of visitors and worshippers for whom the sacred buildings always conveyed something of the divine presence. Today, when public observance of religious belief is not as widespread as it once was, the cathedrals are, paradoxically, popular as never before.

2. For some, the majesty of the buildings themselves is an expression of what might otherwise remain inarticulate, a perception of the holy, an anticipation of eternity. For some, there are historical resonances: those cathedrals which were conceived or adorned as great canopies over the bones of saints, as stone reliquaries on an enormous scale, remain still a witness to sanctity and an insight into fellowship with past believers. Here the least of the world's citizens can experience the dignity of spiritual space; cathedrals are accessible places, where all can see evidence of the effects of Christian truth as living faith. For some others cathedrals are a dimension of heritage, an illustration of historical processes, aesthetically satisfying, the venue of artistic and cultural achievement. They certainly have crucial purposes: they are concerned with education, and with service which attends to social need; they are centres of evangelism, presenting the gospel to many who would not otherwise recognise it, and they are places where witness to the presence of God in the world achieves great spiritual beauty. There are many associations and many responses. But what are they for? Cathedrals may fulfil several functions and meet a number of emotional or spiritual needs – needs, however, which may be, for all their importance, quite separate from their essential purpose. And that purpose has to do with the organisation of the mission of the Church in the world. For the cathedral, in the words used in the first section of the Care of Cathedrals Measure 1990 – which we would

emphatically endorse – is 'the seat of the bishop and a centre of worship and mission'.

3.   The ministry of a cathedral is thus to be recognised as part of the general mission in which all Christian people are engaged, and in the tradition of the Church of England that mission is organised into diocesan units governed by bishops. For historical, and one or two practical reasons, cathedrals as institutions have developed separately from the evolution of diocesan structures. In the nineteenth century the cathedrals, as corporations aggregate with their own property rights – in an age which still assumed a relationship between the possession of property and social function – were reformed independently from the rest of the Church. The instruments of diocesan administration, which hardly existed before the middle years of the last century, grew up with the needs of population growth and mobility in mind, with pastoral provision for a changing world, with popular education and social welfare as its markers, and with a more effective use of manpower and resources. The parallel development of dioceses and cathedrals, as a historical accident, was not of any great note since churchmen themselves, and the public generally, valued cathedrals as self-explanatory monuments to the historical continuity of English Christianity, important, in their way, as indicators of a rich heritage. The few who questioned whether they might have a function beyond that – men like Pusey and Selwyn – tended to see them as an educational or clerical resource.

4.   The relationship between the cathedrals and the dioceses in which they were set did not, in general, appear problematical. As a consequence the real purpose of cathedrals has, until comparatively recent times, received little appraisal – at least within the Church of England. In some other constituents of the Anglican Communion, and in the Roman Catholic Church, cathedrals have an unambiguous and close relationship to episcopal authority. In an episcopal Church, like the Church of England, the representation of Christian truth to the people is something undertaken by bishops, now operating within a synodical structure, and not by individual institutions. Cathedrals and dioceses may have chanced to have experienced separate historical development, but they do not have separate messages to convey to the nation. The cathedral is the bishop's church, the symbol of the unitary nature of Christ's mission in the world.

5.   Deans and chapters, and provosts and councils, have in modern times shown a remarkable responsiveness to the challenges and opportunities of the changing social landscape around them. Their contribution to the Christian presence in England has demonstrated considerable variation – for the cathedrals are all different, and their resources and capabilities

have often been employed differently. Some changes may be appropriate, and in some things a measure of uniformity of practice may be desirable, but the overall impression which must strike the observer is of openness to adaptation and responsiveness to new opportunities by many cathedral authorities. They have transformed their own levels of activity and areas of witness in very many ways: the provision of special services for church, civic, diocesan, charitable and other bodies; the care of the congregations which have attached themselves in such numbers in recent years; the maintenance of expertise in music and liturgy. The older cathedrals have also had to cope with crowds: the gentle musings of antiquarians among the Gothic piers, which once contributed to the tranquil atmosphere of cathedral life, have been exchanged for a mass tourism which has brought its own rewards and problems. In all these activities there are mixed results and sometimes rather elliptical observation of opportunities, but cathedral authorities have in general shown themselves to be vital and adaptive to the shifting context in which they now find themselves.

The Bishop and the Diocese

6.   To say that a cathedral is, by a defining statement, the seat of the bishop, the historic place of his cathedra, does not, however, describe an actual state of affairs except in the most removed symbolical sense. It is not always clear that cathedrals regard their bishop and his authority as a major consideration in arriving at the strategy most appropriate for Christian advance in the geographical area where both are located. Sometimes, in fact, there has been a persistent tendency for cathedral chapters and diocesan synods to devise separate strategies for approaching their service. As cathedrals have become more conscious, in recent times, of the need to use or to develop their resources in creative responses to the general mission of the Church, they have not always – some would say, have not usually – done so in harmony with plans in the rest of the diocese. This is not to say that this has of itself produced conflict. Conflict has, despite a small number of well-publicised cases, not characterised the separate developments of cathedrals and dioceses: the problem here is much more one of wasteful use of resources, duplication of effort, unnecessary isolation in the mission to the world.

7.   We have addressed ourselves to practical ways in which cathedrals should be more effectively integrated with diocesan strategy. Clearly the importance of the bishop's role in relation to his own cathedral needs some examination. The bishop's should not be the determining voice in arriving at a strategy, but a strategy having his approval should play a crucial role as the setting for the cathedral's strategic contribution to the diocese. Replies to questions which we asked, and our experience in visiting

the cathedrals, suggest that many in them have a personal and episodic, rather than a structural, view of the place of the bishop, commenting on the frequency of his attendance at cathedral worship, or his personal disposition in relation to cathedral activities. The non-churchgoing public, for its part, sometimes regards the cathedral as a rather grand parish church, with the bishop as a kind of superior vicar. For regular churchgoers, on the other hand, the cathedral will more obviously appear to be the bishop's church if he attends as often as he can. It is surely plain that existing arrangements, however, do not always express as coherently as they might the essential fact that the cathedral is the bishop's church, and that the mission and ministry of the cathedral are, or should be, an integral part of the local strategy of the diocese.

The Independence of Cathedrals

8.   Adjustments to practice and a degree of structural change in this area need not, and are not intended to, diminish the independence of cathedrals. The purpose is to redirect the use to which independence is put, and to utilise it in ways which are better calculated to serve the ends of Christian mission – to use the cathedrals, popular Christian resources, within the general ministry of the Church of England. There are areas of expertise within the cathedrals which are always going to be otherwise unavailable to, and beyond the practical or financial capabilities of, other churches in the diocese; and there are aspects of Christian witness, in the splendour of great music or experimental worship, for example, which are assimilable in the scale of a cathedral's activity but which a parish church might find inappropriate or beyond its resources. To recognise the cathedral's ministry as an extension of the bishop's, furthermore, is not to suggest that there is a uniform pattern to which all Christian institutions should conform. Much would be lost to the Church if an integrated diocesan strategy were taken to imply that the rich experience of particular dimensions of Christianity had all to be measured according to the same scale. The parochial is not the only model of Church organisation, and the independence of cathedrals, like the independence exercised in parish churches, recognises that specialist styles of witness require particular structures of governance appropriate to them, and a measure of practical autonomy.

9.   The existing inheritance of cathedral independence, in some of its forms, however, perpetuates practices appropriate in earlier centuries for the maintenance of property rights, both in real estate and in office, which no longer have relevance to their mission. In the context of the modern world it can easily be made to appear as if the independence of cathedrals is directed against the 'interference' of the bishops rather than being a

practical device for the performance and exploration of specialist expertise in the service of the Church in general. The time has come for cathedral independence to be, in short, expressed within a structure which involves more precise accountability.

10. The independence of cathedrals is important. It secures space for great celebrations of Christian worship which have reference to areas of public life which do not derive from the immediate diocesan context; space also for local civic activities, and for celebrations and commemorations, like the Hillsborough tragedy, which have a national significance; it enables innovative explorations of different styles of Christian mission; it allows those who serve in cathedrals a degree of flexibility in allocating their resources so that a wider range of people can be reached than may be possible in the geographical or social confines of the parochial organisation; it provides a separate platform from which issues may be raised for public debate; it encourages the development of a number of skills and expert practices in, for example, music and liturgy.

11. But these things describe a practical rather than an ideological independence. There should be no sense in which those who serve in cathedrals enjoy an independence against the authority structure of the Church in general – as if in contrast to the bishop or the rest of the diocese. There is no need for the independence of cathedrals to be regarded as a kind of balance in ecclesiastical polity: there is a single Church, in which a measure of independent action may need to be secured for some of its institutions in order that they may have the practical means of fulfilling specified functions. The cathedral should not offer a sort of scrutiny of episcopal stewardship, a rival point of reference in the diocese. Cathedral clergy should not be appointed, as sometimes in the past, in a kind of rewards system, but in order that explicit functions may be provided for, in worship, evangelism, management, scholarship, and Christian service in the community. These are functions which are best performed within a context of relative independence; the proposals in the present Report are intended to reinforce that independence and to annex it to a more precisely defined context. The sovereign principle of the proposed adjustments, however, assumes the priority of episcopal and diocesan strategy in the administration of the Church.

Symbolism

12. Cathedrals are also shrines of faith. Even the smaller, less-visited ones whose architectural splendours may be more modest can be shrines of the faith for those who live near them, or who regard them as being in some sense a focal point of the diocese, the 'mother church'. It was in 1927 that the Report of the Cathedrals Commission set up by the Church

Assembly stated that a cathedral 'as the place of the bishop's seat is the mother church of the diocese'. The 1961 Report *Cathedrals in Modern Life* referred to cathedrals as 'the visible counterpart of the episcopal system'. The symbolical importance of cathedrals, both to active believers and to society generally, is among the features which most need to be respected in any consideration of their role and purpose. As monumental represent-ations of the truth of Christianity they have a national reference too. They are sometimes understood as visible signs of the higher purpose to which human society is drawn, the consecration of the busy life around them. To very many they represent the timelessness and spiritual beauty of Christ's message; they can evoke serene images of the sublime mystery of God as he dwells among the men and women of the world. Here are recognised points of stability amidst the rootlessness inseparable from a world of permanent change, indicators of eternity, which transcend the conventional limitations of class and culture. There is unanimity about the priority of worship in the function of cathedrals. All the great faiths of the world have their temples and shrines: the cathedrals of England are a spiritual asset available to enormous numbers of people, of very differ-ing spiritual traditions, some of whom do not otherwise encounter the ministry of the Church. These great buildings are descriptions of the majesty of God; places of living faith.

Relationships

13.   For all that, however, cathedrals have an immediate and concrete function as the centres of mission in the local Church in the diocese. Indeed, those who look to them as a valued part of the Christian inheri-tance include many who are not members of the Church of England, but who consider the cathedrals as theirs too, for they are part of the local deposit of Christian witness, established by time and esteemed in popular sentiment. They focus local community consciousness, at county or city level. Any consideration of the future of cathedrals must take this into account. Relationships with other Churches and with local meetings of Christians, such as Churches Together, should be close and regular. Inside the diocesan organisation of the Church of England itself the cathedral community should regard itself as having an integrated role – in representation at synodical bodies, in regularised financial contributions to the diocese, in attendance by the dean at the bishop's staff meetings, and by the presence of the members of the chapter on major occasions in the cathedral attended by the bishop. Sometimes it is in very small things that those who serve in cathedrals can put themselves and their building at the disposal of local Church efforts: it is a matter of openness to opportunity and a preparedness to seek the initiative in a sharing of resources. Numerous good practices of this sort already exist, and we

aspire to encourage them. Yet cathedrals are all different from one another – not in function but in custom and administrative arrangements – and an enhanced exchange of information would considerably assist the vitality of local action, through providing a more uniform and accessible shared reference, which would enable more coherent forward planning and make better use of resources.

14. Relationships between cathedrals and civic authorities are already a valued and well-established feature, and are plainly of enormous benefit to the cities and other authorities concerned, for enriching local identity, and to the cathedrals, for enabling an association with the public life of the place in which their immediate mission is set. But there are also some guidelines which need to be observed. Cities are multi-cultural places, both in social class terms and through a rich varying pattern of ethnicity in many places. Elected civic organs of government have to represent people and interests which have less cultural and religious coherence than they once had. Those concerned with relationships between cathedrals and civic authorities should remember that they are operating in the sphere of Church and State relations, even though it is at the local rather than the national level. Even for an Established Church, as the Church of England is, there are many who would feel that it is late in the day for new links of Church and State to be forged if they could be construed as potential causes of local controversy.

Management

15. There are recent developments in the life of society and of the Church which suggest a reconsideration of the administration and the management of cathedral resources. Many cathedrals have already begun to evolve more professional management in aspects of their finance, properties, fabric, tourism, music and educational activities, and so forth. This is clearly an area of change which is not only desirable in itself but points to future developments. The expertise now required is largely possessed by the laity, and the emergence of lay administrative ministry is perhaps among the most decisive as well as among the most valuable of recent developments. Since all who work in cathedrals, clerical or lay, should be performing clearly defined functions, these changes will of themselves indicate a need for rationalisation of management structures. Lay staff will need to be clear about the structure of accountability, and their relationship to the dean and chapter, in the day-to-day conduct of affairs. In some cases, it may be appropriate for senior lay officials to be themselves canons; certainly membership of decision-making bodies might be given to those who carry a major share in the responsibility of management. One of the great advantages to be derived from the present

appointment of lay cathedral officers is the sense of the cathedral as a microcosm of the whole Church, clerical and lay, operating together for the promotion of Christ's Kingdom in a manner which makes maximum use of talent and experience.

The Cathedral Community

16.   Among the most important aspects of the life of a cathedral is provision for the worship and pastoral care of its own community. Whether it is the dean and chapter or the cleaners of the stalls, whether the attendants in the shop or the craftsmen on the scaffolding, whether the vergers or the choristers, the cathedral community is the place of mutual ministry, an institution whose mission in the diocese at large will only be truly effective if within its own house there is attention to worship and an exchange of Christian service. One of the most remarkable features of recent decades has been the growth in the number of people attending cathedral services, many of whom attend regularly. Here the lines have been blurred between the 'dean and chapter' cathedrals (most, though not all, of the Old and New Foundations – those which are of mediaeval origin and those which were founded or re-founded during the Reformation) and the 'parish church' cathedrals (broadly those established since the later years of the nineteenth century and incorporating existing parishes and congregations).

17.   The older cathedrals now show a measure of diversity in the extent to which they fulfil 'parochial' functions, but increasingly some sort of provision is made for a council or other consultative body to represent the views of the regular congregations. Parish church cathedrals, on the other hand (many of which were set up in centres of population which have since shifted, or in an industrial economy which has since passed away), already had statutory parochial councils, and have now sometimes found that the population which once surrounded them has radically declined, leaving their parish functions in the hands of very much the same kind of regular worshippers who form the substance of the congregations of the older foundations. At the same time, through the incidence of civic identity and a growing public taste for musical expertise, through the growth of symbolic and commemorative services, and because of increased adherence by worshippers who do not live within the formal parochial boundaries, the parish church cathedrals have, in atmosphere, formalism, and worship, begun to resemble the traditional cathedrals in many points of detail. To the extent that cathedral congregations are 'eclectic' – gathered from no clearly defined geographical area or ecclesiastical unit, but self-selected on the basis of individual preferences in relation to styles of worship, and so forth – they are much the same in all types of cathedral.

18.   In fact, in this aspect of their support, cathedrals are not all that different from many other churches. The parish system is one of the most distinguishing features of the Church of England. The time when regular worshippers were drawn to a church because it was their parish church seems, however, in some places to have passed; people now choose their church – and it is often one at some distance from where they work or live (a consequence of near-universal personal transport) – because they like its liturgical practice, or its degree of formality, its level of activism, the sympathy of pastoral care, and perhaps even the beauty of the actual building. The modern growth of cathedral congregations additionally reflects the inclination of some for personal anonymity at worship; they do not want to be involved in the community atmosphere of parish churches. There are some others for whom the splendour of cathedral worship, which is beyond the resources of most local churches, is the determining consideration. Others are drawn to the cathedral because a son or daughter is in the choir, or they have links with educational facilities attached to the cathedral. For some others, again, worshipping in a cathedral represents a distinct sense that cathedrals have a particular function in the ministry of the Church: their choice is explicitly vocational.

19.   We feel that the existence of sizeable congregations in some cathedrals, both of dean and chapter and of parish church types, is likely to be a permanent characteristic of their development, that provision should therefore be made for representative bodies of the regular cathedral community, and that they should have a defined statutory voice in certain aspects of the life of the institution. We also believe that if both existing types of cathedral are assimilated the proposed representative bodies can be made to correspond to a single model, superseding the present historical variations. Recognition of the importance of the views of the cathedral community, and its structural embodiment in the chain of authority internally directed by the dean and chapter, has however to be compatible with the function of the cathedrals as countrywide institutions, fulfilling a vocation as part of the spiritual inheritance in the life of the nation. There are elements of cathedral service which transcend local preferences. Although the views of the worshipping community in cathedral life should not be sovereign in the government of cathedrals, or in the determination of policy, they do nevertheless need to be properly taken into account.

20.   Those responsible for the conduct of worship should recognise that the cathedral's worshipping community is at present drawn from different sources and may have varying emphases in their understanding of cathedral life. They are:

1. the dean and chapter, the statutory foundation of the cathedral, who are, for historical, though hardly for practical, purposes, the formal 'congregation'; they have the responsibility for the conduct of worship and for the stewardship of the cathedral's resources and assets; it is their life together which sustains the spiritual vitality of the cathedral, and furthers its mission purposes;

2. the gathered congregations, the regular worshippers – those whose loyalty and support link the cathedral with the local community; they should not see themselves, or be regarded by others, as refugees from surrounding churches, but as bridges between the cathedral and the rest of the diocese;

3. casual visitors, who may, numerically, be a larger group than the regular worshippers; these are people to whom the cathedral may well find that it has an important missionary purpose, by providing a spiritual presentation in the splendour or variety of its worship and in its preaching office;

4. those of the cathedral community whose work in the cathedral is principally non-liturgical, who occasionally or regularly worship in the place;

5. those who come to the cathedral for diocesan or civic occasions, for special services or ordinations and commissionings, and so forth; in practice these are likely to be the occasions on which the cathedral, as the bishop's church, is most effectively displayed, and which therefore will come nearest to demonstrating to those outside the regular cathedral community something of its essential nature.

21. Some of the better-known cathedrals have become major centres of tourism, and we have been encouraged, during our visits, by the extent to which the opportunities this presents have been grasped. For tourism is not just a valued source of income, and it is certainly not a distraction the cathedral communities could do without: it is a great occasion to welcome the public to the house of God and to display and explain some of the essential purposes of the building. Visitors are encouraged to enjoy the splendour of the cathedral for its own sake, for its historical and cultural associations; they are also able to receive an intimation of the religious reasons why the cathedral was built and why people have cared for it over the centuries, and what it conveys about God's relationship with his people. The management of large crowds of visitors plainly involves the cathedrals in specialist procedures, however, and in this Report we make suggestions about the appropriate courses of action which cathedral authorities might take.

The Bishop and Interdependence

22.   Whatever the existing statutory provisions or the legal realities, the fact is that for most people bishops are closely identified with cathedrals: they have the intrinsic sense that this is where the bishops belong. Since this sentiment corresponds with a set of attitudes which we would ourselves endorse, we have considered ways in which the place of the bishop in his cathedral can be regularised and reinforced, so that the relationship between dean and chapter and bishop can be seen to be one of interdependence. It is also desirable that the bishop, as practically or as frequently as possible, should be part of the worshipping community of the cathedral, so bringing the public perception of his place there, and the reality of it, into greater correspondence. The independence of cathedrals has values which should not be eroded, and the government of the Church and the diocese by the bishop requires a secured provision for his place in the cathedral as the seat of episcopal authority. We believe that the two objectives are not incompatible, and that the relationship of interdependence, which in some cathedrals is even now felicitously practised, can be encouraged by a number of changes.

23.   The notion that the bishop may assume the functions of dean, suggested by a few in their submissions to us, was considered carefully but not favoured. The whole burden of this Report indicates that service in a cathedral requires expertise for the conduct of clearly defined tasks. It is too much to expect that the duties of a bishop, themselves involving particular expertise, will allow time or require the appropriate types of skill, as those needed in a dean. Deans and bishops have different work to do, and the qualities and experience for them demand increased attention to particular knowledge and experience. It is also possible that if the offices of dean and bishop were combined the relationship of interdependence between cathedral and diocese might lose focus. The diocese needs the peculiar resources of the cathedral staff – of people selected and trained specifically for the purpose, and that must extend to the dean who is at the top of the managerial structure. The proposed new governmental structure for cathedrals incorporates the diocesan bishop in a manner which is designed to show that his jurisdiction extends over the cathedral and its clergy, yet leaves them independent in the practical conduct of the cathedral's operation. It also introduces an important new element of accountability.

24. We do conclude, however, that not enough provision is made for the collective episcopal presence in the cathedral: that area and other suffragan bishops need to be recognised in the life of the cathedral. This recognition needs to be more than symbolical (such as having an honorary canonry) – it is only right, in an episcopal Church, that all the bishops who hold stipendiary office in the diocese should receive some honour (for example, of precedence or invitations to preach) in cathedral churches. At present there appears to be no overall code of practice.

Appointments

25. Of crucial importance in the practice of interdependence between bishops and cathedral authorities, between the missions of the diocese and the cathedral community, will be the mode of appointment to senior cathedral office. Recommendations are made elsewhere in the Report about this. But plainly the method and terms of appointment and the nature of the preceding consultative procedures should be intended to reflect a measure of personal sympathy and shared objectives between bishop, dean and chapter. Here, also, the local and national vocations of cathedrals will need to be balanced, and talents and personal resources matched with defined mission priorities. Senior cathedral clergy are among those who may find themselves public spokesmen on national issues or on occasions of national importance. The nature of appointment should recognise this as much as it simultaneously endeavours to secure appointments fully compatible with local and diocesan requirements. Since the cathedral is the bishop's church, however, it is only right that the structure of appointment of deans and canons enables the bishop to express preferences.

Conclusion

26. There has been, periodically down the years, a debate about the extent to which cathedrals should be independent. But it is a sterile debate, for cathedrals and the parish churches of the diocese have distinct and mutually supportive purposes. The functions of a bishop in a diocese, and the chapter of a cathedral, are part of a single Christian ministry, and both have particular contributions which require specialist capabilities and vision. Cathedrals need to be institutionally independent in the sense that their autonomy provides space for the exercise of those functions. In this Report we offer suggestions and make some specific recommendations which are intended to facilitate and improve the use of that autonomy. But cathedrals are nevertheless part of an integrated Christian presence in English society, and we are also concerned that their work should be accountable and efficient. The excellence already evident in cathedral work, both lay and clerical, encourages us to believe that the

changes brought forward here for discussion are likely to be received as suggestions tending to generalise and enhance existing practices. This Report proposes organic change, not a break or a discontinuity with the past. It is our hope that ministry in cathedrals will readily be seen as a distinct vocation to fulfil, and not, as sometimes previously, as a kind of reward or promotion. We also envisage the enlarging of mission opportunity, and a more professional approach to management. Like our predecessors who have examined cathedrals on behalf of the Church, however, our primary emphasis is on worship: the maintenance of a daily witness to the sovereignty of God in the world. Cathedrals have a national role in our society too – our belief is that the maintenance of worship is the supreme way in which that role can receive continuing reality and so be of service to the nation as well as to God.

3

Mission

Introduction

1.   Cathedrals are shop windows of the Church of England. Large numbers of people will derive ideas of the Church from what goes on in them. Cathedrals are frequently seen on television screens, and are the setting for many public occasions; they are visited by thousands each year. Some have substantial resources in their buildings and property, in professional skills and influence in the community. They are, in consequence, vitally important in the total mission of the Church, and an integral part of its overall strategy.

2.   During our visits we were impressed by the imaginative use of these resources and the many examples of good practice and initiative. However, it is still appropriate to stand back and review the work of cathedrals in the light of the general mission of the people of God. A mission perspective might well call, as a result, for some adjustments of attitudes: cathedrals are sometimes misled by their public image into a false grandeur – when the proper response they should make is described by humility without timidity and singleness of purpose without arrogance.

3.   God's mission to his world is displayed in his creation, in his chosen people, supremely in his Son, and through him in the new people of God. That is the context in which the mission of the Church is expressed. Strategy for mission is not like a commercial promotion but a response to what God has done. Mission is discovering what God is doing, and trying to do it with him. In this chapter of the Report there is an examination of the chief ingredients of mission – worship, teaching, service, evangelism, and witness – and an attempt to point to ways in which they may find expression in the life of a cathedral.

Worship

4.   The whole created order is called to worship and it is the Church's privilege and duty to help people to respond. Worship always has a missionary reference – in giving glory to God, the primary purpose of worship, those present may be enabled to catch a glimpse of that glory. At the centre of the life of the cathedral is the daily offering of worship and praise – Eucharist, Morning Prayer and on most days Choral Evensong –

a unique Anglican contribution to Christian spirituality. All that may be suggested about creative experiment in cathedral worship should be understood within the givenness and stability of the daily offering – the central pillar of the Church's prayer and praise down the centuries, and the spiritual heartbeat not only of the cathedral but of the diocese, the community and the nation.

5.   As one might expect, cathedrals are at the forefront of the celebration of the great Christian festivals in the **nation**. At Christmas and Easter many thousands are drawn into the cathedrals who might otherwise not find an expression of their religious instincts. But there are other occasions when cathedrals may play a national role too. From time to time the Church is called upon to articulate the nation's emotions, and on particular occasions to give them an explicit form. The collective joy or sorrow associated with public events, assisted by media coverage, can be focused in the worship of a cathedral in a way which no other institution can provide. Whether it is the enthronement of an Archbishop, or the commemoration of a disaster, great symbolic acts of worship, in which the affairs of men and women are raised to God and sanctified by him, are precisely what cathedrals arrange so effectively. Such occasions reinforce the sense of public 'ownership' of the cathedrals.

6.   Secular authorities and institutions feel that they have a particular identification with their own cathedral – a religious focus for the **city** and the **county**. Cathedrals have become, and increasingly so in modern times, the places for civic, legal and university services, and beyond those there is a constant stream of requests for acts of worship by numerous organisations, from the Chartered Institute of Bankers to the Scouts and Guides. All these groups believe instinctively that there will be a positive response from 'their' cathedral when a service is requested, and that the cathedral authorities will produce a form of worship which will reflect and interpret their own concerns and area of service. They rightly sense that the cathedral 'belongs' to the community and is not the exclusive preserve of a private corporation called a dean and chapter.

7.   The evidence suggests that most cathedrals take this public role very seriously and devote a good deal of time to the preparation of appropriate special services – ones which will celebrate the contributions of each organisation, and give expression to their needs and aspirations. This involves the cathedral authorities in consultation with the representatives of each group; these are occasions which can assist indirect evangelism and witness to the concern of Christ in the daily affairs of his people.

8.   Things can go wrong where there is a confusion of objectives about a particular service, or where the cathedral fails to be imaginative. To

provide a statutory Choral Evensong when two thousand military personnel are present may well be quite inappropriate. If organisations feel that they have to come only on the cathedral's terms, it should not cause surprise if the next generation does not ask to come at all. If worship is taken seriously as an instrument of mission, those who produce such worship will see it as their duty to provide an appropriate vehicle which will help as many as possible to worship effectively 'with the spirit and with the understanding'. This will involve sensitive and sound judgement. In a very 'visual' age it will certainly involve symbolic action; it will mean an imaginative approach to the spaces to be explored, dramas to be enacted, colour to enhance, music to uplift; it will mean the sensitive marriage of the traditional and the modern, the familiar and the unfamiliar, the use of old words in new contexts and new words to describe ancient truths. Too much of the past will be perceived as yesterday's religion, yet if there is too much change worshippers will feel threatened by the unfamiliar. It is a matter of experiment and balance. Cathedrals are the liturgical laboratories of the Church; they have the freedom and the potential flexibility to meet the spiritual needs of many who may not be even on the edge of formal Church life but who may encounter the divine presence when they attend cathedral worship as members of a secular group for a special service.

9.   It is not always easy for cathedrals to be recognised as the 'mother church' of a **diocese**. Geographical location is not always central, and sometimes there are other major town churches in the diocese which form a more obvious local focus. We found, however, that every cathedral is host to the diocese on important occasions each year when the bishop presides at ordinations, confirmations, and special celebratory services. As the bishop's church the cathedral has a particular role in affirming and supporting the episcopal leadership of the diocese. This affirmation should be reflected in the bishop's liturgical role in the cathedral. Great acts of worship in the cathedral, at which the bishops are present, serve to enhance the corporate unity of the diocese, and to communicate a sense of belonging – especially for those who come from small rural or inner-city parishes. It is an antidote to narrow or sectional perspectives and priorities, and can set new horizons in liturgy and worship.

10.   It is sometimes said that diocesan services can be difficult to devise because they highlight the growing divergence between cathedrals and parishes. Thirty years ago the music in most parishes did not differ significantly from that in cathedrals – parishes with good choirs, indeed, aspired to the cathedral style. Today there is a radical difference. Some parishes are progressively adopting a greater measure of informality and spontaneity in worship, with music which matches it: there are songs and

choruses rather than hymns, and sometimes synthesisers and guitars instead of organ accompaniment. Cathedral worship has become a distant experience for many parishioners in the diocese. The acceptance of such a dichotomy between 'cathedral' and 'parish' styles of worship does not prevent some hard work being done to build bridges between the different approaches. Diocesan worship committees could be a common ground for the diocese and cathedral; if the cathedral has a good practical liturgist on its staff (and the worship will be the poorer if it does not) his or her membership of the committee will enable a more ready exchange of practice and experience. It will also help make the liturgical resources of the cathedral more available to the diocese.

11.   When worship for special occasions is being devised we must bring out of our treasure things old and new, not ignoring the rich heritage of the past (as parish churches may be tempted to do) nor being enslaved by it (as cathedrals sometimes seem liable to do). If worship is to have proper meaning in today's world, the decisive voice must be the creative artist rather than the liturgical archaeologist. Yet it may be necessary to have a deliberate policy of establishing a 'core hymnody' for use in cathedrals, dioceses and schools, if the complete abandonment of some of the gems of traditional spirituality is to be avoided.

12.   These considerations also apply in an **ecumenical** dimension. Since cathedrals belong to a common Christian heritage, and in that sense belong to everyone, they are the natural venue for shared Christian worship. Ecumenical occasions may be categorised under four heads: worship devised together (the launch of the Council of Churches for Britain and Ireland, for example); worship devised largely by a visiting group or community (like the two hundred and fiftieth anniversary of the conversion of John Wesley); worship devised by the cathedral at which ecumenical representatives are present (royal occasions, for example); and services that are ecumenical by implication (rotating between various denominational venues). All such visible expressions of our unity in Christ are to be encouraged and are likely to become ever more frequent in the years ahead.

13.   All cathedrals these days have their own **congregations**, although they may well be considerably added to by visitors and tourists. The core of this group will be those for whom the cathedral is treated as their parish church. The existing pattern of Sunday worship varies; 25 cathedrals have two principal morning services, and 17 have one service – almost invariably the Eucharist. Where, in the ancient cathedrals, there are two morning services the pattern tends to be Matins and the Eucharist, whereas in the existing parish church cathedrals there is often a parish Eucharist followed

by a 'cathedral Eucharist' – the distinction largely expressing the amount of music and the level of congregational participation. (We were surprised that at one cathedral the principal Sunday service, a thriving parish Eucharist, took place without a choir, but the Matins which followed had the full musical resources of the cathedral in use even though only a few people attended it – such a divorce between the musical establishment and the community is perhaps atypical.)

14.   The recognition of, and care for, the regular congregations are a notable feature of some existing parish church cathedrals; in some dean and chapter cathedrals, however, the evidence from the laity suggests that the congregations are virtually ignored 'because we are not a parish church'. There are, nonetheless, some encouraging signs, from cathedrals of very different types, that facilities are being developed for their worshippers. In some places educational work with children is now being linked to Sunday worship, and a few cathedrals have crèche and nursery facilities. Some of the laity remark on the absence of adequate consultation and pastoral care, although such a comment is not unknown even beyond the cathedral world!

15.   During our visits to cathedrals we were delighted by the very high standards of liturgy and **music**. When we asked individuals what was specially good about their cathedral, the first answer was invariably the music. Musical standards have probably never been higher, encouraged by the expectations of musical excellence through the availability of studio-produced recordings. We warmly appreciate that such standards are only maintained by the continuing commitment, professionalism and liveliness of directors of music and organists who themselves inspire so many other musicians in cathedrals to give of their best in the service of Almighty God.

16.   The relationship between music and Christian worship has not always been seen in as positive a light as it is today, with music as the indispensable handmaid of great worship with its ability to inspire and to express aspirations and emotions better than words, and its universality able to transcend religious, intellectual and social barriers.

17.   Nevertheless, from time to time there are criticisms of the cathedral music world to which some response ought to be made.

   (a)   *It seems to be an elitist world since, despite efforts by choir schools to recruit from all sectors of the population, the majority of choristers come from the higher socio-economic groups.*

While this may appear to be so with regard to some choir schools, there are 17 cathedrals which succeed in recruiting from all types of schools and sometimes from the poorer areas of our inner cities. The Choir Schools' Association, through its Bursary Trust, has done a good deal of work to ensure that children from low-income families are assisted to attend fee-paying schools. The Trust receives an annual grant from the government. Financial help, however, goes towards school fees and not to other expenses, and so those cathedrals without choir schools receive no government money to assist with their choral foundation. Bearing in mind that cathedrals provide a unique cultural contribution to the life of the nation, much admired abroad, we would hope that consideration could be given to some government funding to assist all cathedrals in their musical and cultural work (see Chapter 5, paragraph 1).

    (b)   *It seems to be sexist since very few girls are involved in cathedral choirs.*

We have been heartened that so many cathedrals have taken thought about this matter, particularly since the publication of *In Tune with Heaven* (the report of the Archbishops' Commission on Church Music 1992), and several are in the process of taking immediate action to introduce girls into the liturgical round of daily services.

    (c)   *It seems to be an expensive luxury at a time of dire financial need.*

The figures in the financial section of this Report (see Chapter 13) speak for themselves. We found that the cost of the music in cathedrals averaged 12% of total expenditure and, whilst there is no room for complacency, the figure is much lower than the common perception.

    (d)   *Cathedral music is exclusive in that such music only speaks to a tiny minority of the nation.*

There may be some substance in this criticism in that, if cathedrals lock themselves into one particular cultural idiom, they can cut themselves off from the majority of the population – although it should be noted that over four million people now tune in to Classic FM. What is important is that a service, including the music, has its own inherent integrity which can be appreciated by those who come, even if it is not to their particular musical taste. There is an appreciation by some cathedral authorities that there is a problem to be faced and there are some attempts at broadening the cultural spread of some special services. It must also be said that cathedrals are probably still in touch with more people beyond the mainstream of Church life than many parish churches, and for those who come there is the same givenness about the style of worship as there is in a local parish church. Whilst we would hope that the cathedrals would accommodate the homely as well as the majestic, they should not accommodate worship which is either off-hand or stuffy.

18.   The choice of music, its style, language and length will be addressed by the director of music and the liturgist (see Chapter 5, paragraphs 16 and 17) so as best to serve the liturgy within the context of the overall mission of the cathedral. The impact of such music within the liturgy can only be enhanced by attention to the balance, pace and flow of each act of worship.

19.   We concur with the relevant recommendations set out in *In Tune With Heaven*, but recognise that the resources needed to maintain the excellence of the cathedrals' musical tradition are considerable and will come under increasing pressure. Those who favour diversity – more than one cathedral choir, for example, or the inclusion of girls in the musical arrangements, or Saturday morning classes for children from the diocese, or more time spent by cathedral musicians in the parishes, or sharing the cathedrals' musical resources with the music specialist departments of local education authorities – should realise that these desirable develop-ments imply enhanced resources and more staff. Otherwise, the very musical excellence that is so widely applauded will be put at risk.

20.   Radical questions may have to be faced in the future. Are there other ways of maintaining the excellence of cathedral music? A letter from the Dean of Carlisle in the *Church Times* challenged the assumption that standards are bound to be higher where there is a choir school. The whole area plainly calls for discussion. Twenty-five cathedrals have schools attached to them which educate choristers, and 17 others recruit boys and girls from a variety of schools. Do different cathedrals require different musical resources? Could a professional octet, say, maintain the excellent standards necessary in a small cathedral? The loss could well be more pastoral than musical. Newcastle estimates that 50% of its congregation is derived in some way or other from its choir. Manchester, which has a statutory choir, a voluntary choir, a girls' choir, and a training choir, would lose contact with innumerable families if a purely professional musical solution to the problem of costs were adopted. Financial con-straints are unlikely to lessen in the future, and this may well lead to more choral foundations seeking sponsorship and setting up trusts (as at Bristol) which might well protect the music of cathedrals in the coming years.

21.   Many cathedrals are centres of creativity. From them we should hope to see new compositions: new hymns, anthems, instrumental pieces, new poetry, new prayers and forms of liturgy – such as the cantor masses of Philip Duffy, which enable large congregations to participate in Eucharistic worship, or the responsorial psalms of Stuart Beer, which

allow complementary participation to choir and congregation alike. We would, in this context, wish to pay tribute to the work of the Liturgical Commission in recent years and we hope that a growing creative relationship between the cathedrals, with their own liturgical expertise, and the Liturgical Commission will be a mutually enriching development for the future.

22.   The ministry of **preaching** is a crucial aspect of the mission of cathedrals, and during our visits we were often impressed at the care taken for its provision. Quite apart from helping the regular congregations – not to speak of the members of the chapter – to formulate the Christian faith in the appropriate language and images of the day, good preaching can speak to many who drift into a cathedral service and are, perhaps unknown to themselves, ready to hear a clear presentation of religious truth. Preaching should be high among the qualities which are considered when appointments are made to the staff of cathedrals.

23.   Many who are of influence in society attend cathedral services at some time or other, and the cathedrals have the opportunity, in giving a voice to the voiceless, to present them with applications of the Christian faith. Cathedral pulpits can open lines of communication between different sections of society, and declare issues which, in other contexts, might be inappropriate or too contentious. The historic independence of cathedrals can, in this regard, be a real gift to the present.

24.   In dealing with the spoken parts of a cathedral's worship it is important to notice that even weekday lessons should be chosen with the public in mind. Many believe that the present lections are too long, and so in consequence are difficult to assimilate. A short introduction might also help a congregation to grasp the essential point of what is to follow – especially since in the modern world personal knowledge of the Bible is rare. We note that a cathedrals' Study Group currently has this under consideration.

25.   Many cathedrals produce their own version of service for regular worship, printed as a booklet. This is a helpful practice, and does not preclude those who want to from bringing their own copy of the Book of Common Prayer or the Alternative Service Book to follow readings. Such a booklet should contain sufficient rubrics to put people at their ease without the confusion of printing all the possible alternatives; it also allows a printed welcome to be displayed in local terms. The quality of the actual printing of such matter is important as is also the size of typeface used. A cathedral may spend enormous sums on the music yet allocate quite inadequate resources for the production of good printing. No cathedral should place in people's hands a production which would be inadequate in a secular context.

26. Given the pluralistic element in modern culture it is perhaps inevitable that worship, too, will express **diversity**. Excellence and experiment have often been spoken of together; the evidence is, however, that there is more excellence than experiment around. The Church had an old tradition of popular 'bridge services', often on Sunday evenings, which did not replace but complemented the statutory services. Seventy years ago, or so, these consisted of hymns and exhortations by a dynamic preacher; today the more appropriate form might be a 'prayer and praise' evening, or a charismatic happening, or a Taizé-type service, or a service of healing, or a multi-media presentation like the well-known nine o'clock service in Sheffield or similar presentations in Willow Creek. Whatever popular forms evolve, it is important that the cathedral is known to be hospitable to a wide spectrum of Christian worship, and that it is not the exclusive habitation of one particular cultural idiom. This will often simply mean making it known that the cathedral welcomes those who wish to use its space for forms of worship not normally associated with traditional formality. Members of the chapter and of the musical establishment, whatever their personal preferences in relation to styles of worship, will be glad to give a lead in extending this welcome. Cathedrals have the freedom to be bold and take risks. Cathedrals are also called to be inclusive rather than exclusive. [In this connection we note the guidance on multi-faith worship recently formulated by the House of Bishops (see GS Misc. 411), as we also note the continuation of the Commonwealth Day Observance in Westminster Abbey.]

27. Cathedrals are well placed to be reconciling centres between the institutional and the charismatic. Because a cathedral so epitomises the institutional Church, however, it will often need to take the initiative in welcoming other forms – to be forever seeking ways of realising its inclusive vocation.

28. The Liturgical Commission has recently raised the whole question of unity and diversity in Church of England worship. What should be the limits to liturgical diversity? Is there to be a common core of Anglican worship? If cathedrals are places where the complete range of worship may be encountered, it is axiomatic that they should be places where whatever makes Anglican worship distinctive can be found too. If no such common core is found to be possible in the parishes, the cathedrals could well become solely responsible for any observable evidence of Anglican identity.

Teaching

29. The regular teaching of the Christian faith continues to be one of the crucial ingredients of mission. Whether it is in the proclamation which attends key events in the Church's calendar, the presentation and

25

analysis of basic Christian themes, or expositions of the biblical text, teaching provides a vital means of communicating Christian belief. This focus on communication through teaching has a long history. Christ himself was a great teacher, who used a variety of methods in order to reach people, both children and adults, with the truth about God, about themselves and about the Kingdom.

30. Throughout the centuries those same teachings have been main-tained and upheld. In each generation the Church has tried to respond to them afresh as new issues have arisen which require Christian insight and wisdom. In our day we have the responsibility also to teach the biblical text and to learn how to understand and apply it to our age and culture at the end of the second millennium. The potential place for cathedrals in participating in this task is enormous. They have both opportunity and challenge to teach the faith faithfully, but in ways which are relevant to those who come to hear.

31. Mediaeval cathedrals did not have a teaching function; they were spiritual corporations which existed for worship, the administration of property, and – a strange notion for modern people – for the enjoyment of their rights. The education of choristers led to the foundation of schools, but their purpose was practical rather than evangelistic: they were concerned primarily with the recruitment of members of a clerical caste. It was the Reformation, and the preceding emphasis on the dissemination of biblical learning, which gave cathedrals the first real impetus to become involved in the direct teaching of Christian truth. The form was the lecture and the sermon. The age of Christian Humanism produced a distinguished company of great preachers, and the cathedral was the place where they found pulpits from which to declare the excellences of theo-logical learning. Nowhere, perhaps, was this better exemplified than in Archbishop Cranmer's establishment of a college of Six Preachers at Canterbury – which exists, in a residual form, to this day.

32. The sermon and the lecture continued, in the nineteenth century, to be the major teaching resource of the cathedrals. In an era which valued the work of mechanics' institutes and working-men's colleges, popular education events found ready support, and it was noticeable that cathedral services which included a sermon or address attracted more substantial congregations than those which did not. Cathedral libraries, too, although not exactly a popular resource, were able to provide some basis for theological reading – in some cathedrals, in fact, the money received from admission charges was explicitly earmarked for book purchase.

33. In society today, however, there is a much greater emphasis on visual skills in learning, and many cathedrals find it hard to equal the

professionalism and high cost of deploying the kinds of educational resources which are now commonplace; nonetheless, we found notable examples of educational work at Exeter and Guildford.[1] But there is a more fundamental difficulty for those anxious to see cathedrals achieve an enhanced teaching function: modern people often do not themselves see the need to be taught religion. There is a widespread assumption today that Christianity is something which is chosen by the individual, or experienced, rather than something which, dependent upon revealed truth, is received at the hands of a teacher.

34.   Despite this the sermon remains an extremely effective and popular means of conveying Christianity, and the cathedral is an excellent setting for teaching – precisely because it has a strong basis in its own community, which is able to welcome the visitors who may come to a special or a regular service. Good preaching is as effective today as it has ever been, and cathedrals can reach those who would not otherwise hear the proclamation of God's word. Many cathedrals also still adhere to the old practice of organising lectures, both for their worshipping community, and for those who may be attracted by an advertisement and come into the cathedral to hear something about a specific topic or a particular dimension of the faith. It is important that these two means of presenting Christianity are cultivated to the full. There are so many in society today who form attitudes towards Christianity without any informed notion of what it is. The popularity of cathedrals makes them excellent venues for representing its authentic nature.

35.   The area least developed in the preaching role of the cathedral is in the teaching offered to the casual visitor. This is inevitably an area of difficulty, because those who come to visit may be there for numerous and very different reasons. The backgrounds, understandings, needs and education of those who sit and listen to the preacher may be not only enormously varied but also incompatible. Whatever assumptions the preacher makes of his or her listeners is bound to be contradicted by some who are there. Yet this 'broadcasting' of the Christian gospel has always been part of our tradition, and the varied nature of the congregation has always produced a challenge to the development of effective and appropriate teaching. It is arguable that the cathedrals are the best placed of all Christian institutions to carry on this tradition today. We would urge cathedrals to look in detail at encouraging those who teach to undergo more training in this kind of communication.

---

[1] The cathedrals named in this and following chapters are examples to illustrate good practice which may also be found in other cathedrals not so named.

36.   Visitors to cathedrals, as emphasised elsewhere in this Report, often sense the acts of faith which have been invested in the very buildings themselves – and this is as true of comparatively recent foundations as it is of the ancient ones. Those who serve in cathedrals, and especially guides, may well be those whose presentation of the Christian purpose of the building will be the most effective conveyance of Christian truth. Their sense of vocation needs every encouragement (see Chapter 9, paragraph 27).

37.   Links with the diocese in the area of teaching are often used to deepen the effectiveness of what a cathedral can offer. Expertise in communication, in work with children and young people, in contemporary methods of teaching, and in the use of multi-media programmes provides an important resource which many cathedral chapters call upon. This is most often the case when a diocesan educationalist has a particular place on a cathedral chapter, or when there is a regular exchange between the two. Co-operation and readiness to learn, even in an area where a cathedral believes that it has its own expertise, is felt to be as important in the teaching aspect of mission as anywhere else.

38.   Some dioceses are also able to supply resources in drama and mime which increasingly play an important part in teaching and in communication. With massive central space, and dramatic context, the cathedral can provide a centre for artistic expression and communication that many other buildings lack. When these media are used as an interesting and innovative part in the teaching mission of the cathedral, they are often found to be very successful.

Service

39.   One of the expressions of God's mission in Jesus Christ is the establishment of a Kingdom. That is a way of living according to the rule of God. It would bring that set of conditions in which righteousness and peace would exist alongside justice; where love would be pure and without ambiguity; where God would be seen to be sovereign and all people would find harmony in him. The Kingdom dawned with the coming of Christ. In him the human race is seen in its perfection and God and his creatures are in complete unity. Yet the Saviour himself spoke of a Kingdom still to be fulfilled. He gives us the ingredients, told in parable and acted out in his compassionate dealings with individuals, but his followers have a role in continuing to discover the realisation of the Kingdom in each culture and generation. Every epoch of Christian history is both an attempt to live out the precepts of Christ and also a looking forward to that fulness of time when all will be at one with him.

40.   Like other institutions of the Church cathedrals struggle with the call to be both icons of a Kingdom which has already dawned and prophets of what has still to be fulfilled. For Christ himself that call led to a way of suffering. It has been the same with the saints and martyrs down the centuries. The dimension of mission which we have called service leads to occasions of sacrifice, and a cathedral's mission is inadequate if it does not have this hallmark of the Kingdom about it. That indicates a particular difficulty. For cathedrals have roles imposed upon them, both by Church and by society, which belie a servant role – which inhibit self-sacrifice, anonymity, and unconditional service. The image of cathedrals is often projected not by the evident sanctity of the individual lives of many who work in them but by material splendour. Sacrificial service is not a quality conventionally associated with the scale of cathedral buildings, or with the neatly trimmed lawns and grand houses of the precincts. Cathedrals do not deserve the charge of superior detachment which is sometimes brought against them, but they have to acknowledge that the charge is nevertheless made by others who are also bearing the heat and burden of ministry in the Church. It implies that some cathedrals have an image which must be changed if they are to be seen as an integral part of a Christian ministry which is characterised by sacrificial service. Our visits revealed that most cathedrals were aware of this tension.

41.   In addition to involvement by individual members of the congregation we noticed a number of examples of good practice of corporate service. Some are mentioned here to encourage others, yet in the knowledge that this list is very far from being exhaustive. Bristol engages in care for vagrants and in ministry to the older generations through a lunch club. Chester supports local agencies concerned with social deprivation. Coventry provides food and funds for those in need; Kennedy House and the Bardsley Trust manage residential accommodation and a centre for young people on behalf of the cathedral, diocese and city. Derby supports a day centre for the homeless. Newcastle is attempting to improve help to the homeless and the hungry in association with the City Centre Council of Churches. Portsmouth has a homelessness action group. Rochester has taken an initiative amongst the unemployed in partnership with local politicians, trade unionists, and voluntary agencies. Sheffield provides breakfasts for the homeless and unemployed. Southwell has a night shelter for teenagers run by Churches Together. Much of this sort of work only touches the fringes of social problems, but it indicates an awareness of the kinds of service to which cathedrals are called and a preparedness to attach cathedrals as institutions to real involvement with social need. So much of a cathedral's life is tied up with permanence and predictability that it requires a particular sort of enterprise to seek involvement with the frontiers of social distress.

42.   In responding to the needs of the local community there is room for a more productive expansion by cathedrals into this sort of work if priority is to be given to service. It will certainly entail sacrifice: some of the work will not be popular with local residents, some of whom may be tenants of the cathedral. Care will therefore need to be taken with regard to cathedral property if it becomes the regular host to those in need. Above all, it will raise questions about the skills and insights required of those who are appointed to serve in cathedrals. It may also call for a preparedness by cathedral authorities to use the resources of their buildings and money in partnership with other bodies, like ecumenical groups, charitable agencies, and local government. The buildings and personnel which a cathedral provides may often be exactly what is needed to extend and deepen work already undertaken by other bodies such as the Diocesan Board for Social Responsibility.

43.   Apart from practical service of this kind there is another sort of service, equally a sign of the Kingdom, for which cathedrals are traditionally well equipped. For they are a good base for prophets who can declare the nature of the Kingdom in the context of the modern world. Authentic prophecy discovers permanent spiritual truths in the transient circumstances of unstable culture; it derives moral lessons from the unfolding events of an uncertain world. Prophetic canons may be uncomfortable members of a chapter, but their influence, on behalf of causes which are extremely unpopular or involve, perhaps, political or moral controversy, may well place a cathedral in the forefront of a generation's idealism and sense of service. Although their occasions of wider service may be an accident of individual appointment, a cathedral should be ready to provide a platform from which the prophetic nature of the gospel can be expressed.

44.   The priority of racial justice within the modern agenda of social concern, both throughout the world and in this country, prompts consideration of cathedrals as places where enormous benefits can be secured in enrichment of service and witness by the appointment of clergy from non-European racial backgrounds. There are far too few appointments from other parts of the Anglican Communion. Some cathedrals do have links, through the diocese or independently, with cathedrals in other parts of the world, and these have proved to be important adjuncts to the universal witness of prayer which sustains those who labour in Christ's name.

45.   At the heart of Jesus' message of the Kingdom are the themes of reconciliation and atonement. The Church is called to live and speak of these distinctively Christian perceptions of the needs of the world. A cathedral is in a strong position to be the place where people of diverse

social origins, different ecclesiastical loyalties, and varied racial roots gather together in mutual service and with common visions.

Evangelism

46. There has, during the past couple of centuries, been a renewed use of the word 'evangelism' to convey something of the vitality and activism which is actually inseparable from the essential message of Christ. Yet some believe – and this was reflected in aspects of the evidence presented to us – that cathedrals are not the appropriate places for evangelism. Some maintained that they should not be; others thought that they could not be because of their very nature. It is our view, however, that cathedrals should be evangelistic in their vocational purpose, and that in many cases they already are.

47. Statistics suggest that cathedrals are more in touch with non-churchgoers than any other part of the Church. The ministry to schools, tourists and pilgrims is discussed in another part of this Report (see paragraphs 58 ff below and Chapter 12) and it is a very complicated area for interpretation and analysis. What is quite clear, on the other hand, is that visitors to cathedrals constitute a body of people to whom the cathedrals can present the plain truth of the Christian faith. To what extent is this opportunity exploited? In many places a great deal of thought and effort already goes into addressing answers to this question: worship and music are an invitation to a personal religious response; tourist facilities and education centres offer explanations and encourage further exploration; where there is a programme of social care people can catch a glimpse of Christianity in action; leaflets, video presentations, and bookstalls provide Christian interpretations of the great truths which the building exists to celebrate. Numerous opportunities and the means to meet them are there; but is there any evidence that, as a result, individual visitors are actually stimulated to take the first steps of a committed faith?

48. We believe that most cathedrals could be more active in their evangelistic mission. They should endeavour to move from implicit to explicit presentation of the gospel in a way which is centrally represented in the mission statement of the cathedral's strategy. Everyone who works in the cathedral should be aware that evangelism is one of its primary purposes: it should feature in individual vocational descriptions, and should be the subject of regular prayer in services of all types. Each cathedral department should ask itself the question, 'In what way is our work an invitation to people to consider the calling of Jesus Christ?'.

49. Cathedrals should each consider establishing an enquiry centre or other suitable facility for those wishing to know more about the Christian

faith. These centres should be staffed by people specifically trained to assist enquirers and to encourage people to ask questions. They should have available literature which relates to personal faith and to the work and witness of the cathedral itself. At Easter, for example, such a centre should be able to provide explanations of the truth of the Resurrection which employ the ceremonies and symbols of the sublime experience of the Risen Christ seen in the cathedral. It should also provide information about pastoral assistance available through the cathedral's ministry – to the bereaved, to those whose lives are dislocated or broken, and to those seeking to make a fresh start. Particular skills and sensitivity are required in those able to offer Christian help in this way, and this may be an appropriate area of service for parishes and the cathedral to combine resources. It can be seen as a partnership between the cathedral and the rest of the diocese through the work of the diocesan mission or evangelism committees.

50.   Cathedrals have a traditional ministry of preaching. Each cathedral might have at least one member of the chapter who would undertake to provide, at regular intervals, sermons which present the basics of the Christian faith and allow occasions for personal responses. Others in the cathedral community could prepare their own work in a manner which helps to illustrate the particular evangelistic themes chosen for presentation by the regular preacher. There are some who visit a cathedral and attend its worship because they prefer its relative anonymity. Many, however, come for a single occasion and may be glad of the chance to be put in touch with a local church in order to experience in a more sustained way something of the religious inclinations or feelings which they may have sensed during their visit. There should be arrangements for those who would wish to be introduced to the priest or minister of a church in the area where they live.

51.   Enquirers will come from different stages in their personal pilgrimage. For some the cathedral will evoke memories of a lost faith; others will come almost completely ignorant of Christianity or with distorted understandings of it; some will come at a moment of personal crisis; others will come with a sense of the needs of the world and a desire to serve. It is already evident, from the observations of those who work in cathedrals, that many in all of these categories come with a need to pray. Votive candles may be a first expression of this need, and it is good to see many cathedrals giving people the opportunity to ask for prayer. It is also important for cathedral authorities to remember that their evangelistic priorities are not applicable only to visitors: they extend to the cathedral community itself, and it will be a poor ministry which neglects perpetual renewal of faith for those who are resident in the house of the Lord.

Witness

52.   The word 'witness', as part of the mission of the people of God, is an indication of something for which cathedrals are supremely fitted. It suggests that Christians are, first and foremost, not called upon to accomplish anything in their own strength and judgement, but simply to point to what God has done and is doing. In St Luke's Gospel 'You are to be witnesses to these things' pointed to the Christian calling to be bearers of the evidence of the Resurrection.

53.   There is no doubt that cathedrals display how this witness to the Risen Saviour worked out for Christians in the past. The history of the building is, quite simply, the story of centuries of Christian witness. That may seem obvious to those whose lives are devoted to the service of the cathedral, but it is not so plain to those who come on a rare visit. Some may see the building as merely a dimension of cultural heritage, a museum which displays the treasures of a distant tradition. The living purpose of the cathedral needs to be made explicit – not just saying that the people of the past built the cathedral because of their faith but saying what the faith was and is.

54.   The tombs of kings and bishops, the stained glass and carvings, should not be located only in national history but described in their context of religious witness. Whatever the frail ambiguity of human motivation, it was the dedicated desire to do God's service which inspired great men and women of the past to create and to endow these buildings, and care should be taken, in explanations of them for modern visitors, to explain the importance of religious faith to people of the past. The modern secular mind often has great difficulty in appreciating the authentically religious element in the motivation of people in other times and places. Cathedrals like other important churches are a surviving and continuing witness to the vitality of a living tradition of belief.

55.   It can be argued that the beauty and the space of a cathedral speak for themselves and are best left to evoke personal reflection in each visitor. But, for many people, responding to a building the size of a cathedral can be a novel and often confusing experience. We believe that it can be part of a cathedral's witness to help people ask questions about how they react to this. What kind of emotions, what kind of questions are evoked? There are some fine examples of how the furnishings of a cathedral can portray Christian witness. Children's literature especially lends itself to this. But, in a secular age, this needs to be made very explicit and nothing taken for granted even for adults. The Cross itself is the central Christian symbol but needs explanation in terms of living faith and historical context. An altar table, a font, a lectern and a pulpit all need description which not

only says, 'This is where the Eucharist is celebrated or the Bible read', but why Christians think that these things are so important. For the casual visitor this may be the only opportunity which they are prepared to take to learn something basic about the Christian faith – without feeling that they are getting involved more than they choose to be.

56.   Apart from the impact of the building and its artefacts, Christian witness will also be demonstrated by the quality of life of the people who make up the cathedral community. There are some common divides which tend to militate against the concept of a community with a partic-ular style of life. The divides of clergy and laity, of paid employees and volunteers, of those who know their way about and the relative stranger, the insiders and the outsiders, women and men, white and non-white, young and old – all these divisions find their way into cathedral life at great cost to the effectiveness of Christian witness. It is our concern that Christian virtues of community should be clearly demonstrated. All people within the cathedral community should be aware of the impact of their corporate witness.

57.   Some cathedrals have commendable induction courses for their staff and volunteers (see Chapter 9, paragraphs 32-34) but too often these focus on a good marketing image and stop short of cultivating a common Christian witness to the faith. It would be an encouragement to all involved in the cathedral's service to the public if they met together on a regular (but not necessarily frequent) basis in order to rekindle the concept of Christian community whose main objective is to say something about their faith. In this way people from different departments and with different levels of commitment in terms of time would be reminded of their interdependence on each other and corporately of their dependence on God. Many who belong to the cathedral community come from parish-es in the diocese, and some from different Christian traditions. An impor-tant dimension of witness will therefore be to make it evident that the cathedral is not a ghetto but a part of the Universal Church.

58.   The question of staff attitudes leads to the consideration of tourism as an aspect of hospitality and witness. In Christian theology, faith is often characterised as journeying, being on the move, and the image of travelling with the God whose Son came among us as one who serves seems particularly appropriate for those who must minister in cathedrals to people who are also on a journey, as pilgrims or tourists.

59.   For some people in the Church, there are mixed blessings to be found in becoming embroiled in the tourist industry. They fear that human beings will always destroy or threaten what is special and set apart, and sense that the ethos of certain places can only be preserved by

restrictions. It is true that modern tourism can suggest images of uncultured busyness, overcrowding, the spoliation of natural beauty and a carelessness of encounter with people and places. But the freedom to travel, and at relatively low cost, to famous and accessible places is now such a part of our lives that it would be difficult for cathedrals to limit the numbers of visitors, even if that was their aim. Moreover, for all its potential dangers, mass tourism and travel ought to be welcomed as an often powerful means of opening closed minds, of breaking down irrational barriers or fears, and of confronting us not just with human complexity and variety, but with our shared humanity. And any theology based on the Incarnation, any Church interested in ministry and mission, cannot but be interested in all kinds of people on the move, and be willing to face the reality that people inevitably affect places.

60. In earlier times, Christian pilgrims visiting holy sites committed themselves to a long journey, for what was looked for in the holy place was not to be had without arduous travelling. Modern tourists, however, travel with much greater ease, and with a less complex agenda. And although they come to a place for a whole variety of reasons, and in different states of mind, they are in most cases just passing through, unable, or unwilling, to invest too much time and energy in individual encounters with places, and thus with people. For them, and for those who minister to them, it is inevitably a brief encounter, and so there is work to be done if the tourist is to be drawn into the life and meaning of a place in a way that is fruitful.

61. In one sense, a cathedral, like any place, must be allowed to speak for itself, on its own terms, and yet buildings, like people, need help if they are to speak in a language which communicates. In this decade we can no longer assume that this is a common or natural language, and there will be many who arrive unskilled in holy things. As tourists ourselves, we are all used to being informed, directed, by others when we travel to a place. But we also reserve the right to direct our own eye, emotion, imagination, in a way which complements the official direction of those who have local wisdom to share. For all cathedrals in their dealings with people, there is then a balance to be struck between a letting be and direction, between accepting the tourist's own agenda and offering our own. It is a balance, we might say, which reflects the way God himself deals with his creation.

62. The challenge of tourism raises for cathedrals the question of what a call to hospitality means. To provide a ministry of service to tourists is not to offer hospitality in its more usual sense. But it is a calling to exercise a level of professional care which as far as possible enables each

visitor to make the best use of time and place. In this context, the word 'professional' is a coded way of expressing a theology of carefulness.

63.   There are of course tensions for those who are stewards of a place, when they welcome strangers who are nevertheless guests. There is a desire to interpret the building and its life on our own terms, to maintain and control the environment which the visitors will encounter. These desires arise out of that feeling of belonging to a place which is a spiritual home, and which generates a sense of shared purpose by its liturgical rhythm and common life. But there is also the need to acknowledge that any form of hospitality involves a disruption of personal rhythms which is not always easy to accept. Anyone who has experienced as a 'resident' the effects of large-scale tourism on a place recognises that particular form of ambivalence which the stress of numbers can generate. And yet any theology of tourism will direct us to see that, if we are to serve visitors in this way, then we need a certain abstinence from private expectation, from that tendency to see the building as our possession, and the visitor as intruder rather than guest. These tensions reflect of course those which exist in the wider Church. But if service, evangelism and witness mean anything, and if cathedral ministry is in a very special sense a 'service industry', then it is vital that the tourist is seen as guest rather than intruder.

64.   Those who are stewards and ministers in the life of a cathedral are part of an ancient Church, and our history reminds us that, as stewards of the architectural and liturgical benefactions of those who have gone before us in the faith, we too are merely sojourners. And if we are passing through, then graciousness in the way we respond to those who are passing through as our guests must be the antidote to any desire to privatise what is not our possession.

65.   It is a commonplace to observe that those who enter a cathedral as tourists are sometimes beguiled by place, mood and size into a mode of wonder. They can acknowledge a desire to understand, to question, even to confront the God whose inspiration has made possible both the building and the moment. In this way, the tourist may indeed be transformed into a pilgrim. But if such transformations are to take place, if we are to have a theology of tourism which sustains us in our vocation to service, then we need wisdom to see how best we can prepare a building to speak, how best we can prepare people to be guides and servants of need, how best we can encourage every visitor to experience our ministry as a reflection of God's concern for people, people who are always on the move.

66.   There are opportunities in some cathedrals for hospitality to those who are more than passing visitors. Such is the quality of music, liturgy and environment that cathedrals are ideal for residential retreat and reflection. Holy Week is a good example. During this period most cathedrals present daily liturgies of high quality. The numbers of people benefiting from them could be extended if residential facilities were available, perhaps in partnership with local hotels and guest houses.

67.   The cathedral has, indeed, many opportunities of demonstrating its bridge-building role and welcoming, not as guests but as part of the wider Christian family, those who look to the cathedral as an important centre of Christian activity within the region as a whole. The existence of Christian disunity hampers witness more than any other consideration, and the cathedral has the opportunities to show the world that Christians love one another and can work with one another. Other partnerships in which Christian witness is possible are those with the local authorities, educational institutions, health services and statutory bodies, thus engaging the world of public service and care with imperatives of the gospel.

68.   In the course of our visits we became aware of the contribution made to the lives of cathedral communities by the cathedral bells and their ringers. Most of our cathedrals have peals of bells and they include some of the largest and best rings in the country. In most cathedrals an eager and enthusiastic team of ringers ensures that the bells are rung regularly to call worshippers to service and to remind the city of the continuing role of the cathedral. In a few cathedrals ringers are short in number, and in one or two cases bells are no longer rung on a regular basis. We would encourage all cathedrals to ensure if possible that their bells are rung regularly.

Recommendation

We recommend that in their strategic planning of their mission cathedrals address the questions in the following paragraphs.

WORSHIP

1.   In what respect is the cathedral developing an imaginative and creative approach to its worship? (paragraph 8)

2.   Is the cathedral bridging the perceived gaps, musical or liturgical, between cathedral and diocese? (paragraph 10)

3.   In what ways is the cathedral taking ecumenical initiatives in its worship? (paragraph 12)

4. Does the cathedral affirm its congregations both liturgically and pastorally? (paragraph 14)

5. Are the dean and chapter satisfied that the resources for worship and music are of the right order for their cathedral? (paragraphs 15 ff)

6. Is the cathedral encouraging the composition of new liturgical and musical material? (paragraph 21)

7. When did the cathedral last review its policy about preaching and reading the scriptures and to what effect? (paragraphs 22 ff)

8. Is the cathedral seeking to include a wide spectrum of Christian worship? (paragraph 26)

TEACHING

1. Is the preaching ministry of the cathedral capable of being extended through public lectures or other methods of presentation? (paragraph 34)

2. Are those who work in the cathedral trained and able to respond to the expectation that they will be mediators of the essential purpose of the building? (paragraphs 35 and 36)

3. Are all the opportunities for teaching, especially to the young, and using new forms of media being fully exploited? (paragraphs 37 and 38)

SERVICE

1. Is the cathedral so planning its resources as to include the meeting of immediate human need locally and regionally? (paragraph 41)

2. Is the cathedral developing partnerships with other churches and caring agencies to meet human need? (paragraph 42)

3. In what ways does the cathedral carry out a prophetic role in the context of a needy world? (paragraph 43)

4. How is the cathedral forging links with the world Church? (paragraph 44)

EVANGELISM

1.   Is evangelism explicit in the cathedral's strategy? (paragraph 48)

2.   Is the evangelistic purpose of the cathedral known by all staff and volunteers and included in their training programmes? (paragraph 48)

3.   Should consideration be given to the establishment of an enquiry centre in the cathedral? (paragraph 49)

4.   Does the job description of at least one full-time member of staff include the development of the ministry of evangelism in preaching and teaching? (paragraph 50)

WITNESS

1.   Are the beauty, the space, and the furnishings of the cathedral explicitly used to evoke questions of meaning and faith? (paragraph 55)

2.   Is it explicit that the cathedral as a building is a witness to the Resurrection which has been lived out in history? (paragraph 55)

3.   Are all cathedral staff and volunteers taught and inspired to a corporate witness? (paragraph 57)

4.   Is the theology and practice of hospitality in the cathedral capable of further development? (paragraphs 58 ff)

5.   Are the cathedral's partnerships with other churches and statutory and voluntary agencies showing signs of growth and development? (paragraph 67)

EVALUATION

Are there, built into the cathedral's life, mechanisms by which regular evaluation of the cathedral's mission can take place?

4

Education

Introduction

1.   As historic buildings of great architectural, artistic, literary and social significance, and as living Christian communities, cathedrals have considerable potential as an educational asset both of the Church and of society. They offer insights into the nature and development of the Christian faith and its relationship to historical and social change. Cathedrals also have the advantage of accessibility: they are within reach of schools, colleges and universities; they are open most days of the year; .they are spacious enough to accommodate large groups; most have gone to much trouble to provide facilities for their inquiring visitors by establishing centres, historic trails, and library access; some have developed good links with local education authorities.

2.   The Church's traditional role in education, and its concern for the transmission of basic skills (and their relation to moral and spiritual education), have encountered new problems in modern society. The resourcefulness of Christian teachers in county schools, and the dedication of those entrusted with Church schools, both primary and secondary, are unable to win against the increasing secularisation of educational processes. Professionalism itself has for various reasons given educational work an autonomy whose practice often leaves little space for Christian dimensions; the present functional view of education tends to exclude just that attention to the transcendent aspects of human life which the Church exists to preserve and to interpret. In higher education the Church often lives on borrowed time: the academic study of theology itself is left almost entirely to the universities, which are in practice secular institutions, and the surviving Christian pastoral and spiritual presence in many universities is, despite the seriousness with which the ministry is treated there, in some measure a minor feature of the work of those institutions. Even the Church Colleges of Education (Voluntary Colleges), which are institutions directly under the control of the Church or of Anglican trusts, are in practice usually run on secular professional lines indistinguishable from the secular colleges – as indeed they must be to attract professional respect and achieve required standards.

3. Cathedrals, on the other hand, can be seen as direct educational resources of the Church. They are well placed to participate in the development of an educational strategy which is based on a theological view of the person, and on witnessing to the religious dimensions of human culture. Cathedrals are themselves integrated monuments to the past development of faith: they can speak, therefore, to those who seek an integrated view of human life in the modern world.

4. Cathedrals will thus need to work not only in the educational areas which presently concern them; they will need to be active in contributing to Christian reflection about the whole process and direction of education.

Primary and Secondary Education

5. We recognise that cathedrals have varying resources at their disposal in the area of education. Most of them see the potential of their building, their history, their site and their resources for education. But there are some differences in the way in which they approach their educational work at primary and secondary level. Those which are most effective have forged good links with the local education authorities, have established education centres, are enjoying good relations with teachers in local schools, are able to provide resource materials and handbooks to accompany visits, hold regular exhibitions for younger children, take seriously the need to co-ordinate and guide school parties, and have developed historic trails through and around the building.

6. Many cathedrals which we visited fell into this category, but some were struggling to find the money, personnel and interest to develop resources, often against a backcloth of discouragement. One cathedral (Bristol) reported that school visits had become much rarer after the 1988 Education Reform Act. Another (Derby) said that financial problems had led to a reduction in the number of schools' visits. These assessments, however, need to be set against those cathedrals which have experienced a growth of educational visits as part of the new National Curriculum (see paragraph 8 below). Many cathedrals have no education centre; one of them (Gloucester) noted that lack of space had made this development difficult. Others have no personnel specifically allocated to make key educational links. Many rely on untrained volunteers. Lack of financial resources, diocesan provisions, and established links are all cited as reasons for being unable to participate in educational projects for primary school children.

7. On a number of our visits the civic representatives told us that they saw education as offering greater potential for co-operation between the cathedral and the locality. One city council chief executive saw the

cathedral's role as an educational resource as one of its three main roles, and felt that it could do more to develop its resource for schools. Another council representative felt that the cathedral targeted mainly Church schools with which it had existing links, but could also look more widely.

8.   We noted a large number and a great variety of good practices.

(a)   VISITS AND TRAILS

Bradford's relatively recent developments now include tours which are adapted especially for the needs of individual schools. A Cathedral Adviser in Development and Education visits schools beforehand to assess these needs. Canterbury Cathedral Education Department, staffed by an Education Officer, a small team of employees and a number of volunteers, welcomes 6,000 children a year. In addition to several historic trails there, a full range of educational materials is available in several languages. The cathedral has an annual Schools Day, which in 1992 attracted pupils from 37 schools. Chelmsford has experienced a marked increase in school visits in recent years, despite not being a natural place of pilgrimage or tourism. Coventry is visited by about 17,000 schoolchildren per annum, and the trip includes a visit to the audio-visual theatre. Exeter, which stresses that its aim is to focus on a living place of worship rather than a historical building, caters for 5,000 children a year as part of school groups. Lincoln is visited by 15,000 children in school parties each year, using the cathedral as a study focus. 3,000 children pass through Lichfield's study centre annually. Norwich liaises regularly with the local authority and with the many school teachers who bring groups from all over East Anglia to its topical exhibitions. Wakefield used the enthronement of a new bishop as the opportunity for a week's schools programme.

(b)   CORE CURRICULUM

A significant number of cathedrals have developed courses and study days which relate to the school curriculum. Study areas, audio-visual materials and handbooks are available to help pupils to work on a number of relevant topics. Many of these include projects in history, geography, music and dance, English and drama. Amongst many cathedrals, Canterbury and Guildford are active in developing these connections in a wide variety of innovative ways. The potential for cathedrals to work with the curricula for primary schools and GCSE syllabuses is considerable. Where teachers themselves are enthusiastic the relationship between cathedral and school is a very positive one. Where the contribution includes a specific Christian contribution this is to be especially encouraged. Wells ends each of the three days of a summer teaching programme with an act of worship.

9.   There are also, however, two less optimistic notes to be sounded.

(a)   In some places local schools do not seem to think of involving the cathedral at all in their educational programmes.

(b)   Sometimes even the cathedrals which are active in their educational work fail to use the opportunity to integrate it with the belief and worship life of the cathedral, or with teaching on the Christian faith.

Whilst being delighted at the developments already in existence, we are aware that much more work needs to be done both in developing links with schools and other bodies, and in relating other areas of education, and especially of adult education, to the Christian faith.

10.   We believe that, in view of the considerable potential for education within the cathedral context, it is important to maximise the resources available. We therefore commend the exchange of material and ideas which has taken place between many cathedrals, with the aim of providing a common resource base and avoiding unnecessary duplication of effort.

Choir Schools

11.   Many cathedrals have their own choir schools, a situation which allows them (in theory at least) to have a greater influence in the education of young people. In practice the picture is rather more complex, with many choir schools enjoying a level of relative autonomy. The schools themselves differ from each other in their relationship with the cathedral and with the local education authority. No cathedral choir schools educate only choristers; all have non-chorister pupils.

12.   In most choir schools the deans and chapters have a prominent role on the governing body and as owners of the sites or buildings. Otherwise, educational links between schools and cathedrals do not appear in general to be close. The choir schools do attend some statutory services en bloc and many candidates are offered for confirmation. In each of these areas, however, attention should always be given to a creative relationship.

13.   We would wish to pay tribute to the choir schools – for the way they maintain the balance between the academic pressures on young children and the demands made by the cathedral music department. Many of the schools are energetic and contented communities, in which the choristers and other pupils are given a sound musical and academic education.

14.   The governance of choir schools involves the cathedrals, and through them the Church of England in general, with wider issues about independent education. This also affects the public schools which are

attached to some cathedral foundations – sometimes, as at Canterbury, even situated inside the precincts – and which are to many observers the most obvious sign of the cathedrals' relationship to education. For some, both inside the Church and outside, this raises questions about the political or professional desirability of the Church being involved at all in independent (fee-paying) education. The political issue latent here is not within our terms of reference: what concerns us is the proper relationship between cathedral and school. This relationship is often embodied in part in the presence of cathedral representatives on the governing bodies of such schools. In some cases the head of the chapter is ex officio chairman of the school governors. A wide range of practice prevails, but queries are legitimately raised as to whether deans and canons are invariably the best qualified to serve in an area in which a variety of backgrounds as well as a knowledge of and feeling for educational issues are essential. Some cathedral clergy may have these attributes, but others may not. Other areas of disquiet concern the potential conflict of interest between the chapter and the needs of the school, especially over finance and property.

15.   We believe that it is possible to explore models which might introduce a measure of flexibility into existing statutory provisions and practices; which will preserve close links between cathedrals and schools, yet simultaneously allow for variations of available expertise to be recognised and catered for. It might be thought proper, for example, for the chairman of the governing body of a school to be elected from among the membership of the whole governing body; or for deans and chapters to nominate members to governing bodies without having the statutory obligation to serve on them themselves; or to provide that governors' decisions are not subject to revision by the chapter. There is a range of possibilities which plainly will benefit from exploration (and the cathedral's Greater Council (see below) may be able helpfully to assist in this process). In considering them, the need is to find that set of arrangements which will make certain that school governing bodies contain the wide range of skills and experience necessary to help ensure a successful school, while retaining the right relationship between cathedral and school.

Sixth Form Programmes

16.   A small number of cathedrals make special provision for sixth form work, and this is an area which can be developed far more. Work with A-level syllabuses in drama, music and religious studies can be areas for co-operation, as well as hosting debates. Worcester, for example, is particularly involved with sixth form students and encourages them to study sources in its library.

Higher Education

17.   For many people their student years are a time when they reject or reconsider the Christian faith, or come to it for the first time. With the focus on learning, rather than on the minutiae of routine work or domestic life, there is often opportunity for them to be introduced to the Christian gospel by friends or chaplains, or by professing lecturers who teach them. We are glad to note that some cathedrals see their own role in this process to be a significant one.

18.   A number of cathedrals foster good structural relations with institutions of higher and further education, including Church Voluntary Colleges. In some cases the dean is a member of the governing body of the local college (for example, Chester), or a member of the university senate (as at Durham).

19.   Other cathedrals hold regular or annual events specifically aimed at students. These include a Lent or Advent lecture series. We found many examples of good practice. The Open Lecture series at Wells explored a *Theology of Creation*, and invited well-known Christian academics to participate. Chester's Autumn Cathedral Lectures explored Christian ethics. Bristol hosted the Annual Universities Sermon, at which the Vice-Chancellors of both universities in Bristol were present along with a significant number of students, faculty and alumni.

20.   Many cathedrals reported good relationships with university theology departments, archaeology faculties, Church Voluntary Colleges and centres for extra-mural studies: Canterbury, Durham and Manchester all have viable joint programmes. Some have their own student theological group. Chelmsford has established, in conjunction with the Anglican chaplaincy, a Centre for the Study of Theology at the Anglia Polytechnic University. This focuses on theological research, teaching and publication. Rochester is involved in setting up a chaplaincy at the new Chatham campus of the University of Greenwich.

21.   Many of the excellent projects designed by the cathedral for the local college or university rely on some measure of external funding, and when this is not available even the most carefully designed programme can be in jeopardy. Coventry mentioned that its Student Guide Programme was a victim of the first wave of recession.

Libraries

22.   Cathedral libraries are a varying source of educational material. A few of the most valuable cathedral collections are no longer kept at the cathedral itself, but are stored in university libraries: Ely's collection is

stored at Cambridge University Library. We applaud this important way of ensuring that the books are being used and looked after. (We do not feel, however, that the valuable historic collections of most cathedral libraries should be separated and placed in less appropriate surroundings.) Some cathedral libraries were very dated and, although their volumes had considerable historical or antiquarian interest, there were few contemporary theological books which would be useful to the academic or the student in a modern theology department.

23.   The library areas in cathedrals are often in the oldest part of the buildings; although they are sometimes found to be in need of refurbishment and repair, much has been done to keep the books in an appropriate environment. The need to allocate financial resources to the maintenance of the library has to be weighed against other pressing needs. In some cathedrals the library occupies valuable space which members of the chapter believe could be better used in some other way. The need also to allocate staff time as librarians was a further issue which, some chapters represent, constrains cathedrals in making fullest use of library resources.

24.   Many libraries are an important location of archives and records. Those working on family histories, or local histories, frequently consult them. They remain a valuable asset to many archivists. We record with pleasure the service to Christian scholarship performed by so many cathedral librarians and archivists. It is thanks to their expertise and enterprise that so many cathedrals have been able to retain a place in the increasingly professional world of historical research.

Centres of Theology

25.   It is not only students and those involved in higher education who have theological interests or concerns. In taking its educational responsibilities seriously the Church will need to include those whose educational background and needs are very different: cathedrals have a part to play here, too, in developing programmes for public lectures and courses which address profound theological and religious issues in varying levels of presentation, and for Christians and non-Christians alike. Some cathedrals have already begun 'teach-ins', devotional series, exhibition centres, seminars and lectures, which present the faith and the issues of the modern intellect with sensitivity and effective use of popular formats.

Theological Colleges

26.   There is no evidence of large-scale use of cathedrals as a training base for ordinands. Most theological colleges who placed their students either as ongoing Sunday placements or on block placements did not

usually incorporate cathedrals into their scheme. We felt that more could be developed along these lines. In some places – at Lincoln, for example – the theological college has strong links with the cathedral, of the sort which might be encouraged elsewhere (where geographical location is favourable).

Diocesan Board of Education and Chapter Educationalists

27. The level of co-operation between Diocesan Boards of Education and cathedrals varies very much from diocese to diocese. The lack of an overall structural pattern means that there is a patchiness in the provisions made and in the way resources are used. Some cathedrals enjoy a close relationship with their Diocesan Board of Education – for example, a cathedral canon is the secretary to the board – and this allows the potential at least for co-operation and coherence in the development of educational policy, and a wider use of the cathedral resources by the diocese. In other cathedrals there is little liaison with the diocesan board and few joint projects. Sometimes this leads to an uncomfortable duplication of effort, or to events being placed on the same night and therefore being seen to compete with each other. Projects sometimes get abandoned when the chapter members with responsibility for them leave the service of the cathedral: an overall structure would assist continuity.

Conclusion

28. We believe that more cathedral chapters should give collective thought to education. It is evident that in some cases education does not occupy a high proportion of discussion time at chapter meetings; in some very large cathedrals there is little or no provision made for a paid professional to work in this area. Sometimes this key work is left to unsupervised volunteers who have to use a great deal of personal initiative to get any project off the ground. Then, because it is not seen to be a high priority for the dean or residentiary canons, those wanting to use the cathedral for an educational purpose might be tolerated rather than welcomed by the vergers or other employees of the cathedral.

29. Those cathedrals which are most effective in the area of education have been able to allocate a trained member of chapter or a full-time professional educator to oversee, develop and promote this whole area of cathedral involvement. Financial constraints may well inhibit further expenditure on the employment of personnel, desirable though that is; yet all cathedrals should look for ways of creating educational priorities in their overall ministry.

Recommendations

1. Cathedrals should be active in contributing to Christian reflection about the whole process and direction of education (paragraph 4).

2. Work carried out in developing links with schools and in relating other areas of education to the Christian faith is of great value and could be enhanced (paragraph 9).

3. The resources available for education should be increased by the continued exchange of material and ideas between cathedrals (paragraph 10).

4. Attention should always be given to a creative relationship between the cathedral and its choir school (paragraph 12).

5. The future governance of choir schools needs to be carefully explored, and any potential conflicts of interest between chapter and school, particularly in the areas of finance and property, need to be resolved (paragraphs 14 and 15).

6. Involvement between cathedrals and theological colleges can be most fruitful (paragraph 26).

7. Cathedral administrative chapters should give collective thought to education with a view to creating educational priorities in liaison with diocesan resources (paragraphs 27-29).

5

Music

Introduction

1.   As we mention in Chapter 3, paragraph 4, 'At the centre of the life of the cathedral is the daily offering of worship and praise – Eucharist, Morning Prayer and on most days Choral Evensong'. The offering of daily choral worship in cathedrals is one of the most significant contributions made by this country to European culture. The fact that music and worship of a generally high standard are being offered regularly with little or no financial support from the government or arts funding bodies should be recognised. In view of the importance of the contribution made by cathedral musicians to cultural life in this country and abroad, it is to be hoped that the Arts Council, the Association for Business Sponsorship of The Arts, the National Lottery and local authority arts funding organisations will give serious consideration to ways in which they might support this unique facet of English musical life.

2.   Cathedrals and their musicians deserve much praise, encouragement and continued support for their work. The report of the Archbishops' Commission on Church Music, *In Tune with Heaven*, (published in 1992) both recognised cathedrals' musical achievement and made a number of recommendations for strengthening it further. We do not think it appropriate to repeat those recommendations here but we comment briefly on a number of points which struck us as significant as we visited cathedrals.

Resources

3.   The size of a cathedral and its acoustic characteristics will determine what size of choir is appropriate. As also mentioned in Chapter 3, paragraph 20, a professional octet of singers could be used in some cathedrals. Authenticity of performance, however, has some importance and a choir consisting of some sixteen or so treble/soprano voices and at least two each of alto, tenor and bass is likely to produce a sound which is more fitting to the standard cathedral choral repertoire. The training and direction of the choir will be in the hands of the director of music; he or she will have an assistant, whose main task will be that of accompanying the services.

51

4. English cathedral organs are, in general, of considerable importance both musically and historically. Maintenance and repair are very costly and, here again, cathedrals deserve praise for the way in which they have made sure that these instruments are preserved for future generations. When rebuilding is necessary the best advice both local and national should be sought.

5. Many cathedrals call on a group of orchestral players to accompany the cathedral choir from time to time. There is considerable scope for the use of instruments other than the organ in cathedral worship (cf. *In Tune with Heaven,* Recommendation 41).

6. It is important that the library of printed and manuscript music should be efficiently catalogued, well cared for, and appropriately housed.

Choirs

7. There continues to be much discussion about the provision of cathedral chorister education for girls. Those opposed to opening choirs to girls argue that the sound of girls' voices is different and that the authenticity of performance demands that boys' voices should be used. Furthermore, it is claimed that, when girls join choirs, boys tend to leave and that, if two choirs are used, there will not be enough for either the boys or the girls to do; funding for two choirs would also be difficult or impossible. It is our belief that the musical arguments are not strong. The evidence is tending to show that there is not a vast amount of difference between the sound made by boys' and girls' choirs: it appears that the training of the voices is the critical element in the sound made by a choir of children. Even if the girls' sound was completely different, this would not preclude it as a vehicle for worshipping God. The authenticity argument is one which could be applied to many areas of cathedral music: organ wind pressure; vocal techniques; quality of vocal sound; pitch etc., and so there seems little reason to highlight this one particular area.

8. The social argument is one which does need careful consideration. The anecdotal evidence comes from the world of parish music where, in a mixed treble/soprano line, boys can become disenchanted with singing as they tend not to become the senior singers in a mixed choir – because girls can continue to sing after the time when a boy's voice changes. Evidence given to the Archbishops' Commission on Church Music, however, suggested strongly that it is possible to run a mixed parish choir, and its success depends on the skills of its director. We know of no plans to institute a cathedral choir which includes both boys and girls. Those cathedrals which have started providing chorister education for girls have done so on the Salisbury model which requires a boys' choir and a girls' choir, in

addition to the lay vicars (lay clerks). This has meant that the boy choristers sing six services each week and the girls sing three. The reduction in the boys' singing workload has meant that the children are less pressured, and they have more time for academic, cultural and sporting pursuits.

9.   While recognising that the subject of girls singing in cathedral choirs is an emotive one, nevertheless we hope that all cathedrals will give careful consideration to the possibility of providing chorister education for all children.

10.   Over the last fifty years or so there has been a significant decline in the number of children being presented for chorister voice trials. The reasons for this are varied: unwillingness to be committed to regular singing, particularly at weekends; the national decline in boarding, particularly at an early age; greater sporting and recreational possibilities; the perceived decline in primary school singing teaching; the lack of good parish choirs from which to recruit cathedral choristers. Along with all these problems, however, has gone a marked improvement in musical standards so that, while greater numbers of applicants would be desirable, it must be recognised that their lack has not led to a musical problem in cathedrals.

11.   Twenty-five cathedrals have choir schools at which their choristers are educated. (No cathedral has a school which educates choristers only.) Of these schools 23 are independent and two (Peterborough and Southwell) are in the maintained sector. For some choristers at independent schools there is no charge at all; on average, parents pay less than half fees. The Choir Schools Bursary Trust, run by the Choir Schools' Association, helps parents who have problems in finding sufficient money to pay for chorister school fees. The Bursary Trust receives an annual grant from the government under the provisions of the Music and Ballet Scheme (cf. Chapter 3, paragraph 17(a)).

12.   Those cathedrals without choir schools recruit choristers from a variety of schools in the locality. This puts an added burden on the organist /director of music, who has to be proactive in recruitment and, because his or her choristers are all volunteers, has to make sure that the interest, enthusiasm and commitment of the children and their parents are maintained. In both types of system, the choir is a tightly knit social organisation which at its best involves children and their parents in the wider life of the cathedral.

13.   Recruitment of lay clerks (songmen, lay vicars, etc.) is becoming a serious problem. The newer cathedrals tend to operate a system whereby the men are amateur volunteers; in the older cathedrals, the singing men are part-time salaried employees. The recruitment and training of amateur volunteers lays a considerable burden on those cathedral directors of

music who operate within that system. They are warmly commended for their work.

14.   There are various problems connected with the employment of adult singers: the work is part-time and does not pay a living wage; with the present employment situation it can be difficult for men to find suitable other employment; fewer men are prepared to make the commitment to sing on such a regular basis, particularly at weekends; there can also be a perception that a lay clerkship can be combined with a career as a professional concert or session singer. In London this is sometimes possible, but demands from cathedral choirs make this sort of combination difficult outside the large metropolitan areas.

15.   Where institutions of higher education are near the cathedral, there is the possibility of developing a scheme of choral scholarships. This sort of scheme operates successfully in various places, but it needs to be realised that choral scholars are not cheap lay clerks. The point of using choral scholars is twofold: to fill the choir stalls with young men who might go on to be lay clerks elsewhere, and to be part of the cathedral's ministry of teaching in a specific department. Some cathedrals have extended the choral scholarship system to include recruits from overseas, and this is commended.

Music Department Management

16.   The policy concerning music will be determined partly by tradition and partly by the dean and chapter and their advisers. Although for many people it is the music which draws them to cathedral worship, it has to be stressed that music together with architecture and movement need to be perceived as integral parts of the liturgy. We therefore recommend that one member of the chapter should have executive line management responsibility for the liturgy (see Chapter 7, paragraphs 14 ff), and that he or she should be the member to whom the director of music specifically refers. It is important that the policy concerning liturgy and music should be agreed by all concerned, and that it should not be subject to various preferences of canons 'in residence'. One of the key liturgical tests of any cathedral service is that it sends people out inspired and uplifted, not frustrated by something which is irritatingly different from what they are used to in their local church.

17.   The liturgist (for the purposes of this chapter the canon/dean in charge of liturgy and music will be referred to as the liturgist) should ensure that the music of the services is of a high standard, that the repertoire should be representative of the best of English church music, and that it should incorporate music from European and other traditions. The

liturgist will be advised by the director of music on the specific choice of each piece of music. The development of a creative and mutually responsive relationship between liturgist and director is essential, and requires constant attention.

18.   In addition to his or her musical and liturgical activities, the liturgist should take an active pastoral interest in the members of the music department and their families. He or she should be the member of the chapter to whom they can turn for help and advice.

19.   The senior practical musician is the director of music. Titles differ from cathedral to cathedral – Master of the Choristers; Master of the Music; Cathedral Organist, etc., but the director is the man or woman responsible for training and directing the choir and instrumentalists. Traditionally this work has been done by an organist but, over the last forty years or so, there has been a considerable change in the role; whereas in the first half of this century the director of music played the organ for virtually all services and the choir looked after itself, current practice is for the director of music to conduct the choir and for the assistant to play the organ. Given that expertise as a keyboard executant is not foremost amongst the skills required to teach singing and to train a choir, we recommend that cathedrals consider carefully the roles of director of music and assistant organist – in order to utilise to the full the talents of those musicians who are not professional keyboard players but who might be expert choir directors (cf. *In Tune with Heaven,* Recommendation 39).

20.   The job specification of the director of music needs to be drawn up carefully, and the remuneration needs to be set at a level which will attract candidates of a high calibre. We recommend that his or her salary should be comparable to that of a residentiary canon. While it is undoubtedly true that the work of cathedral musicians benefits from musical experience outside the immediate cathedral work, it is important that musicians should not be forced into accepting extra musical engagements outside the cathedral merely to enhance their incomes.

21.   While parish churches should not seek to follow cathedral styles, cathedral musicians should be seen as a resource for the diocese: a role which will require particular skills in addition to those of a traditional cathedral director of music. This role will also require the expenditure of time and effort. One possibility may be to link the role of cathedral director, where appropriate, with that of an assistant director of music in the diocese. We commend those cathedrals whose musicians go out to hear and to contribute to music in the rest of the diocese, and we recommend that organists', singers' and directors' 'surgeries' should be a regular part of the musical life of the cathedral. Deans and chapters will need to take this

additional commitment into account when preparing a job specification and setting a salary.

22.   There are undoubtedly personnel and management problems of career structure in cathedral music. Directors are frequently appointed at an early age, and there is little sideways movement. This inevitably means that some musicians are in their posts for a very long time. Consideration should be given to the length of time of service specified in contracts of employment. There is some in-service training organised by the Cathedral Organists' Association but we suggest that more could be done. Directors and organists could be sent on courses in this country and abroad; assistants could be seconded to other cathedrals for a period; directors could exchange jobs with other directors for a period; outside experts could be brought in for training days. There should be a system of regular appraisal.

23.   Many cathedrals are making organ scholarships available. Holders of these posts are sometimes school leavers who have a free year before taking up a university or college place; sometimes they are post-graduate students who are gaining experience of the cathedral world. As with choral students (see paragraph 15 above) organ scholars should not be perceived as inexpensive second assistants; they should be part of the music department's teaching programme.

Recommendations

1.   Cathedrals should seek to provide chorister education for girls as well as boys (paragraphs 7-9).

2.   Where possible, a system of choral scholarships for altos, tenors and basses should be established (paragraph 15).

3.   One member of the chapter should be the liturgist, in charge of worship (paragraph 16).

4.   Careful consideration should be given both to the role of director of music and to the musical and management expertise needed to perform the role (paragraphs 19 and 20).

5.   Cathedral musicians should be adequately and appropriately remunerated (paragraph 20).

6.   The musical resources of the cathedral should be seen as a resource also for the rest of the diocese (paragraph 21).

7.   There should be regular appraisal of members of the music department and in-service training should be encouraged (paragraph 22).

6

The Governance of Cathedrals

Introduction

1.   Having looked at the role of cathedrals, their place in mission and education, and their music, we turn to consider how best they can be organised to meet the expectations upon them. We look first at the governance of cathedrals: at how the responsibilities for their overall direction are allocated and how those to whom they are allocated are held accountable. In the following chapters, we go into their internal management in all its various aspects.

Analysis of the Present Arrangements

2.   We have set out later in this Report an account of the historical background to the different types of Church of England cathedrals. The existing structure of governance of the cathedrals is a product of long history and local needs. Although there are common threads, and the 1963 Cathedrals Measure achieved much, each cathedral has its own particular statutes, character and organisation.

3.   It is right that arrangements should suit the needs of the particular situation. And justifiable differences in organisational structure can witness to a creative independence acting in the service of the local community and the wider Church.

4.   However, many of the organisational differences between cathedrals appear to have no contemporary justification. Long-standing organisational arrangements have in many cases ceased to meet contemporary needs. The legislative framework within which cathedrals operate is inflexible and discourages the adaptation required to accommodate the changing demands of Church and society. Their independence can cease to be a source of creative strength and instead result in an unacceptable gap between cathedral and bishop/diocese.

5.   Further, authority can come to be wielded without accountability. Structures and processes are complex and confusing. They place a good deal of authority in the hands of particular office holders, especially members of the chapter. They work as long as there is goodwill and trust

among those concerned. But when this breaks down, paralysis and embarrassment ensue. So the arrangements for governing cathedrals can come to absorb rather than release energy. Frustration and disillusion can result.

Principles

6.   In what follows we suggest a model framework on the basis of which the governance of our cathedrals could be restructured. In compiling it, we have had in mind the desirability of arrangements which are:

- supportive of achieving the desired roles and relationships for each cathedral, particularly in bridging any gap between the cathedral and the rest of the diocese;

- transparent, i.e. clear to all who is responsible, for what, to whom;

- effective, i.e. they enable cathedrals to fulfil their many roles in the most efficient way possible;

- accountable, i.e. those who are given responsibility not only have the necessary authority to discharge that responsibility but are answerable for their use of it;

- responsive to changing needs.

7.   In compiling this framework, we have tried to build on what is best in the existing arrangements (and we have seen much that is good) while avoiding existing deficiencies.

One basic framework

8.   As we have indicated in Chapter 2, paragraph 19, we see no need to perpetuate the present distinction within and between 'dean and chapter' and 'parish church' cathedrals. The distinction is justified only by the origins of the cathedrals concerned, not by any contemporary feature of their role. In practice, there are as many different types of cathedrals as there are cathedrals. So, as the table below shows, some dean and chapter cathedrals have a sizeable parochial responsibility while many parish church cathedrals have virtually none:

Selected Cathedrals: Parish Populations (October 1993)

Cathedral (Those marked * are parish church cathedrals)	The extent of the parish in terms of population	The percentage of the regular worshipping community which is drawn from the parish
Birmingham*	456	Negligible
Blackburn*	2,443	5-10%
Bradford*	354	10%
Chelmsford*	3,500	15%
Coventry*	10	Negligible
Derby *	72	Negligible
Leicester*	20	Negligible
Manchester	900	Negligible
Newcastle*	Non-residential	None
Portsmouth*	4,000	31%
Ripon	7,617	75%
St Albans	2,773	3%
St Edmundsbury*	250	Negligible
Sheffield*	637	Negligible
Southwark*	150	Negligible
Southwell*	5,500	95%
Truro	130	Negligible
Wakefield*	2,200	3%

9.   Instead we propose a single broad system of governance for all cathedrals, which can be flexibly adapted to suit local circumstances. The chief elements in this system are described below. We see them being embodied in a revised Cathedrals Measure, which would set out a framework of constitutional arrangements for all cathedrals, within which each cathedral would, subject to sensible checks and balances, both settle the detail to suit its own circumstances and more easily than at present amend that detail to reflect its changing needs. Guided, as we believe reform should be, by the desire to simplify and clarify existing organisation wherever possible, such a development would help both to make the arrangements for running cathedrals more easily understood by those inside and outside them, and to identify where responsibility and accountability for their operation rest.

10.   In the proposals which follow, we seek to take the best from the existing different types of cathedral structure and to work them into a single, broad, new arrangement. This does not involve parish church cathedrals becoming dean and chapter cathedrals, or vice versa, but rather the creation of a new uniform model of cathedral organisation. In keeping with that approach, we refer to both provost and dean in what follows by the single title 'dean', for we recommend that the title 'provost' should disappear and that in future the senior clergy member of the Administrative Chapter (see below) should be known in all cathedrals by the title 'dean'.

The Cathedral Greater Council

11.   Each cathedral should have a Greater Council (although this would not be the same as the council of an existing parish church cathedral). The role of the Council would be to reflect the different communities of interest which the cathedral exists to serve, and to be the body to whom the dean and chapter would account for their stewardship of the cathedral. The membership of the Council would accordingly embrace the various interests touched on by the cathedral (see paragraph 14 below). A secular analogy is with the Council of a university. It would be chaired ex officio by the diocesan bishop unless in exceptional circumstances he chose to delegate the task to another person, not being a member of the Administrative Chapter, appointed by him, in which event the bishop would remain a member of the Council. The Council would meet at least twice a year.

12.   Under the arrangements we envisage, the administration of the cathedral would be the work of a body we call hereafter the Administrative Chapter. (This would not have precisely the same composition as currently found in some dean and chapter cathedrals – see paragraph 17 below.) The Administrative Chapter would be legally responsible for the administration of the cathedral and its properties, but would be accountable to the Greater Council for the way it discharged those responsibilities. The specific functions of the Council would be to:

(a)   approve statutes relating to the cathedral within the constitution established under a revised Cathedrals Measure (see paragraphs 41 ff below);

(b)   advise on the long-term policy of the cathedral (see below);

(c)   receive the annual budget plan;

(d)   approve the annual report and accounts of the cathedral (which should be published);

(e)   call for reports from the Administrative Chapter on any matter concerning the cathedral;

(f)   have the right to petition the bishop for the removal of the dean or any member of the chapter.

As regards (b) above, the Council's task would be to advise on the dean and chapter's proposals for the overall direction and mission of the cathedral. It would not be for the Council to get involved in the detail of the preparation and execution of policy proposals, which remain the responsibility of the dean and chapter. So, for example, the Administrative Chapter would be expected to seek the Council's views on proposals, say, for a substantial financial appeal or for articulating the cathedral's role in the mission of the diocese. The Council would consider the proposals and give the Chapter its advice on them. But it would be for the Chapter to finalise and to execute them. A major task of the Council would be to ensure that the plans and objectives of the cathedral and the diocese complement and support one another. It would not be the Council's purpose to second-guess the dean and chapter in the running of the cathedral, but rather to advise and support them in carrying through their policies for the overall mission and direction of the cathedral.

13.   The bishop (as chairman) and the dean would consult about the preparation of the agenda for meetings of the Council, and any other matters to do with the Council's operation. In exercising its right of petition under paragraph 12(f), a majority of two-thirds of the members of the Council (excluding the dean and chapter) would be required.

14.   The members of the Administrative Chapter (up to a maximum of, say, five) would be members ex officio of the Council. Other members might include representatives of:

–   the cathedral community, elected thereby;

–   the College of Canons, elected from among themselves;

–   the wider diocese (these should include representatives of the rural deans, parish clergy and laity, appointed by but not necessarily themselves members of the Bishop's Council); and

–   the local community, appointed by the bishop after consultation with the dean and the administrative chapter.

In addition, there should be room for the bishop to appoint, after consultation with the dean and the administrative chapter, up to two independent members to meet the particular needs of his cathedral. Where appropriate, the regional, national or international dimension would be served by up to two additional people, appointed again by the bishop after consultation with the dean and the administrative chapter. It would also be open to the Council to invite others to attend its meetings as its business required. Members of the Council would clearly be expected to be supportive of the aims of the cathedral and would normally be communicant Anglicans. This should not, however, be an absolute requirement as, in appointing independent members or representatives of the local community or the wider national dimension of the cathedral, we hope that both bishop and dean and chapter will have in mind the desirability of appointing some member or members who could also reflect the interest of other Christian Churches in the cathedral and its ecumenical role.

15.   The precise composition of the Council would fall to be determined in the circumstances of each cathedral, although we would expect it to reflect the categories set out in the preceding paragraph. Some of its members would become members by election, others by appointment by the bishop after consultation with the dean and the administrative chapter. Members would be elected or appointed for overlapping terms of from three to five years so as to ensure continuity. Terms would be renewable for up to two additional periods after the initial election or appointment (i.e. no one, other than the ex officio members, should serve for more than a maximum of three terms). We do not think it sensible to lay down a precise number of Council members for every cathedral because the circumstances of individual cathedrals vary. But total Council membership should not exceed, say, twenty-five or so. We offer in the Annex to this chapter an illustration of what we have in mind.

The College of Canons

16.   Under the arrangements we envisage, the present Greater Chapter (to be called the College of Canons) would be a college of residentiary and non-residentiary canons, lay as well as ordained. Ordained honorary canons would relinquish their canonries, although not their emeritus title, on ceasing to be beneficed or licensed in the diocese: lay canons would be appointed for a term (renewable at the discretion of the diocesan bishop) and would normally be members of the Church of England or of a Church in communion with it, or be otherwise qualified under the Church of England (Ecumenical Relations) Measure 1986. The College of Canons' formal role in the government of the cathedral would be limited to the election of two of its members to the Greater Council and it would retain the former Greater Chapter's, now purely honorific, role in the election of the diocesan bishop. In practice it would have two main functions. The first would be to provide a two-way link through its members with the parishes in the diocese and with the wider community, although its

members might also be given specific tasks e.g. as chaplain to cathedral visitors. This latter question would be for local decision, as would whether its members were given any liturgical task in the cathedral. Secondly, it would provide a forum in which the dean and the administrative chapter could, as appropriate, seek the views of an experienced body of clergy and lay people on matters affecting the cathedral.

The Administrative Chapter

17. We recommend that every cathedral should appoint a suitably qualified administrator who would be a member of the Administrative Chapter, be expected to play an appropriate part in the spiritual life of the foundation and, together with the dean and residentiary canons, make up the Chapter's executive group. They would be joined by up to three independent members (who could be lay or clergy although at least one should be lay) appointed by the bishop after consultation with the Greater Council and with the consent of the dean. They would be full members, normally appointed for a period of three years (which could be renewed for no more than two additional terms), and would be there to bring additional expertise and an external perspective to the Administrative Chapter's deliberations. It would be for the Council, through its power in relation to the cathedral's statutes (see below), to approve the size and make-up of the Administrative Chapter depending on the particular circumstances. In former parish church cathedrals, for example, the Council might decide that some or all of the independent members should come from those elected at the cathedral AGM (see paragraph 24 below). In the exercise of this power by the Council, and of his power of appointment by the bishop, care would need to be taken to ensure that the Chapter was limited to a size which would ensure effective decision making; that a balance between inside and outside interests was secured (so that it was not dominated by the latter); and that the breadth of traditions within the Church was reflected in its membership.

18. The Administrative Chapter would carry legal responsibility for the ownership and administration of the cathedral and its properties, would hold and have authority to affix the cathedral seal to documents, and would be seen as exercising those responsibilities in a position of trust for the benefit of the Church as a whole. It would be responsible to the Greater Council for proposing and executing the overall policy and direction of the cathedral and for ensuring arrangements for its proper management and administration. The Chapter's members would share responsibility for the spiritual life of the cathedral. The Chapter's management duties are spelled out more fully in the next chapter on Management. It would meet approximately monthly, although its executive members might well meet more frequently.

19.   The members of the Administrative Chapter would be accountable to the Greater Council for the discharge of their responsibilities. They would report at least annually to the Council, and the members of the Council would have the right to petition the bishop for their removal from office if for any reason they failed in their responsibilities (see paragraph 12(f) above and Chapter 8, paragraph 30).

The Dean

20.   The dean would be the chairman of the Administrative Chapter and a member of the Greater Council. In lay terms, he would be the 'executive chairman'. We very much hope that he would continue to be a member of the bishop's staff meeting, and that he would give that membership high priority.

21.   As chairman of the Administrative Chapter, the dean would have a casting vote. The Administrative Chapter would seek throughout, however, to work on a collegial basis. It is to be hoped that votes would rarely, if ever, be necessary. Where they were, however, the members of the Chapter would be bound by the collective decision.

The Residentiary Canons

22.   Together with the dean, the residentiary canons are at the heart of the spiritual life of the cathedral. They are expected to worship, to teach and preach, to pastor and to serve. In addition, they may have management tasks within the cathedral – their function in this context is spelled out in the next chapter on Management – and may have substantial diocesan responsibilities outside the cathedral. Provided that any diocesan responsibilities are not too substantial, we believe that two full-time canons or their full- or part-time equivalent is the irreducible minimum number of canons required to work with the dean and suitable lay or other ordained staff. This assessment is reflected in the present arrangements under which the Church Commissioners fund two canonries in each cathedral. How duties are allocated between canons is for local decision. Precisely how a cathedral is staffed is, we believe, also a matter for local decision, as is the extent to which the canons take on diocesan and extra-diocesan roles, although in principle we believe that it is sensible for everyone to have at least some duties which take him or her outside the cathedral. If a cathedral or diocese wants to appoint more than two full-time 'working' canons, or their full- or part-time equivalent, it should be for them (as now) to make the case for and finance these posts.

The Cathedral Community

23. We use this term to describe all those people who are actually involved with the cathedral, not only as regular or habitual worshippers but, for example, as guides, bell-ringers, stewards or in any other capacity, including as employees.

24. The cathedral community should meet annually to elect up to four representatives to the Greater Council of the cathedral, two of whom could, if so desired, be known as Cathedral Wardens. Those entitled to vote would be defined in terms of membership of a roll made up of those recognised as regular or habitual worshippers or who are otherwise regularly involved in the work of the cathedral.

25. The annual meeting would receive a report and financial accounts, as approved by the Greater Council, from the dean and relevant subordinate bodies, and those present would be able to ask questions on any matter concerning the cathedral. Cathedrals should in addition create a Cathedral Community Committee which would be involved in those matters which relate to the purely domestic activities of the cathedral (such as the pastoral care of its congregations, crèche and nursery, Sunday School and youth group provision). The elected members of this Committee would also be identified at the annual meeting. The dean should normally share the chairmanship of this Committee with an elected representative of the cathedral community.

Cathedrals and Parishes

26. The parochial responsibilities of cathedrals vary considerably and take a variety of forms. The parish church cathedrals have the usual territorial parish, and their parishioners and others on the church electoral roll of the parish have rights corresponding to those in any other parish (save that the powers of the Parochial Church Council will usually have been transferred to the Cathedral Council). However, as the table accompanying paragraph 8 makes plain, the actual number of resident parishioners may be very low indeed. Other cathedrals have parishes associated with them in a variety of ways; for example, a residentiary canon may be priest in charge of the parish which surrounds, or is near to, the cathedral, or which comprises only the area of the cathedral close, and this parish will have all the usual apparatus of churchwardens and PCC. On the other hand, a cathedral with no associated parish may nonetheless have a strong commitment to the local area in which it is situated; it may, for example, be a part of an ecumenical grouping of city-centre churches.

27. In some cathedrals, Southwell being the most obvious example, the parish is central to much of the cathedral's life and work. But in others,

however strong may be the cathedral's pastoral role in relation to its city or county, the formal parochial role has become more apparent than real. Where this is the case that role, and the formal legal arrangements for governance which go with it, should end. Where it is not, some adjustments will still be necessary in those arrangements to reflect other recommendations in this Report. At the same time, all cathedrals should be given a recognised place in the structure of synodical government, the annual meeting electing representatives to a deanery synod, which would complement the financial relationship between cathedral and Diocesan Board of Finance recommended in Chapter 13, paragraph 43.

The Diocesan Bishop

28.   The diocesan bishop would be ex officio chairman of the Greater Council, unless in exceptional circumstances (for example, where a visitation is in progress, see paragraph 30 below) he chose to delegate the task to another person (other than a member of the Administrative Chapter) appointed by him (in which event he would remain a member of the Council). He should be available to give advice informally to the dean on a regular basis, and should be consulted by the dean on strategy, policy, plans and major developments or other critical matters affecting the cathedral, and relations with the diocese or the wider community. The day-to-day responsibility for the running of the cathedral would, however, rest with the dean and the administrative chapter.

29.   The diocesan bishop should both be in a position and be prepared to counsel and advise on matters affecting the cathedral. Many if not most matters should be capable of resolution in this way. We have considered whether he should retain his existing formal powers of visitation. On the one hand, it can be argued that these may occasionally be valuable as a means of enabling either a comprehensive review of the functioning of the cathedral or a specific inquiry into a particular circumstance. On the other hand, the quasi-legal nature of the visitation process may be felt to impede the desirable relationship between bishop and dean and chapter, and it could be argued that the new arrangements which we propose (including the bishop's position as chairman of the Greater Council and the Council's power to call for reports on the running of the cathedral) overtake the need for a specific visitation power.

30.   While we hope that our proposals will lessen the possible need for visitations, on balance we believe that the power to visit should be retained. We are fortified in this view by the role which the bishop's visitorial powers have now assumed in relation to the enforcement of the Care of Cathedrals Measure 1990. The bishop should, however, be enabled to delegate the task of undertaking a visitation and, where he is

chairman of the Greater Council, he should so delegate in any case of dispute between the Council and the Administrative Chapter. We understand that a bishop can already delegate his power of visitation to his Chancellor, and we believe that he should do so whenever a visitation is carried out primarily for legal rather than pastoral reasons. In pastoral cases, the bishop should consider whether a review should be undertaken by himself assisted by others as appropriate or by a group (consisting, for example, of a bishop from another diocese, a dean and an appropriate professional person) which would report to him. Following such a review, its recommendations might be implemented informally by agreement or become the subject (with or without modification) of an episcopal charge.

Inspection Arrangements?

31.   One suggestion we have heard is for the creation of a regular system of inspection of cathedrals. Each cathedral would be inspected not less than once every ten years. Such inspections would look into all aspects of a cathedral's life and operation. They would be undertaken by members of an inspectorate bringing together people of different skills and experience relevant to the work of cathedrals. The inspectorate would also be available to offer informal advice at all times. Its formal reports would be made to the cathedral's Greater Council. Copies of the reports would go to a restructured Cathedrals Commission (see below) and to the Archbishop of the Province.

32.   We do not favour this proposal. There is a real risk that such an arrangement would become over-centralised and bureaucratic, and that cathedrals would see it as the task of the inspectorate to solve problems rather than tackling them themselves. Nevertheless, the idea of an identified body of people with different sorts of expertise on which cathedrals could draw is attractive. We believe that such an advisory function could well sit with a restructured Cathedrals Commission.

Continuing Central Responsibilities: A Cathedrals Commission

33.   The cathedrals have a number of agencies through which they can co-operate. These include the meetings of the Deans and Provosts' Conference and the Association of English Cathedrals, as well as a number of specialist bodies. There is, however, no single body carrying out central Church responsibilities in cathedral matters, and to which the cathedrals can relate. Some central responsibilities lie with the Church Commissioners, in respect of their financial support, and others with the Cathedral Statutes Commission. The latter has a strictly limited role and is concerned with the minutiae of cathedrals' constitutions and statutes; as we shall shortly indicate, the legal framework within which the

67

Commission operates should be substantially reformed and simplified, and in that process the Commission could be abolished.

34. We do, however, see a clear need in the revised arrangements which we are proposing for a Cathedrals Commission of modest size. This would provide a reference point in the central Church structures for cathedral matters; it would advise the Archbishops and bishops and the General Synod; it would keep under review developments in the governance and management of cathedrals and their finances, and advise the cathedrals accordingly; it would oversee the constitutional changes in cathedrals which would follow from the implementation of this Report; and it would exercise the limited continuing central responsibilities for cathedral constitutions which would survive from the present powers of the Cathedral Statutes Commission. We envisage a body which would be available to respond helpfully to developments, but one which would in no way duplicate the work of the existing voluntary bodies or that of the Cathedrals Fabric Commission for England.

The Legal Framework

35. As a corporate body, a cathedral needs some form of constitutional framework to provide it with a legal structure. Since the earliest days of the Church of England's cathedrals, this has taken the form of a separate set of statutes for each cathedral, and that approach has been upheld by successive reviews. It recognises that each cathedral has its own life and ethos, and that a certain degree of flexibility is essential if they are to be preserved and to develop in a way which is suited to local needs. However, there has been a gradual process of increasing central regulation and some degree of standardisation, reflecting the generally held view that cathedrals and their governance are not matters of purely internal or local concern but are of importance to the Church of England as a whole and, indeed, to the nation.

36. That process, so far as it has gone, culminated in the 1963 Cathedrals Measure, which requires certain basic provisions to be included in the constitution and statutes of every cathedral, while allowing a certain degree of flexibility in the way they are set out in detail. It also lists a number of other provisions which may be included, indicating their content in some detail. However, the 1963 Measure also gives a very large degree of freedom to add other provisions 'for the good government of the cathedral church'.

37. Constitutions and statutes can be changed, following a procedure set out principally in the Cathedrals Measure 1976. It involves local initiative, a role for a central church body (the Cathedral Statutes

Commission), the publication of a scheme with opportunity for representations, with the scheme being eventually laid before the General Synod and confirmed by the Privy Council. The procedure is similar to, but if anything more complicated than, some of those concerning parish churches operated under the Pastoral Measure 1983.

38.   The resulting position is unsatisfactory on a number of grounds. The fact that the legislation permits such a wide range of optional and additional material has resulted in constitutions and statutes which contain a mass of detail on minor matters. This tends to obscure the basic structure for the governance and management of the cathedral. Although most cathedral statutes make provision for bye-laws, little use is made of this power. The detailed nature of the material means that regular review and amendment are needed, but where cathedrals have tried to bring points of detail in their statutes up to date, they have found that the procedure, which is designed to deal with major matters, is protracted and time-consuming. It is also quite expensive, a typical scheme requiring upwards of £2,000-worth of the time of staff at Church House, Westminster in addition to significant local costs. The result is that most cathedrals' constitutions and statutes have not been updated since they were originally brought into line with the 1963 Measure and contain a large amount of out-of-date material on minor matters.

39.   The overall result seems to be that rather than go through the procedure under the 1976 Measure some cathedrals simply treat their statutes as a dead letter until problems arise in practice (as they can be expected to do if the basic legal requirements are not being followed). Thus the system which was meant to combine flexibility with a degree of central control is now, in practice, failing on both counts.

40.   Our recommendations as to the future governance of cathedrals will in any event require primary legislation replacing the 1963 and 1976 Measures, and the present constitutions and statutes will require wholesale amendment. The procedure adopted in 1963 – when the Cathedrals Measure legislated in an indirect way, by providing that certain matters had to (and others might) appear in every set of constitutions and statutes, after which every cathedral had a new constitution and statutes prepared and approved – would be time-consuming and expensive. A reforming Measure must be more direct in its method.

41.   A way forward would be to set out in a Schedule to the new Measure a standard constitution applying to every cathedral (perhaps capable, like the Church Representation Rules, of future amendment without the need for further primary legislation) within which statutes are to be made and amended by the appropriate body in the cathedral (the Greater Council)

with minimal central involvement for prescribed issues. In effect, much of what is now in the form of statutes, while still so described, would be amendable in much the same way as existing bye-laws are intended to operate; there seems no need for three distinct levels of legislation, and bye-laws as such would cease to exist.

42.   Inevitably, the statutes of every cathedral would have to be revised and it might be necessary to provide a uniform interim set of statutes under which the cathedral could operate from the coming into effect of the new Measure, the expectation being that each cathedral would amend the interim statutes so as to express local needs and traditions.

43.   The model constitution would need

(a)   to preserve the corporate body of the cathedral church and define its membership;

(b)   to provide for the offices of

visitor

dean

residentiary canon, whose number could be expressed as two or such greater number not exceeding six as might be fixed by statutes; and

administrator;

(c)   to provide for a Greater Council and its powers, and to provide a prescribed outline membership, details to be supplied in statutes;

(d)   to provide for an Administrative Chapter comprising

the dean as chairman

the canons

the administrator

up to three persons having no executive responsibilities in the cathedral church, appointed by the bishop after consultation with the Council and with the consent of the dean;

(e)   to provide for the administration of the cathedral church in its worship and mission and for the ownership and administration of its property and revenues to be in the hands of the Administrative Chapter, and to deal with the common seal and patronage rights vested in the Chapter;

(f) to provide for any committees required by statute, including the Fabric Advisory Committee (see Chapter 10, paragraph 10) and for the creation and role of a Finance and Investment Advisory Committee (see Chapter 7, paragraph 27), including its function in determining or advising on appropriate levels of remuneration, including clergy expenses and lay benefits;

(g) to provide for an annual meeting of the cathedral community, those entitled to vote being prescribed in statutes, and for the election of representatives to the Greater Council;

(h) to provide for a College of Canons (lay and ordained) and their appointment and tenure of office;

(i) to provide for the making of statutes by the Greater Council with the consent of the bishop. The new Cathedrals Commission would be empowered to advise Greater Councils on the making of statutes, and Councils would be under a duty to inform it of any which they made. Any statutes which fell outside the provisions of the model constitution would require the Commission's approval before they could be effective. Statutes could deal with various specified matters including the other offices in the cathedral and its services, and other matters required for the good government, peace and order of the cathedral church;

(j) to ensure appropriate interim or transitional arrangements.

44. We do not seek to diminish the national interest in the good governance of cathedrals, but the Privy Council's present involvement in the procedure for confirming cathedral constitutions and statutes entails delay and expense to Church and State. In view of this we recommend that the Privy Council's role in respect of cathedral constitutions and statutes should cease.

Cathedrals and the Creation of New Dioceses

45. An issue presented to us in evidence concerned the current legal requirements as regards cathedrals in the creation of new dioceses. The last occasion on which a new diocese was formed in England was 1927. There have of recent years been an increasing number of calls for more new dioceses to be created, rather than add to the proliferation of suffragan bishoprics which has occurred since the 1920s. (In 1930 there were 28 suffragan sees, in 1994 there are 66.) Legislative provision already exists (in the Dioceses Measure 1978) for the creation of new dioceses. We have received evidence from the Dioceses Commission, the body created by the 1978 Measure to vet proposals made under the provisions of that

legislation, drawing attention to one factor, relating to cathedrals, which is perceived by some as inhibiting proposals for new dioceses being brought forward. That factor is the expense and complexity which would, these days, be entailed in establishing a new cathedral as part of the proposals for a new diocese.

46. When the last group of new dioceses was formed, the present cathedrals legislation was not yet enacted; the provisions of the Cathedrals Measures 1931, 1934, 1963 and 1976 were not in force. The impression is current, whether justified or not, that the setting up of a cathedral in the late 1920s was a much simpler and less complicated matter than would now be the case. The existing parish church cathedrals largely evolved in a flexible way over a period of years after the diocese was founded. A typical example would be Chelmsford where 'the diocese was established in 1914 and Chelmsford Parish Church became Chelmsford Cathedral. But it was only in 1935 that the Rector and Sub-Dean became the Provost and that a Cathedral Council was actually established as a governing body. The first residentiary canon was not appointed until 1957.' Such a gradual and flexible evolution would be precluded by the 1978 legislation currently in force. The expense of providing stipend, housing and support for senior cathedral clergy would be entailed from the outset.

47. The suggestion is made that some arrangement by which a particular church might be designated as the cathedral for a new diocese, leaving fuller organisational provision to follow gradually as the new diocese became established, could be a more appropriate model than the assumption inherent in the Dioceses Measure 1978 that the fully developed cathedral establishments which have evolved since the 1920s would be created, ab initio, for any new dioceses.

48. We recognise that amending legislation would be required if the present provision were to be modified. We also recognise that the question of whether or not new dioceses should be created is a larger issue, outside the scope of our terms of reference, which has been addressed in the 1990 report of the Archbishops' Group on The Episcopate (*Episcopal Ministry* GS 944). We would, however, hope that any moves for the creation of new dioceses which won general support would not be hindered or inhibited merely because of the expense and complexity of establishing a fully-fledged cathedral from the outset. We would support any moves to amend legislation to allow a more gradual evolution of cathedral establishments, such as that which, in fact, was the case for cathedrals created in the late-nineteenth and early-twentieth centuries.

Recommendations

1. The distinction between 'dean and chapter' and 'parish church' cathedrals should be ended and a single broad system of governance for all cathedrals introduced, capable of flexible adaptation to suit local circumstances (paragraphs 8-9).

2. The senior clergy member of all Administrative Chapters should in future be known as the 'dean' (paragraph 10).

3. Each cathedral should have a Greater Council. This would be the body to which the dean and chapter would account for their stewardship of the cathedral. Its membership would embrace the various interests touched on by the cathedral (paragraphs 11-15).

4. The present Greater Chapter should become a College of Canons, residentiary and non-residentiary, lay as well as ordained (paragraph 16).

5. The Administrative Chapter would be legally responsible for the administration of the cathedral and its properties (paragraph 12). In addition to the dean and residentiary canons its membership should include an administrator and up to three independent members (of whom at least one should be lay) (paragraphs 17-19).

6. The dean should be executive chairman of the Administrative Chapter (paragraphs 20-21).

7. Precisely how a cathedral is staffed is for local decision but two is the minimum number of full-time residentiary canons or their equivalent required to work with the dean and suitable lay or other ordained staff in running a cathedral (paragraph 22).

8. The cathedral community should meet annually to elect up to four representatives to the Greater Council, as well as the members of a Cathedral Community Committee which would be involved in the purely domestic activities of the cathedral (paragraphs 23-25).

9. Where the parish is no longer central to a cathedral's work, the formal parochial status of the cathedral should be ended. All cathedrals should be given a recognised place in the structure of synodical government (paragraph 27).

10. Other than in exceptional circumstances, the diocesan bishop should chair the Greater Council. He should be prepared to advise on matters affecting the cathedral. The bishop's right of visitation should be retained but may be delegated (paragraphs 28-30).

11. A Cathedrals Commission of modest size should subsume the functions of the Cathedral Statutes Commission, to which should be added certain other advisory duties (paragraph 34).

12. There should be a simplified and streamlined system for approving and amending the constitutions and statutes of cathedrals, embodied in a revised Cathedrals Measure. The Privy Council's role in the present procedure should cease (paragraphs 35-44).

13. The Dioceses Measure 1978 should be amended to allow a more gradual evolution of cathedral establishments in the event of the creation of new dioceses (paragraphs 45-48).

ANNEX

Illustrative Composition
of Cathedral Greater Council

Bishop	1
Dean and Administrative Chapter	up to 5
Cathedral Community	up to 4
College of Canons	2
Wider Diocese (appointed by the Bishop's Council)	up to 6
Local Community	up to 2
Regional/National/International Dimension	up to 2
Independent members	up to 2
Total	24

7

Management Structure and Process

Introduction

1.   To adapt the methods appropriate in the management of enterprises in the secular world to the conduct of ecclesiastical institutions is not, in itself, a secularising undertaking. Jesus, in several of his parables, spoke of good stewardship in terms of professional expertise; the materials of the Kingdom begin to be assembled among the men and women of the world.

2.   Cathedrals, which are sometimes large organisations, can only benefit by drawing upon current management thinking in public, commercial and other sectors. In modern circumstances, they are increasingly professionalised through their need to exercise good husbandry of their resources, and to accommodate practices and legislative provisions relating to such things as terms of employment, safety, and health. Regarded in this perspective, the visits which we made to the cathedrals of England indicated an uneven pattern of responsiveness by the cathedral authorities to existing management techniques and structures. In some places, there had been an impressive openness to change, and a recognition that complicated organisations require clear and well-defined structures and processes: many of the suggestions which we would wish to make are already in place there. In some other cathedrals, however – and they are not necessarily the smaller ones – management styles are under-developed or even inappropriate to the ends sought.

3.   Cathedrals make use of both clergy and lay staff, paid and volunteer. Their internal balance of management has to be extremely sensitive to spiritual and vocational priorities as well as to sound financial and per-sonnel considerations. Viewed as ministry, the function of lay expertise in the management of cathedrals will be at its most effective, and so better serve the purpose of Christ's Kingdom, when the professional skills deployed are both of the highest quality and used in the most efficient manner – according to a scale of excellence which the secular world of business and enterprise would recognise. It is, indeed, one of the most encouraging features of present developments that lay service in cathedrals provides a clear example of lay ministry, while at the same time it releases the clergy to attend to the historic purposes of worship,

evangelism, teaching and so forth. Precisely because, in a Christian institution, the human relationships of those who work in it are so important, getting the right management structure becomes not an adjunct to the function of the cathedral, but something very near to its essential purpose.

4.   Over recent years many cathedrals have successfully adapted their methods in order to make better use of resources. It has been a time of development even for the smaller foundations. For example: market rents are levied on capitular properties; trading activities are made more profitable; internal management is improved; educational provision is enhanced; and tourist income and facilities expanded. There is, nevertheless, room for further improvement in virtually all cathedrals in at least some aspects of their managerial operation. In some there might be more attention to the provisions for management itself, or to more managerial expertise, or greater willingness to learn from good practice elsewhere (including other cathedrals). With the reduction in the Church Commissioners' grants, the falling yield from investments, and the finely balanced state of most of the cathedrals' finances, the case for a close reconsideration, by each cathedral, of more efficient and effective use of resources is incontrovertible.

5.   Each of the cathedral foundations is different and is staffed by men and women of different gifts, confronted with local circumstances: structures of management accordingly need to show some differences in adaptation to circumstance. However, certain basic principles and guidelines still apply, and the suggestions which follow illustrate how these can be applied everywhere.

Management Structure

THE ADMINISTRATIVE CHAPTER

6.   It is of the greatest importance that the management arrangements of a cathedral are precise and clear, and that they can be seen to be such by all who work there. The consequence of incoherence is simply division and personal unhappiness, even in those whose sense of dedication and service is of the highest order. To that end, the responsibility and accountability for each function within the cathedral should be known.

7.   The Administrative Chapter, which is itself accountable to the Greater Council, has responsibility for the affairs of the cathedral, and its members should properly see themselves as the ecclesiastical equivalent of a board of directors. They are collectively responsible for the overall policy concerning the management and administration of the cathedral and for superintending its execution. Decisions made by the Chapter are col-

lective decisions and once taken, whether unanimously or not, they must be supported by all its members.

8.   In their responsibility for the cathedral the Chapter should:

(a)   propose policy on which the advice of the Greater Council would be sought;

(b)   determine plans and budgets within that policy;

(c)   define a management structure and responsibilities for the execution of policies, plans and other decisions;

(d)   appoint senior management and key advisers;

(e)   establish personnel policies and oversee their practice;

(f)   set the authority limits within which delegation can take place;

(g)   monitor performance and general developments in society and the economy of the nation;

(h)   initiate policy changes to meet unanticipated events;

(i)   resolve conflicts between functions;

(j)   prepare an annual report and audited accounts for approval by the Greater Council;

(k)   undertake other functions under the statutes and provide reports requested by the Greater Council.

9.   The Chapter may also decide to reserve specific matters to itself – decisions of principle, for example, concerning the use of the cathedral.

THE DEAN

10.   The position of the dean should be unambiguous as the head of the management structure of the cathedral. In some of the existing cathedral statutes, the dean is described as 'primus inter pares'; others are silent on the matter. We are clear that the dean should have sufficient authority to be able to exercise effective leadership, should if present always occupy the chair of the Chapter and, to avoid deadlock, should have an additional casting vote. The dean moreover, from the chair, embodies the collective view of the Chapter and should thus, subject to sensible safeguards, interpret Chapter policy in relation to particular matters which may arise. When it is not in session, it is the dean who has day-to-day responsibility for executing the decisions of the Chapter and managing the cathedral's operations. He or she is, in lay terms, the 'executive chairman', and should have authority to deal with any emergencies.

11. As such, the dean should delegate much of this day-to-day management responsibility (in accordance with the management structure agreed by the Chapter) to the lay administrator, as chief operating officer, and to those canons with executive line responsibility (see paragraphs 14 to 20 below) for specified departments or functions. Delegation is reciprocal: delegation downwards of responsibility, and accountability upwards for the results.

12. If the dean has to be absent for significant periods (through illness, for example), he or she should name a deputy to act during his or her absence: either a canon or the administrator. This provision should be regarded as totally unrelated to any rotation of canons 'in residence' – whose duties are more analogous to those of a 'duty officer' than to an executive head. The nomination of a deputy does not affect the dean's position in the chair of the Chapter, nor does it relieve the dean, even temporarily, of ultimate responsibility for the cathedral.

13. The dean will be, ex officio, a member of the Greater Council which the bishop would normally chair. However, in addition to that formal link, the dean should have such a relationship with the bishop that informal advice is sought over cathedral affairs and that there should be mutual consultations on critical matters touching the policy and life of the cathedral and Chapter.

RESIDENTIARY CANONS

14. Residentiary canons are members of the Chapter and bound by its decisions: they are accountable both for the decisions of the Chapter as a whole and for any delegated functions for which an individual has responsibility. The nature of a canon's responsibility for functions can vary, although there are clearly two categories under which it may be represented. A canon may have what in secular terms would be called executive line management responsibility, or, alternatively, the canon may be an adviser with essentially oversight responsibility – executive line responsibility in this second case rests with another, usually the administrator. Oversight responsibility involves an advisory, counselling and representational role to support the management of the department involved; an executive line management responsibility, on the other hand, additionally carries full accountability for the department and responsibility for decision taking, and the issue of instructions after consultation. A canon precentor, for example, will usually have executive line management responsibility for liturgical and musical matters, with the director of music or organist reporting to him or her. The canon custos, in contrast, may have oversight responsibility for the care of the fabric (possibly including chairing an internal maintenance committee) while the clerk of works reports directly to the administrator.

15. The title or terms of appointment may imply a responsibility which is not precisely defined and a canon may, for historical reasons, bear a title for which either there are or he or she has been given no management responsibilities. In such circumstances, in order to clarify the actual arrangements for management of the cathedral, this is a practice which might in future be abandoned. The management responsibilities of canons should not, anyway, be regarded as immutable: the Chapter should be in a position to change responsibilities among its members as available personnel change and as needs develop.

16. We would not wish to prescribe in detail for every cathedral on these matters as circumstances and resources vary, but we do believe that a canon should be given executive line management responsibility only if the person concerned has the time to provide effective leadership, possesses the appropriate expertise in the area concerned, and is ready to accept responsibility for the designated function and its results. If these conditions cannot be met, then the canon concerned should be an adviser with an oversight role (the administrator or another having executive responsibility), or should receive no managerial responsibility. The Chapter should state clearly who has executive responsibility for each function and who, if any, has oversight responsibility – and should ensure that all who work in the area of the cathedral's operation involved are acquainted with the management arrangements.

17. It should also be possible for particular residentiary canons to be free of administrative responsibilities within the cathedral so that they can hold diocesan or national positions or attend to other duties for which ordained clergy are required. Decisions here will plainly depend upon local needs and resources.

18. Furthermore, just as we distinguish the 'canon in residence' role from any encroachment on the dean's authority (see paragraph 12 above), so too do we distinguish the 'in residence' role from any delegated responsibility (executive or oversight) for particular functions to the administrator, individual canons or others. Executive (or oversight) authority should not therefore rotate with 'residence'; it should remain with the relevant member of the Chapter as determined by the Chapter.

LAY ADMINISTRATOR

19. Many cathedrals, in recognition of the increasing complexity of their operations, have appointed senior lay administrators known variously as the administrator, receiver general, chapter clerk, etc. but referred to here as the administrator. Some are former officers retired from the military service; other appointments are made of people with senior management

experience in business. We believe that the efficient and effective management of a cathedral and its many activities, some of a commercial nature, now justifies the appointment of a senior lay administrator in all cathedrals. Defining the responsibilities, the recruitment of candidates with appropriate managerial skills and experience, and determining the remuneration of this post are of the greatest importance. Recommendations in relation to those matters are made in Chapter 9.

20.   The position of the administrator is such that the person who is appointed should have the same status as a residentiary canon and be a full voting member of the Chapter participating in all the Chapter's deliberations and activities (including worship).

HEADS OF DEPARTMENT

21.   Each of the functions fulfilled within the cathedral should be headed by a suitably qualified and experienced person who should be responsible for implementing the policies, plans and budgets determined for the department concerned by the Chapter. Each head of department should report to the member of the Chapter who has been designated with executive line responsibility for the particular function of the department. Each head of department, ordained or lay, should be responsible for the staff, both salaried and volunteer, in the department. Where the departmental head also happens to be the senior professional in his or her field working in the cathedral, he or she should normally also advise the Chapter generally on matters of his or her professional expertise, and should similarly advise other heads of department where the head concerned has executive line responsibility.

PROFESSIONAL ADVISERS

22.   Every professional adviser to the cathedral – for example, architect and lawyer – should have the right of access to the dean and chapter on matters concerning the areas of their professional expertise. However, for the purposes of managerial efficiency and clarity, each professional adviser should be responsible to a specified member of the Chapter. Written terms of reference should be approved by the Chapter.

23.   Experience has shown that it is vital that the working relationships and lines of communication between each professional adviser and the cathedral's staff with whom they work are wholly clear in every respect. Particularly is this the case if the Chapter wishes the adviser to fulfil an executive role when it is imperative that the terms of reference, limits of authority, chain of command, obligation to 'consult and inform', and accountability are unambiguous and understood by all concerned.

LAY PAID STAFF AND VOLUNTEERS

24. Lay paid staff and volunteers are vital to cathedrals, and during our cathedral visits we were deeply impressed by their dedication and service. But effective management, including their support, is essential, and this does not always happen. Our views and recommendations on this matter are set out in Chapter 9.

FINANCIAL MANAGEMENT

25. Good financial management sustains all the practical activities of a cathedral. The administrator should have direct executive responsibility for finance except where there is a canon with appropriate experience and the time and willingness to act. The head of finance should be a qualified accountant (unless the administrator is himself or herself a qualified accountant), with the duty of attendance at all Chapter meetings at which finances are to be discussed. In smaller cathedrals, where it is not possible to make a full-time appointment as head of finance, a part-time appointment should be made or a suitable firm of accountants employed.

26. Section 7 of the Cathedrals Measure 1963 permits (but does not require) a Chapter to appoint a committee with delegated powers to administer the finances and property of a cathedral. While few have followed the Measure to the letter, some have formed Finance and Property (or similarly named) committees comprising members of the Chapter and others, including independent external specialist advisers, to help with investment policy, budgets, and financial, investment and property management generally. These committees are sometimes chaired by the dean, sometimes by the canon treasurer, and sometimes by the administrator, and usually meet monthly: they are executive sub-committees of the Chapter. It has been the experience of those cathedrals which have these arrangements that they work well, and we seek to encourage the practice.

27. We also believe, however, that each cathedral should additionally have a Finance and Investment Advisory Committee (FIAC) of completely independent lay specialists – charged with commenting to the Chapter, and advising it upon its overall investment and financial management. Lay members of the FIAC should not provide paid services to the cathedral. The Committee should normally meet quarterly and appropriate members of the Chapter would usually be expected to attend. The FIAC could also have a role in establishing appropriate levels of remuneration (including benefits) paid by the cathedral.

28. The Cathedrals Measure 1963 requires the written advice, consent or confirmation of the Church Commissioners in respect of various actions concerning the disposal or acquisition of capitular land and invest-

ments (sections 20-25). We are advised that these provisions are not closely followed and that when they are they are sometimes found to be cumbersome. If the Measure could be amended so that, instead of the Church Commissioners, the FIAC should be required to ensure that proper advice is taken in respect of investment decisions, we believe that a more effective and less cumbersome scheme of supervision could result.

Associated Matters

IMPLEMENTING THE ORGANISATION STRUCTURE

29.   Most cathedrals would benefit from some changes in their management structure: in some cases radical changes are needed, in others relatively minor adjustments only may be necessary. We recommend that each cathedral should review its structure, following the principles indicated here. This review should be guided by those experienced in management, lay volunteers or professional consultants, and there should be full discussion and consultation with each department.

30.   The new management structure will need to be fully explained to all staff, and it must be rigorously followed in practice. Senior members should resist the temptation to bypass their subordinates, and they should avoid allowing any direct access by those who ought ordinarily to go first to other members of staff. However, cathedrals, above all, are places where God's service is done, and the atmosphere in which a management structure operates needs to reflect this. There is no place in God's house for a bureaucratic mentality and most cathedrals would benefit from more informal contact between members of the Chapter and the staff. Relationships must be at the personal level in all circumstances and communication is always improved by 'walking the floor'.

31.   Management structures should be kept under constant review and changes considered periodically and whenever a new dean, canon or administrator is appointed.

ACCOUNTING AND FINANCIAL PLANNING AND CONTROL

32.   The Cathedrals Measure 1963, which requires each cathedral to prepare audited accounts of its capitular funds, is silent on the basis on which those accounts should be prepared. The accounting bases employed differ widely from cathedral to cathedral and do not, in many cases, comply with best current professional accounting practice. As a result, some cathedral accounts may be in danger of not showing a true and fair view. Furthermore, the Measure only requires capitular funds to be included although, as the financial survey (see Chapter 13) reveals, non-

capitular trust funds held for the benefit of cathedrals account overall for 16% of aggregate net assets and 20% of aggregate income and expenditure. Without the inclusion of those trust funds, an incomplete picture of cathedral finances would be portrayed. The financial accounts are an important part of exercising improved accountability and should be the basis of the management accounts needed for effective financial planning and control and for inter-cathedral comparisons.

33.   We recommend, therefore, that cathedral accounts should show a true and fair view and be based upon best current professional accounting practice, that they should be audited in accordance with such practice, and that the audited accounts should incorporate, in an appropriate manner, information on non-capitular trust and other funds held for the benefit of the cathedral.

34.   We have recommended that accounting guidance on the preparation of cathedral accounts should be developed under the aegis of the Association of English Cathedrals (AEC) and that all cathedrals should follow this guidance. This is already in hand, financed by charitable trusts associated with and supported by the Institute of Chartered Accountants in England and Wales. We further recommend that cathedral accounts should also be published to the diocese and made available to the general public. It was a matter of frequent unfavourable comment by those who met us during our visits to cathedrals that accounts did not seem to be available. They are in fact required to be published and are supplied to the Church Commissioners under the terms of the Cathedrals Measure 1963, but the Measure is silent on what form publication should take. The Church Commissioners can hardly be considered an accessible source for most people, and steps should be taken by each cathedral to see that their accounts are more widely available locally. We also recommend that cathedral accounts are filed regularly with the new Cathedrals Commission (see Chapter 6, paragraphs 33 and 34).

35.   Most cathedrals prepare monthly management accounts comparing actual expenditure and income with budget. Some are produced only quarterly but, to ensure proper budgetary control, all but the smallest cathedrals should produce management accounts monthly. There should also be an annual long-term financial projection, looking three to five years ahead and forecasting trends of expenditure and income so that a potential deficit can be recognised and necessary steps taken.

DIRECT LABOUR ORGANISATIONS

36.   A number of cathedrals employ direct labour groups – stonemasons and other craftsmen, for example – some of whom work exclusively for the

cathedral and some also for outside bodies. Some cathedrals, however, have hived off a direct labour group into a separate company. Such groups raise real problems of cost-effective management, and we strongly recommend that all cathedrals employing direct labour groups should examine their management arrangements and ensure that customer-supplier relationships are properly defined and controlled.

TOURISM AND TRADING ACTIVITIES

37.   Our visits to cathedrals, supported by analysis of cathedral accounts, confirm the importance of (but showed the extent of the major variations in the effectiveness with which cathedrals manage) their tourism and their shops, catering and other trading activities. Detailed consideration of these activities is set out in Chapters 11 and 12 on trading and tourism.

INFORMATION TECHNOLOGY

38.   Some cathedrals now make extensive use of information technology (IT), such as word processing, accounts and diary maintenance. Personal computers are inexpensive and their benefits considerable; training in their use is readily available, as are personnel with the necessary skills. All cathedrals should make use of IT and we expect that those cathedrals with the greater skills and experience would want to help others gain the maximum benefits.

COLLABORATION AND EXCHANGE OF INFORMATION

39.   There is some exchange of information between cathedrals, which occurs at meetings of the Deans and Provosts' Conference and of the AEC and in the large number of special interest groups, such as the Pilgrims' Association, the Cathedrals' Finance Conference and cathedral vergers. This exchange is in the nature of things, however, rather episodic, and not all of the groups are used by the cathedrals for this purpose. There needs to be some provision for a routine exchange to help cathedral authorities to identify good practices, to avoid duplication, to share problems, and to establish benchmarks of performance. There is also a strong case for cathedrals to be able to speak with one voice when the need arises, and especially when dealing with secular bodies.

40.   We therefore recommend that the AEC should formally foster greater exchange of information and collaboration between cathedrals, including matters such as tourism, shops, catering, education, finance and IT. Already they have circulated among themselves detailed financial data, obtained from our enquiries, which provides information about the financial performance of cathedrals and bases of comparability. Other

topics for improved collaboration and exchange of information have been identified throughout this Report, for example, in the chapters on education, trading and tourism. The AEC should also play a wider representational role on behalf of cathedrals generally.

41. Improved collaboration (e.g. in purchasing, IT and training) and exchange of information (e.g. financial performance, best selling lines, terms negotiated with franchisees) will only come about if groups of interested individuals are tasked to do so and given the necessary support. This requires either the creation of ad hoc groups or enlisting the support of existing bodies. A number of such bodies exist, for example, the Pilgrims' Association, the Cathedrals' Finance Conference, the Church Shops Association. Some have interests outside cathedrals; some do not see themselves yet fulfilling such an active role. None has yet been asked by the AEC to do so. We believe that the AEC should, where possible and appropriate, formally make greater use of existing bodies to achieve the necessary increased collaboration and exchange of information. Where that proves not to be possible, then alternative arrangements should be made.

42. In making those recommendations, we do so in conjunction with a wider recommendation that the AEC should consolidate and broaden its role as the body which represents the interests of cathedrals and through which appropriate collaboration and other joint initiatives (such as those illustrated above) can be pursued. We recognise that this will require the AEC to extend and modify its present objectives, constitution and mode of operation which have been appropriate for the initial phase of its existence. However, we believe firmly that the opportunities for and benefits of an enhanced role for the AEC now urgently justify such changes. Such changes would have the added advantage of enabling the AEC to rationalise the position and role of subsidiary bodies, such as the Cathedrals' Finance Conference and the Precentors' Conference, and to clarify their terms of reference, responsibilities and working relationships.

43. We recognise that there will be financial implications if the AEC undertakes this wider role, but we believe that the necessary finance should be found. We also believe that, in most cases, the additional funds required should be justified in terms of the benefits which will be gained.

Recommendations

1. The management arrangements of a cathedral should be precise and clear, and the responsibility and accountability for each function known (paragraph 6).

2. The dean, as 'executive chairman', should exercise effective leadership, should always occupy the chair of the Administrative Chapter, and should have an additional casting vote (paragraph 10).

3. Residentiary canons should have oversight responsibility, executive line management responsibility or be totally free of executive responsibility depending on their talents and the particular local circumstances (paragraphs 14-18).

4. A senior lay administrator should be appointed in all cathedrals and he or she should be a full participating and voting member of the Chapter (paragraphs 19 and 20).

5. Each head of department and professional adviser should be responsible to a specified member of the Chapter (paragraphs 21 and 22).

6. The head of finance should be a qualified accountant (paragraph 25).

7. A Finance and Property Committee and a Finance and Investment Advisory Committee should be appointed in every cathedral (paragraphs 26 and 27).

8. Clear-cut management structures should be established, fully explained to all staff and kept under constant review (paragraphs 29-31).

9. Cathedral accounts should show a true and fair view, be prepared and audited in accordance with best current practice, incorporate (in an appropriate manner) non-capitular trust and other funds held for the benefit of the cathedral, and be published (paragraphs 32-34).

10. Annual budgets, annual long-term financial projections and monthly management accounts should be produced (paragraph 35).

11. The AEC should extend its role and formally foster greater collaboration and exchange of information between cathedrals (paragraphs 39-42).

8

Cathedral Clergy:
Appointment and Terms of Service

Introduction

1.   Sound organisation can help a cathedral fulfil many of its roles but it is the quality of those who work in it which will ensure whether or not it does so effectively. Among the staff of the cathedral, the leadership and direction given by the dean and the other members of the administrative chapter are of especial importance. In this chapter, we look at the processes for appointing clergy to cathedral posts, at the basis on which they hold those posts, and at other aspects such as their training and development. In what follows we have tried to have regard to other studies, recently completed or in hand, on these matters, notably the report of the Working Party on Senior Church Appointments chaired by Sir William van Straubenzee (GS 1019) and the work of the Steering Group on Clergy Conditions of Service, chaired by Sir Timothy Hoare.

The Appointment of Deans and Residentiary Canons

2.   Earlier in this Report we have noted the artificiality of the distinction between 'dean and chapter' and 'parish church' cathedrals and have recommended the introduction of a single system of governance for all cathedrals (see Chapter 6, paragraphs 8-10). Similarly we believe that the processes for appointing the dean and residentiary canons of every cathedral should in future take, so far as possible, a common form. We take this view for several reasons, including the desirability of ensuring that the procedures for such important appointments are readily understood and because we believe it to be desirable that the body of cathedral clergy appointments is seen and dealt with as a whole.

3.   We note that the van Straubenzee Working Party reached a similar view. We also endorse the emphasis in the report of that Working Party on open and structured appointment processes which ensure effective consultation with interested parties before appointments are made. We hope that the Church will now move firmly to implement, if not the precise detail of the Working Party's proposals, then processes which at least meet these tests.

4.   Of course, the aim of a single, comprehensive appointment process cannot be carried through fully so long as the responsibility for appointing deans (of whom there are 28 in number) rests with the Crown and that for appointing provosts (of whom there are 14) rests with the appropriate diocesan bishop (as to 12) or independent trustees (as to 2). Responsibility for the appointment of residentiary canons is similarly split between the Crown (some 26 posts) and diocesan bishops (about 135 posts). As we can see advantage in a single point of oversight for the total process in making these appointments, we have considered whether to recommend the transfer of the Crown's appointing power to diocesan bishops, or indeed vice versa. We have also considered a middle course in which the Church would cede to the Crown its responsibility for the appointment of provosts, and the Crown would cede to the Church the appointment of canons. The present division of responsibilities reflects, however, the current balance in the relationship between the State and the established Church, and we hesitate to make a recommendation in isolation which could have implications for all the other appointing processes involving Church or State. Indeed, some may hold that such recommendations should be placed in the wider context of the established status of the Church of England and the form which that might in future take.

5.   Nevertheless, we would like to see the process leading up to the making of a recommendation as to a particular appointment being as uniform as possible. Like the van Straubenzee Working Party we see the common steps in that process being:

   (a)   a structured process of consultation leading to the drawing up of a job description for the post in question, and a description of the particular qualities, experience, etc. to be sought in the person to be appointed;

   (b)   making known that a vacancy has arisen, the receipt of suggestions as to potential appointees, and a search using the good offices of the Prime Minister's Appointments Secretary and the Archbishops' Appointments Secretary for the names of suitable candidates;

   (c)   sifting of the names received leading to a recommendation to the appropriate appointing person or body. The results of ministry development review or appraisal should be one input to that sifting process.

6.   We note that the Working Party on Senior Church Appointments recommended, in the case of the appointment of deans or provosts, the setting up of so-called appointing groups to act as a focus for the process which we have outlined. We believe that, in the case of appointments

made by a bishop, it should be for the bishop concerned to decide whether a group is set up precisely as envisaged in the van Straubenzee report or whether the principles and objectives set out in that report are best met in some other way. If each cathedral has a Greater Council as we recommend, the members of the Council should be consulted when the job description and person specification for a post are being drawn up, and they should be invited to offer names of potential appointees. Indeed, if, in any case, a bishop does decide to set up a small appointing group to assist him, the Council would be one obvious pool from which members of any such group might be drawn.

7.   As regards appointments by the Crown, we appreciate the difficulty of the Crown's prerogative in these matters being put into commission. In other words, if the Crown's right to appoint is to be real, it cannot cede the effective decision to an appointing group, however distinguished the members of that group may be. But we would hope to see as close an integration of the processes in the two types of appointment as possible. To that end, we recommend that the Church should seek to open discussions with the Crown about the prospects for the introduction of a single system of appointment to cathedral posts or, failing that, enhanced integration of the existing processes. Matters which might be considered in such discussions include the possibility that, where a bishop makes the appointment of a dean (formerly provost), the Crown should be given the opportunity to be represented or involved (through the Prime Minister's Appointments Secretary if appropriate) in the earlier stages of the appointment process. Conversely, where the Crown is making the appointment, Crown and Church would both benefit considerably if the Crown's representative would be willing to engage in a structured process of consultation (drawing in to that process the Archbishops' Appointments Secretary), and to share information with the Archbishops' Appointments Secretary and particularly with the relevant diocesan bishop as part of that process. What we are suggesting here is mutual openness within a confidential process, whether the final appointment be made by the Crown or by the diocesan bishop. We are glad to recognise the steps which the Crown has already taken in the direction of greater openness and consultation.

8.   There is openness in one further sense which we consider important. We believe that the other members of the administrative chapter should have the opportunity to comment on and, in appropriate circumstances, meet any leading candidates for the office of dean. This practice is increasingly followed in filling senior posts in the secular world, and would give the potential dean the opportunity to view the post for which he or she is under consideration and those with whom he or she would be working. It

would also give the other members of the administrative chapter the opportunity to see their potential future leader. We believe that a gradual move in this direction would be sensible, although (subject to the outcome of the discussions between Church and Crown mentioned earlier) the appointments themselves would continue to rest with the bishop or Crown as now.

9.   In the case of residentiary canons, the procedure for their appointment need not be so elaborate as that for a dean. Nevertheless, before appointments are considered, careful thought should be given to clarifying the role to be filled and to how long the appointment should be for. Can the post be used to help develop the ministry of clergy by means of a limited term appointment or secondment (see paragraphs 12 ff below)? It is particularly important that anyone appointed should be able to fit in well with the other members of the chapter and, if they are to have a wider diocesan responsibility, with their colleagues in that context also. So we envisage that the dean and other members of the chapter should be involved in the selection of any residentiary canon or other chapter member.

10.   The principles of openness and consultation to which we have earlier referred should apply. We endorse the views on the procedures for the appointment of residentiary canons set out in paragraphs 6.50-6.52 of the van Straubenzee report.[1] As regards canonries in the gift of the Crown,

---

[1] Note: Paragraph 6.50 of the report of the Working Party on Senior Church Appointments reads:

'What we have in mind (in relation to those canonries in the gift of the diocesan bishop) is that when a vacancy arises the diocesan bishop should initiate a process under which:

   i.   after discussion with the diocesan bishop, the dean (or provost) and chapter should consider and prepare for his agreement a statement setting out the needs in the post for the next phase of ministry and the kind of gifts that should be looked for in the person to be appointed. Where, however, the canonry in question is linked with a diocesan post, the diocesan bishop should take the lead in preparing this statement, but in consultation with the dean (or provost) and chapter;

   ii.   in the light of i. a job description would be prepared and agreed, together with a profile of the kind of person it would be appropriate to appoint and for what tenure;

   iii.   the diocesan bishop would then gather potential names for appointment, including any put forward by the dean/provost and chapter;

   iv.   the diocesan bishop, having identified the person he felt it appropriate to appoint, would consult informally with the dean/provost concerned before extending an invitation to the candidate in question;

   v.   before the appointment is offered to the preferred candidate, he or she would meet the bishop, and the members of the cathedral chapter and other senior colleagues with whom he or she would work.'

we hope that, as for suffragan bishops, the Crown would be prepared to consider appointments on the basis of two names put forward by the diocesan bishop following a process led by the diocesan along the lines sketched out in the van Straubenzee report. This would leave the right of appointment in the hands of the Crown but ensure that all appointments of canons were considered in accordance with the same basic process, so helping the Church to use such appointments imaginatively and flexibly in the way we later describe. Again, this is a matter which should be considered with the Crown as part of discussions about a single system of appointment to cathedral posts.

Advertising and Interviewing

11. As the van Straubenzee report noted, secular processes of advertising and interviewing cannot be applied willy nilly to senior Church appointments, particularly in view of the Crown's involvement in a number of them. But the existence of vacancies can be made known (which is in effect a form of advertising), and interviewing may be to the point in some cases. Advertising and interviewing may be more appropriate in relation to more junior posts (and this would reflect a good deal of experience in the secular world). Residentiary canonries where the power of appointment rests with the bishop are already advertised on occasion, particularly if they include diocesan responsibilities. (Crown-appointed posts are not advertised.) We believe that these matters are best left to be decided locally in relation to the particular post in question. Whether or not a post is advertised and interviews held, in every case confidential information and references should be obtained and the services of the Prime Minister's Appointments Secretary or Archbishops' Appointments Secretary as appropriate should be used by the appointing person or body.

Succession Planning and Secondments

12. The emphasis which we have put on mutual openness between Crown and Church and on as uniform a process of appointment as possible derives from our wish to see the best people identified for and appointed to cathedral posts in ways which match individual talents to particular needs. We believe that it is in the wider interests of the Church to establish arrangements which involve conscious forward planning for filling cathedral posts, not only in order to ensure that the best people fill those posts but to make the best possible use of the posts in the priestly growth of those who are to move on to fill other demanding ordained roles within the Church.

13. Cathedral posts provide opportunities to stretch and develop individual clergy in new ways. While in some cases they may be the final

stipendiary post occupied by clergy during their ministry, we should like to see a proportion of them used to nurture the ministry of younger clergy who may then move to more senior posts or into particularly demanding posts in the parochial ministry. We examine the implications of this for tenure and stipend later in this chapter.

14. If some cathedral posts are to be used in this way, it will be necessary to develop arrangements which encourage flexibility and forward planning, and which also engage diocesan bishops in accepting responsibility for developing the ministry of those in cathedral posts. One device which could help in this would be to envisage appointment to some cathedral posts as involving a secondment rather than a transfer to a new diocese. A priest on secondment would occupy a cathedral post for, say, three to five years. During that time, he or she would owe canonical obedience to the diocesan of the cathedral. However, the bishop of the diocese from which the priest has been seconded would continue to have a residual responsibility for the priest, and in particular for ensuring, with the diocesan of the cathedral, their re-absorption into the rest of the ministry at the end of their secondment. Such an arrangement:

(a) could produce flexibility in cathedral appointments;

(b) would extend the range of cathedral appointments, which could be open-ended, or for a limited term, or on a secondment basis;

(c) should ease the movement of clergy in and out of cathedrals by clearly indicating who the priest's continuing Father-in-God is and who, therefore, should have regard to the totality of his or her ministry pastorally.

15. The flexibility could arise in a number of ways. For example, the duration of a secondment could be directly related to the needs in a particular post at a particular time. It could also be related to the needs of the chapter the priest would be joining; and his or her needs in terms of the continuous growth and development of their ministry. It might also be useful in relation to some posts which are combined with a diocesan responsibility. If a particular seam of work had been completed by a secondee, then the secondee could be replaced by another to enable a new piece of work to be taken on. None of this precludes the appointment of some canons on an open-ended basis, and it would be particularly appropriate to make those sorts of appointments of priests who were in the later stage of their ministry and for whom the period in the cathedral would be their final stipendiary post. It might also be right for priests who had some particular gifts or specialism that ought to be exercised in a cathedral context. Nor does it exclude using younger clergy e.g. as minor canons and chaplains to fill posts other than those of residentiary canons on a limited

term basis as a means of extending their knowledge and developing their ministry. Indeed, we believe that this is a practice to be encouraged in the interests of cathedrals, of the clergy concerned and of the Church as a whole.

Tenure

16. Our view of the way in which cathedral appointments should be used leads us to call into question the freehold basis on which the majority of cathedral clergy are currently appointed. The freehold – which in essence means that clergy appointed to most cathedral offices hold them at their own pleasure until they reach retirement age – prevents a regular pattern of movement among the members of the administrative chapter, can effectively impede the transfer to another post of a member who has long since ceased to contribute positively to the life of the cathedral, and inhibits the flow of individuals between parishes or diocesan posts and cathedrals, or from one cathedral to another. The advantages of, not to say the need for, freehold in a cathedral setting today seem even less clear-cut than in the parochial ministry (where they are themselves often questioned). For these reasons, we would like to see the freehold in cathedrals abolished, although we recognise that this may have to be linked with changes in the freehold elsewhere in the Church.

17. While noting that some thirty cathedral canonries are already held on a leasehold basis, we have doubts about whether the freehold should be uniformly replaced by a leasehold arrangement i.e. appointment for a term of years. Appointments to posts for a certain term might become the practice for many cathedral posts and, in so far as term appointments build in opportunities for regular review, there is much to commend them. A certain degree of continuity in the life of an institution is, however, also desirable. So within cathedrals we might expect to find a mix of appointments, some open-ended, some for a term of years. However, we believe that all appointments (whether open-ended or for a term of years) should be capable of termination after a period of notice given by either party. This should include the appointment of deans as well as canons. It might be, say, six months (or even possibly one year) when given by the bishop to the member of the chapter, but three months by the priest to the bishop.

18. The ecclesiastical freehold is being examined by the Clergy Conditions of Service Steering Group set up by the Standing Committee of the General Synod and we understand that a consultation paper is likely to be published soon. We hope that the opportunity of reform will be taken and that a pattern will soon be achieved in which it will be normal for some clergy to spend a period as a residentiary canon and then to move to more senior appointments, to other cathedral posts or into

parochial ministry without any sense of demotion. These changes will, of course, require the Church to follow good and caring personnel practices, and mean that she will need to be more professional and more energetic in this area.

Stipends and other Conditions of Service

19.   At present the stipend received by residentiary canons is about 25% higher than the stipend for incumbents. In addition, further significant payments are made to deans and residentiary canons in six cathedrals under the discretionary power in section 28(3) of the 1963 Cathedrals Measure. These payments have been of long standing and are normally justified by the additional costs incurred on housing, etc. in the ancient cathedrals.

20.   We believe that a distinction should be drawn between stipend and the additional costs, whether of housing or incurred for other reasons in fulfilling a role in ministry in a particular cathedral. We believe it right that such costs or expenses should be reimbursed, and that the Greater Council of each cathedral should be responsible for ensuring that suitable arrangements are in place to achieve this. The Finance and Investment Advisory Committee which we have recommended establishing (see Chapter 7, paragraph 27) would be a suitable independent body to determine the basis of reimbursement for expenses, founded on objective criteria and subject to an appropriate system of control.

21.   As regards stipend, in the case of the dean we believe that, in recognition of the greater responsibilities of that office, there should continue to be a differential as now in the stipend level. We have considered carefully whether to recommend that the differential between the stipend of a residentiary canon and of an incumbent in the diocese should be removed i.e. whether, in respect of future appointments, residentiary canons should be remunerated at the incumbent rate, together with expenses appropriate to cover any additional costs which they incur in carrying out their role. Such a step would, it could be argued, encourage greater ease of movement between parochial and cathedral ministry and recognise that cathedral posts are not necessarily more demanding than some parochial appointments. On the other hand, when this matter was last reviewed in 1977 (see *The Differentials Report*, GS 333), we understand that an erosion of the differential was perceived to have led to difficulties in recruiting to cathedral posts. With this in mind we do not think that this issue can be examined in isolation from stipend levels and differentials generally. Such a re-examination will, we hope, flow from the work of the Clergy Conditions of Service Steering Group and we therefore make no recommendation ourselves for change.

22. Stipend rates for all deans and canons should, we believe, be set nationally by the Central Stipends Authority and should not be exceeded. Expenses should be reimbursed by the cathedral on a basis to be set by the Finance and Investment Advisory Committee. Other additional payments made to deans and canons in certain cathedrals (see paragraph 19 above) should be abolished in respect of future appointments.

23. So long as the differential between cathedral and parochial stipends continues, we endorse the continuation of the arrangement introduced in 1990 under which deans, provosts and residentiary canons moving to parochial ministry maintain their stipend on a mark-time basis until their new parish stipend (assuming that this is lower) catches up with their former cathedral one.

Appraisal and Ministry Development

24. A number of dioceses and some cathedrals already have in place a system under which there is an annual appraisal of members of the chapter. The details of these systems vary but their object is to help each chapter member review his or her ministry over the past year and consider how it might be further developed in the year ahead.

25. We believe that such arrangements should be introduced in all cathedrals and that it should be the responsibility of the diocesan bishop – as diocesan and as chairman of the Greater Council – to see that they are in place. The diocesan bishop should himself conduct a ministry development review with the dean: the dean should conduct such a review for each of the other chapter members (with appropriate input and oversight by the bishop). Suitable training should be provided on how to conduct such a review, which might helpfully include an element of review by those lower in the hierarchy. Where a canonry has both cathedral and diocesan responsibilities, the review should embrace and include input on both aspects of the role. Where the closeness of relationships is felt as in any sense an inhibiting factor, it may be helpful to include an element of external input to the review process.

Induction and Training

26. If cathedral clergy are to be helped adequately to develop their ministry for both the immediate benefit of the cathedral and the wider benefit of the Church, appropriate training opportunities ought to be provided. We are particularly concerned that there is no regular system for inducting and training deans, provosts or residentiary canons when they first take up their new role; nor is continuation training provided

other than through the continuing ministerial education arrangements in each diocese for the parochial clergy.

27.   We are aware that the House of Bishops has recently established a Training Committee to oversee the work of a half-time Archbishops' adviser on bishops' ministry, and that the Committee has in mind that the adviser might turn his attention in due course to the training needs of senior clergy other than bishops, including deans and provosts. We regard the development of a coherent set of arrangements for the training and development of clergy in senior posts in the Church of England as of considerable urgency and importance, and we encourage the Archbishops' adviser to work closely with the Association of English Cathedrals in developing an induction and training package for deans and provosts and, thereafter, other cathedral clergy. We give an indication of some 'management' topics which we feel should be covered in training in the next chapter of the Report (paragraph 15). Help in coping with the challenges and opportunities of working in teams is particularly important, as a group of deans' and provosts' wives has emphasised in evidence to us. Training in liturgical and pastoral issues is also important, although here it may be less a question of 'training' than of structured opportunities for mutual reflection on experiences and problems. One possibility to be examined in that context would be the development of an arrangement whereby the clergy of one cathedral might be attached to another for a period as a mutual learning opportunity.

Ending a Cathedral Clergy Appointment

28.   Through good systems of appointment, of induction, training and ministry development, cathedral clergy will be helped to fulfil their roles effectively, as the very great majority in fact already do. Occasionally, however, circumstances will arise in which it is necessary to bring a cathedral appointment to an end, either because of some misdemeanour or because the person appointed has proved or becomes unsuited for the ministry in question.

29.   Arrangements exist under the Ecclesiastical Jurisdiction Measure 1963 for disciplining clergy who commit a misdemeanour, and under the Church Dignitaries (Retirement) Measure 1949 for securing the retirement of deans, provosts, and cathedral clergy if incapacitated by age or physical or mental infirmity, or if guilty of unbecoming conduct or neglect of duty. So far as we have been able to establish, the provisions of the 1949 Measure have never in fact been used, and they do not cover any situation in which cathedral clergy simply prove unsuited to their posts.

30. The 1949 Measure should, we believe, be reviewed, and workable and fair arrangements established for encouraging and helping the ineffective; or, if insufficient improvement is made, for terminating after due warning the appointment of such people in cathedral posts; or simply to enable action to be taken when the members of the chapter are no longer working together effectively. We envisage that in the case of a residentiary canon such a process would involve:

– a recommendation by the dean;

– reference to a tribunal appointed by the bishop (the membership of which should include at least one residentiary canon of another cathedral), which would make a recommendation to the bishop;

– a decision by the bishop.

In the case of a dean:

– the bishop would recommend;

– there would be reference to a tribunal appointed by the Archbishop (the membership of which should include at least one other dean). The tribunal would make a recommendation to the Archbishop;

– the Archbishop would decide.

We do not envisage that, in either case, the Greater Council would have a formal role in the process. It would, however, have the right to initiate the process by petitioning the bishop for the removal of the dean or any member of the administrative chapter (see Chapter 6, paragraphs 12(f) and 19). The members of the Council would also be available to be brought in to the process as the interests of fairness might dictate e.g. to offer the benefit of their experience of the work of a member of the administrative chapter whose future in the cathedral was under question.

31. The precise form of any such termination procedures will be affected by progress (or lack of it) on reform of the freehold. The proposals which we have set out above are based on the assumption that the freehold continues. As we have noted earlier, the future of the freehold is already under study by a General Synod group. Any changes in arrangements for cathedral clergy should, it will be argued, be mirrored in those applying to other clergy groups. Close consultation with the General Synod's legal advisers will certainly be necessary in devising any new arrangements, with careful attention not only to the requirements of the law but to devising procedures which adequately ensure natural justice and safeguard individuals against arbitrary action. Thought will also need to be

given to counselling and supporting those who have to move on to a new phase of ministry or out of the stipendiary ministry following any such process.

Recognition of Area and Other Suffragan Bishops

32. In Chapter 2, we mentioned our conclusion that insufficient recognition is sometimes given of the place of area and other suffragan bishops in the life of the cathedral (paragraph 24). We believe that cathedrals should do proper honour to area and other suffragan bishops, although precisely how this is done may vary from place to place. We recommend that each area or other suffragan bishop should have their own separately designated seat in the quire. As regards the precedence to be accorded them, this is defined in the statutes of many cathedrals: where it is not, it should (at least as an interim arrangement pending inclusion in the statutes) be settled in discussion between the diocesan bishop and the dean. A possible starting point in such a discussion would be:

(a)   if the suffragan were representing his diocesan bishop, he would walk where the diocesan would walk;

(b)   if the suffragan were accompanying his diocesan as part of the episcopate in the diocese, he would walk immediately in front of the diocesan;

(c)   in any other circumstance, the suffragan would walk immediately in front of the dean and chapter.

We recognise, however, that much will depend on individual circumstances; hence the need (where the matter is not laid down in the statutes) for discussion between dean and diocesan bishop.

Recommendations

1.   The Church should seek to open discussions with the Crown about the prospects for the introduction of a single system of appointment to cathedral posts. The processes of appointment should be characterised by openness and a structured approach to consultation (paragraphs 2-10).

2.   Issues of advertising and interviewing are best left to be decided in relation to the particular post in question (paragraph 11).

3.   A proportion of cathedral posts should be used to stretch and develop clergy who then move to more senior posts or into particularly demanding posts in the parochial ministry. A system of secondment could help in this respect (paragraphs 12-15).

4.   The freehold of cathedral posts should be abolished. Within cathedrals there should be a mix of appointments, some open-ended, some for a term of years. All appointments should be capable of termination after a period of notice (paragraphs 16-18).

5.   Stipend rates for all deans and canons should be set nationally. Expenses should be reimbursed by the cathedral, on a basis to be set by the Finance and Investment Advisory Committee. Other additional payments to deans and canons in certain cathedrals should be abolished in respect of future appointments (paragraphs 19-23).

6.   Appraisal or ministry development review of cathedral clergy should be introduced in all cathedrals (paragraphs 24-25).

7.   The Archbishops' adviser on bishops' ministry should work closely with the Association of English Cathedrals in developing an induction and training package for deans and provosts and other cathedral clergy (paragraph 27).

8.   The present arrangements for ending the appointment of a dean or canon because of a misdemeanour or unsuitability for the post in question should be reviewed (paragraphs 28-31).

9.   Cathedrals should do proper honour to area and other suffragan bishops, who should each have their own separately designated seat in the quire (paragraph 32).

9

Lay Paid Staff, Volunteers
and Cathedral Friends

Introduction

1.   The dependence of cathedrals upon lay personnel – comprising paid staff, volunteers and cathedral Friends – for their management and operation is considerable. Compared with the 190 residential clergy posts in the 42 cathedrals in October 1993, there were 1,030 full-time, 800 part-time or seasonal lay paid staff, and 9,900 volunteers. Indeed, one of the current glories of the English Anglican cathedrals is the extent to which they retain the loyalties of such large numbers exercising so many different forms of lay ministry.

2.   But this dependence by cathedrals and the willingness to serve on the part of lay people require that the cathedrals are conscious of the need for, and are seen to exercise, sound management of lay help. Failure to do so means that God's gifts are being wasted; people become dispirited and drift away, and the tasks which they are set may be less well done than they could be. As many of these tasks affect those using the cathedral - worshippers and visitors alike – then the effectiveness of the cathedral's mission will be diminished.

3.   In this chapter, we look at the issues affecting lay personnel management in the cathedrals – dealing first with paid staff and then with volunteers and cathedral Friends.

LAY PAID STAFF

4.   Cathedrals have always been large employers of craftsmen and other staff but in recent years have increased the number of lay staff employed in management and administrative positions. In addition, we noted the very important contribution made by organists, lay clerks and vergers to the life, work and public face of cathedrals. From our visits and the submissions made to us, it was clear that, despite obvious strides forward in recent years, the quality of personnel management in many cathedrals left much to be desired. Not only does this mean that cathedrals can be represented as 'poor employers', but it is also certain that the cathedrals

may thereby not always be making the best use of the gifts offered by the staff.

5.   This need for change on the part of some cathedrals has arisen mainly from the improvements made in personnel management in lay employment generally, some of which is in response to changes in employment legislation. It is also in part due to the clergy not being employed in the lay sense of that word and, generally speaking, having little personal experience of employment issues. In this section, therefore, we set out the principal areas in which improvements in personnel management may be achieved. In making our recommendations we have been mindful of the conclusions of earlier studies in this context, for example, *The Verger's Role in Today's and Tomorrow's Church* (1990).

Job Descriptions

6.   As for the dean and other clerical members of the chapter (see Chapter 8), job descriptions for all heads of department and senior staff posts should be prepared. They should be amplified by a person specification defining the requirements of the post in terms of qualifications, training, experience, background and personality.

Qualifications

7.   The need for appropriate skills and experience is usually self-evident and should be spelled out in the job descriptions and person specifications. The administrator in particular needs to be skilled in general management, financial control, and concern for a wide range of people, as well as leadership. Previous experience in running an organisation with a number of activities connected with the public is important.

8.   While those appointed to senior posts should clearly be sympathetic to the Church of England, the demands of each particular undertaking should predominate.

Appointments

9.   All senior appointments should be made following a proper recruitment process including:

(a)   the review and updating of the job description and person specification;

(b)   the use of an appointment panel, with an external assessor, chaired as appropriate. For example, the dean should chair the panel for the administrator and either the dean or the administrator for the head of finance;

(c) the appointment panel should include one or more lay people with appropriate specialist knowledge;

(d) the panel should review the advertisement and approve the procedure for screening candidates. Sometimes executive selection consultants may be used;

(e) a final report from the appointment panel to the chapter recommending the appointment.

Contracts and terms of employment

10. Employment legislation requires that all lay staff have a contract of employment; disciplinary rules, grievance procedures, and sickness regulations should be published.

11. Despite the financial burden, cathedrals should offer terms of employment sufficient to attract and retain suitably qualified and experienced staff of all levels. Proper rewards for critical posts should improve efficiency and achieve net economy.

12. Many organisations have formed a Benefits Committee, including external members with appropriate experience, to advise on appropriate levels of senior staff remuneration, including benefits. The Committee's membership and procedures should be designed to avoid any conflicts of interest. In Chapter 7, paragraph 27, we have suggested that the Finance and Investment Advisory Committee could fulfil this role. The Committee should also consider benefits and allowances paid for clerical appointments.

13. The provision of, and charging for, housing is important. Both the chapter and the employees benefit if accommodation can be provided. Current personnel 'best practice' requires such an employee to pay a market rent, setting his or her remuneration so that he or she can pay it. This may appear to be self-cancelling but it enables the cathedral to manage the cost of providing accommodation and helps the employee to appreciate the cost of housing which will have to be faced when he or she leaves the cathedral's employment. Proper remuneration and market rents ensure equity between employees who occupy cathedral property and employees who do not. However, in applying this recommendation, cathedrals will need to be mindful of housing legislation pitfalls concerning 'tied housing'.

Training

14. Two kinds of training should be provided for those newly appointed to posts in cathedrals: training in specific skills and induction into the

ways of cathedrals. We recommend that the Association of English Cathedrals (AEC) sponsors the development of appropriate courses either alone or in conjunction with other bodies, for example, the Guild of Vergers. It is especially important that there should be appropriate training for administrators, heads of finance and other heads of department on appointment. Much of this training would be common with that recommended for cathedral clergy (see Chapter 8, paragraphs 26 and 27) and some common with that for volunteers (see paragraphs 32-34 below).

15.   Training should include:

(a)	awareness of the spiritual aims of the cathedral;
(b)	leadership and team working;
(c)	cathedral legislation;
(d)	cathedral finances and accounting;
(e)	property maintenance;
(f)	management of volunteers;
(g)	visitor management and customer care;
(h)	personnel management.

Appraisal

16.   All lay staff should be appraised annually by the head of their department or the responsible member of the chapter. The job description is the best starting point; objectives should be set and progress on attaining them discussed, and appropriate advice should be given. Training in appraisals should also be provided.

Staff Communication

17.   There should be regular (at least monthly) meetings of all staff to ensure that there is good internal communication between members of staff and between departments; these are an essential part of good personnel management. Staff meetings should include:

(a)   one for chapter members and heads of department reporting to members of the chapter. This should be chaired by the dean;

(b)   one for each department, chaired by the head of department. The responsible member of the chapter, if he or she is not the department head, should occasionally be present.

Personnel Management

18. The administrator is the person to whom the chapter would usually look to oversee, and revise as necessary, the various aspects of personnel management. These should be ratified by the chapter, which should define policy and establish procedures.

19. Each head of department should remain responsible for managing his or her staff within the chapter's personnel policy, and within the procedures approved, supported as necessary by the administrator who should provide specialist advice, ensure consistency and provide central personnel management administration.

20. Some cathedrals have well-developed personnel management policies and procedures; others do not. It would make considerable sense for the former to help the latter on some co-ordinated basis. The AEC could facilitate this self-help.

Vergers

21. On our visits to cathedrals we were aware of the particularly significant contribution made by vergers. These men and women are very often in the front line between the cathedral and its public. They carry considerable responsibility for the security of the building, its contents and the people who visit it, and they are often the recognisable members of the cathedral community to whom the visitor turns for advice or, indeed, to make complaint. It is essential that vergers are encouraged to undertake appropriate training and that they are affirmed by the dean and chapter by means of proper management and remuneration.

22. The personal security of vergers and other employees needs to be addressed more seriously in many cathedrals; the provision of radio intercoms would be an advantage.

VOLUNTEERS

Introduction

23. The contribution to the life and work of English cathedrals by volunteers can hardly be overestimated. It is in no way an overstatement to say that without them cathedrals could not function. Chaplains, guides, welcomers, maintenance staff, 'holy dusters', servers, bell-ringers, stewards, cooks, caterers, shop assistants, crèche and child minders, Sunday School teachers, financial, property and investment advisers, and members of Fabric Advisory Committees: the list is long and not exhaustive. Each summer, too, groups of young people provide free labour for a variety of tasks under the 'Cathedral Camps' scheme. All are numbered

among the many volunteers who make a 'gift of time' to cathedrals. The numbers involved at each cathedral are considerable, ranging between 200 and 700, and they by no means all come from the locality of the cathedral. One cathedral has 90 parish groups and 60 parish volunteers. Neither the economics, nor the sheer numbers of people involved, would enable cathedrals to undertake the work they do, particularly in the reception and care of visitors, if it were not for the volunteers. They give freely of their time and talents to help maintain the cathedrals as the centres of excellence and beauty which they rightfully claim to be.

24.   Together with the dean and chapter, the permanent staff and the congregations, the volunteers make up the cathedral community. Some travel many miles to fulfil their duties and provide an invaluable link with the diocese. They exchange ideas and concepts with the parishes. Some cathedrals augment their paid staff (such as vergers, lay clerks and choristers) by the use of volunteers on a regular part-time or occasional basis. We were impressed during our visits by the numbers, skills and dedication of volunteers who work for cathedrals, and by the depth of the goodwill which exists for them.

25.   In this section we look at the role of the volunteers, their recruitment, training, management and care, and finally make recommendations on how the value of their service can be maximised.

The Role of Volunteers

26.   The tasks which volunteers undertake are usually self-evident from their titles: welcomers welcome, guides guide, chaplains minister; but their role in performing these tasks must be carefully established and then explained to them. It has to be recognised that not all volunteers will automatically interpret their role exactly as the dean and chapter might wish and, as a high proportion of volunteers are in frequent and close contact with visitors to the cathedral, it is of paramount importance that the impression which volunteers make on those visitors is positive. Most of the visitors to a cathedral will never see a member of the chapter, but almost all of them will meet a volunteer of one sort or another. Volunteers, therefore, represent to a very large extent the public face of the cathedral, and it is by their demeanour and actions that the cathedral, and consequently the dean and chapter of the cathedral, and by association the Church as a whole, will be judged.

27.   The increase in exposure to people of all ages and many nationalities experienced by cathedrals as a result of tourism offers both an opportunity to promulgate the Christian message and a prospect of augmenting income. The former lies at the very heart of the cathedral's role, and the

latter can help to meet the growing demands for money to finance such things as fabric repair, staff and insurance. Many cathedrals recognise these two opportunities either in their mission statement or by their procedures in the management of visitors. All volunteers have a role to play in these two areas, but guides, welcomers and stewards can have particular influence. It is essential for guides to realise that the historic story of the cathedral, its architectural features and its beauty must be set in a Christian context. Some cathedrals insist that guides must be Christians, but we suggest only that all guides should be crystal clear of the need to explain the cathedral against a Christian background (see Chapter 3, paragraphs 36 and 49). One cathedral certainly avers that one of its best and most persuasive guides in imparting the meaning and purpose of the cathedral is not a Christian. Welcomers by their very presence (and the distribution of leaflets) can encourage visitors to donate money, but they should understand clearly that their presence forms part of an overall Christian warmth of welcome and that their task is not merely to extract money from visitors. Stewards assist the public to join in services; they are not there to forbid entry to children or those who perhaps are not dressed conventionally.

28.   The roles which cathedrals wish volunteers to fulfil should determine recruitment and training, and so it is essential that deans and chapters establish with great clarity what those roles are. We formed the impression during some visits that, although chapters were totally sure in their own minds of the purpose of volunteers, they had not always gone through the necessary process of translating that purpose into particular roles and communicating them to the volunteers.

Recruitment

29.   There is inevitably a tension when considering volunteers between wanting to support all those who are moved to offer themselves and wishing also to apply criteria of suitability. Volunteers inevitably present themselves with differing levels of personal skills, sensitivity and awareness; some, it must be recognised, are, if unconsciously, seeking pastoral comfort for themselves as much as offering their services to the cathedral. This is not in itself disadvantageous, but it needs to be identified. However, if the roles have been carefully established and care is taken in allocating people to tasks, there is almost certainly an area of activity where a willing volunteer can be used.

30.   The determination of the most suitable task should be worked out at an interview with a member of the chapter or a head of department. Recruitment should not be left exclusively to other volunteers who are already employed at the cathedral; it is not enough, for example, that a

guide has a friend who wishes to be a guide too. At some cathedrals, we became aware that most important, high-profile, and visitor-sensitive areas of volunteer activity were staffed entirely by a process of internal volunteer recruitment; it resulted in the perpetuation of an inward-looking, defensive ethos in the area of service concerned. Recruitment should be specific, and appointments made subject to successful completion of training and review after a trial period. Sometimes, as a consequence, the persons themselves will quickly realise that they are not best suited to the task to which they originally felt drawn.

31. Although volunteers are traditionally thought of as fulfilling the more conventional roles of guiding, welcoming or flower arranging, an interview can often identify an expertise or talent which the cathedral needs and of which the volunteer is unaware. Maintenance of inventories, cataloguing books or photographs and even filing may be ideally suited to a particular person who approaches with a 'gift of time'. And if those requirements are identified and known about by the cathedral management, advertising can take place in circles perhaps less obvious at first sight. The local NADFAS, learned societies, schools and universities are all examples of places where there are people with particular interests who might well be more than willing to help if asked, but who would not necessarily offer their services without first being approached.

Training

32. As cathedrals have increasingly come to terms with the need to assist their visitors and provide for the higher standards of service and facilities which today's visitors expect, many have introduced training for their volunteers, particularly for guides. In some cases such training seeks not only to impart knowledge about the cathedral, but also to teach the techniques of guiding. We applaud and welcome such training provision, but believe that it should be extended to cover all areas of volunteer activity. We did not, for example, find much evidence during our visits of systematic training for stewards, wandsmen or sidesmen, and yet these volunteers have a major impact on the image which a cathedral projects. This is particularly important for those cathedrals which are hosts to large transitory congregations. Too many cathedrals leave their stewards to learn solely by experience, but we recommend that specific task-orientated training be introduced for all volunteer activities. It is recognised that the introduction of training for some volunteers, who have been carrying out their duties for many years in a way which they believe to be totally satisfactory, could be misunderstood. We believe, nevertheless, that, properly explained, the rationale of training for the task, and the concept of professionalism which lies behind it, will be readily acceptable.

33.   The management of change is always difficult and many chapters will flinch at the thought of introducing training for – to give one example – the flower arrangers, but even in this sensitive area the provision of periodic lectures by professional flower arrangers would probably be met with surprising approval. The very suggestion of training should make volunteers conscious of the value which chapters place on them and the services which they provide. If all areas of volunteer activity receive training, none will feel that they are being singled out for implied criticism. We believe, and found evidence to support our belief, that there exists today a great awareness amongst volunteers of the need to place themselves within a professional team of which they are an integral part and where training for the task is the accepted norm.

34.   In addition to task-orientated training virtually all volunteers will need general instruction on how to act in emergencies such as fire, bomb scares, electrical failure, accidents to visitors or illness; and what to do when faced with difficult or even abusive visitors. Volunteers should not be left to act on their own initiative, and clear-cut procedures should be established and promulgated. We became aware of one cathedral which publishes a 'Blue Book' for volunteers covering these issues. This aspect of general training can be assisted by the distribution to all volunteers of a small book where the procedures are listed. A major aspect of general training which all volunteers should receive is 'customer care' to make them aware of the need to project a welcoming, positive, Christian image to all who come to the cathedral. One way of doing this (which we observed) is the production by the cathedral of a low-cost video shown to all staff, paid and volunteers, emphasising their individual responsibilities for presenting the message of the cathedral.

Management

35.   We acknowledge that the management of volunteers can be some-thing of a challenge. We occasionally encountered an unhelpful disposi-tion among both the clerical and the lay managers of cathedrals who suppose that volunteer workers offer their services conditionally, and would simply withdraw them if they were encouraged to review their efforts. We do not believe that such an attitude is acceptable. There are many organisations equally dependent on volunteers, notably the National Trust, where management of volunteers is such that volunteers happily place themselves within the professional management structure of the organisation. Occasionally management may have to indicate to a volunteer that he or she will be 'rested', either because of a refusal to co-operate with chapter policy with respect to the duties required, or, sadly, because the volunteer has become tired, slow or infirm. The ultimate

sanction of informing a volunteer that his or her services are no longer required need seldom be used, but should not be discounted if it really becomes necessary.

36. The point has been made elsewhere in the chapter on Management (see Chapter 7, paragraphs 16 and 30) that volunteers must know who within the structure is responsible for them, and to whom they are accountable, so that they have proper access at appropriate decision-making levels and are confident that their particular concerns will be acknowledged. For example, many cathedrals have appointed a lay director of visits or a visitor officer and others allocate the task to a member of the chapter. In the former case we believe that the chapter should still have an oversight of all volunteer spheres of activity, and many volunteers like to feel that they can relate to a member of the chapter.

37. Each volunteer activity should have a volunteer co-ordinator or representative appointed by the chapter (not elected). Some cathedrals form such co-ordinators or representatives into a group or committee which meets regularly together with appropriate members of the permanent staff under the chairmanship of a member of the chapter. We believe that this is a valuable arrangement, allowing the dissemination of information and instructions from the chapter, and also promoting the reception of responses to the chapter. The individual groups of volunteers, guides, welcomers, chaplains, etc. should themselves meet at least annually when policy and training matters can be promulgated, issues (like how to cope with schoolchildren) discussed, and lessons learned. Many cathedrals make those general meetings opportunities to offer hospitality to the volunteers and, if different types of volunteer are combined into one meeting, it helps to create cohesion and a sense of belonging to one cathedral team with a fully understood mission. Interaction between the different volunteer groups fosters respect for and recognition of mutual areas of responsibility and the need for them.

38. No matter how good and comprehensive the training given to volunteers is, not all of the points made will be remembered, and so good management demands that a set of instructions for each group of volunteers should be drawn up and published. These instructions need not be long, but should set down clearly what the duties are, and if all are published in one volume it can include those general emergency procedures (see paragraph 34 above) and make all groups aware of what others do. There will also, however, be information of a temporary or immediate nature which most volunteers will need to know in order to fulfil their role. Guides need to know, for example, when, why and for low long a particular part of the cathedral is closed. Welcomers should be

aware what makes up the programme for an evening concert; chaplains the time and place for interviews. Such necessary but ephemeral information can be made available on a notice-board in the volunteer office or rest room, or promulgated through the pages of a periodic news-sheet for volunteers. Such publications can also be used to promote a lively ethos of management amongst volunteers and enable them to see that they are valued and wanted.

Volunteer Care

39.   The need to impress on volunteers their responsibility for 'customer care' has already been emphasised; the chapter has a similar responsibility for 'volunteer care'. This can be shown in many ways: the provision of parking, payment of a mileage allowance, the availability of rest rooms, discounts perhaps in the cathedral shop, invitations to major services, concern for their safety. These are all obvious ways in which volunteers may be made aware that their service to the cathedral is equally valued with the service of paid staff. But perhaps the most important means of creating in volunteers a climate of support for the cathedral, and enabling them to recognise the need for a management structure, is for the members of the management team, clerical and lay alike, to 'walk the floor', to know and be seen by the volunteers, to talk to them and listen to them so that they understand the extent to which they are valued. They will, too, serve all the better if they are made aware of the spiritual dimension of their work, the opportunities for witness which it provides, and if they come to feel part of the total corporate mission. Given the dependence of cathedrals on their volunteers, care for them is imperative and will help to create a love for the cathedral and a sense of the priority of its religious mission. Some suggestions for the care and training of volunteers are given in the Annex to this chapter.

CATHEDRAL FRIENDS

40.   The figures in Table 16 of Chapter 13 illustrate the enormous contribution made to cathedrals by their Friends' organisations. On the latest information the sum of £1,039,000 was given to the Anglican cathedrals by their Friends, an average of over £25,000 per cathedral, and we learned of several cathedrals which regularly receive over £100,000 each year. Those who belong to Friends' organisations do so entirely from a feeling of affection, and in support of their cathedrals; they receive very few benefits from their membership. Table 16 of Chapter 13 indicates a total expenditure of only £22,000 on member benefits or 41p per head. Over 53,000 people belong to Friends' organisations, and many serve the cathedrals in other ways as guides, welcomers, 'holy dusters', and advisers.

Additionally, many Friends provide a welcome link with the diocese, and the practice observed in some cathedrals of seeking to nominate a cathedral Friend in each parish where he or she can provide an individual and personal link with the cathedral is applauded. Furthermore, the more active Friends' organisations contribute towards an active community based around the cathedral.

41. It was also clear to us that some cathedrals had far more active and larger Friends' organisations than others. Size and activity were not necessarily correlated with the age of members or the income of their cathedrals, but more related to the quality of leadership of the organisation and the support which it received from the dean and chapter. Clearly, cathedrals have much to gain from a large and active Friends' organisation.

42. We observed that the annual subscriptions asked of Friends were often surprisingly low and, whilst we would not wish to preclude membership through over-pricing, it does appear that subscription rates could in many cases be reviewed upwards for new members. It is clearly important to recruit new Friends continually, and in particular to seek ways of encouraging a younger membership. We welcome the initiative of Cathedral Camps in encouraging those young people who attend the Camps to become long-term members of cathedral Friends by means of a subsidised subscription. An obvious way to promote recruitment is by the provision of a Friends' presence in the cathedral, and we noted with approval the number of cathedrals which have a Friends' desk often combined with an illustrative display of the projects funded by the Friends. As for the volunteers, deans and chapters should seek explicit and frequent opportunities to acknowledge their debt of gratitude to their Friends and take every opportunity to affirm them and their contributions.

43. We would also encourage chapters through the AEC to sponsor greater collaboration and exchange of information between Friends' organisations.

Conclusion

44. We believe, in summary, that cathedrals are very reliant on volunteer helpers who should be incorporated within a professional management system. The roles expected of them should be evaluated and explained carefully. Volunteers together with the paid staff represent the public face of the cathedral and, to a very large extent, their attitudes have a major influence on the cathedral's image. Their recruitment, therefore, should be task-orientated and carried out by a head of department with chapter involvement. All volunteers should receive training for their tasks,

and in view of their frequent contact with visitors the importance of 'customer care' should be emphasised. The volunteer's 'gift of time' to cathedrals must be recognised, applauded, appreciated and rewarded. Of equal value to their cathedrals are their Friends whose major valuable contribution and general support deserve similar affirmation.

Recommendations

1. Job descriptions and person specifications defining the requirements for each job should be prepared for all heads of department and senior staff posts (paragraph 6).

2. Procedures for the appointment and personnel management of lay staff should be improved in many cathedrals, with all such staff having contracts of employment and being appraised annually (paragraphs 9-12, 16 and 18-20).

3. Training in specific skills and induction into the ways of the cathedral should be provided for all employees and the AEC should sponsor the development of appropriate courses (paragraphs 14-15).

4. There should be regular (at least monthly) meetings of all staff to ensure good communication (paragraph 17).

5. The role of volunteers in performing their various tasks and the spiritual dimension of these must be carefully established and explained (paragraph 26).

6. Guides should be clear that the historic story of the cathedral must be set in a Christian context (paragraph 27).

7. Specific task-orientated training should be introduced for all areas of volunteer activity (paragraph 32).

8. Volunteers must know to whom they are accountable and each volunteer activity should have a volunteer co-ordinator (paragraphs 36 and 37).

9. The contribution of cathedral Friends should be acknowledged, encouraged and affirmed, and opportunities provided for recruitment by a 'presence' in the cathedral (paragraphs 40-42).

Care and Training of Volunteers

1. Define the role of each type of volunteer with precision and ensure an awareness of the spiritual and mission role which their task entails.

2. A member of the chapter and the appropriate head of department should be involved in the recruitment of volunteers.

3. Training should be designed and given for every type of volunteer activity, not just for the obvious high-profile ones.

4. General training (such as emergency techniques) should be included in specific-type training.

5. 'Customer care' should be emphasised to all volunteers.

6. Volunteers should be incorporated into the overall professional management of the cathedral and have appropriate lines of accountability and reporting.

7. A volunteer co-ordinator should be appointed for each type of activity and those co-ordinators formed into a group which meets regularly.

8. Written instructions giving guidelines for each volunteer group should be published and made generally available.

9. Volunteers should be constantly nurtured.

10

Fabric

Introduction

1.   Many of our cathedrals are among the greatest historic buildings in the country – indeed in the world – and are valued as buildings of both beauty and significance by huge numbers of people. At the same time, unlike ancient monuments, cathedrals are buildings still in use for the essential purpose for which they were originally built; and this continuing purpose gives their care a special perspective. They have always adapted themselves to contemporary requirements, and must continue to do so: indeed, much of what we now value in them results from changes and additions which have been made over the centuries. The need to keep moving forward can sometimes seem to be at odds with the concern to preserve the historic fabric – therein resides a tension which is plainly unavoidable. Yet the obligation of simultaneous preservation and adaptation does not in fact involve incompatibilities: both are essentially creative, as the care and repair of a cathedral require a creative outlook just as much as its embellishment.

2.   The evident readiness of all concerned with the fabric to achieve a transcendent dimension may sometimes be inarticulate but nevertheless expresses a real sense of doing God's service. In this it parallels the liturgy offered by the worshipping community or the music offered by the musicians.

3.   Cathedrals are, therefore, buildings where the creativity which is the lifeblood of the arts has an integral part to play in the worship and mission of the Church, and they have a great ability to draw men and women who have something creative to offer; through them this creativity may find a voice in the nation as a whole. Cathedrals also have considerable scope for commissioning new works of art or craftsmanship, and a remarkable ability to command a very wide range of talent; they thus have a duty to set the highest standards in the visual arts and in works of craftsmanship, as in repair and conservation techniques.

4.   One of the greatest qualities many cathedrals possess is that of space. An ordered sense of space is in itself of value, and is widely appreciated.

Cathedrals therefore have a duty to guard their spaces and to avoid clutter. Space is also a valuable asset for many liturgical and artistic activities; and cathedrals should recognise the importance of making space available for events of all kinds of activity which will further the mission of the Church.

5.   In its liturgical ordering a cathedral should seek clearly to express and articulate its liturgical purpose. The Liturgical Commission has recently set up a 'Cathedrals Group' to help and advise cathedrals in co-ordinating experience in this particular field.

The State of the Fabric

6.   We have made no attempt to carry out a comprehensive assessment of the condition of all cathedrals, as this considerable undertaking has recently been completed by English Heritage as a basis for its grant aid programme. Its report, prepared by Harry Fairhurst in 1991, has kindly been made available to us. The findings reveal that most cathedrals are taking responsible steps to carry out repair and conservation works. This is corroborated by the findings of our financial survey (see Chapter 13, paragraphs 25 and 34).

7.   A significant finding of the Fairhurst report is that most cathedrals may be considered to be in a generally sound state; and many have in hand programmes of ongoing works indicating that problem areas are being addressed on a planned basis. However, the report draws attention to a significant number of requirements for future works at nearly all cathedrals, indicating that fabric matters are likely to continue to require considerable sums within the coming decade and beyond. The provision of government grant aid has enabled a number of cathedrals to embark on programmes of work which they had been previously unable to fund; but there is a backlog of work which may take some time to clear, and not all cathedrals have been in a position to take up the full amount of grant aid offered. It is also clear that some cathedrals require significant expenditure to address problems of post-war construction (Blackburn and Sheffield, for instance), and that these pose difficulties of a different order from most older cathedrals.

The Care of Cathedrals Measure 1990

GENERAL

8.   The Care of Cathedrals Measure 1990 came into operation on 1 March 1991. It was formulated in response to the recommendations made by the Faculty Jurisdiction Commission (published in 1984 as *The*

Continuing Care of Churches and Cathedrals). It establishes a formal system of control of works affecting the fabric of cathedrals, and lays down requirements for many aspects of their care and conservation. The principal purpose of the Measure is to ensure that the Church is conforming to legislative constraints on work to cathedrals no less stringent than those applied to secular buildings; and the process of gaining formal approvals has been established to satisfy this public interest.

9.   Section 1 of the Measure provides that: 'Any body on which functions of care and conservation are conferred by this Measure shall in exercising those functions have due regard to the fact that the cathedral church is the seat of the bishop and a centre of worship and mission.' In this way the Measure addresses at its outset the tension described in paragraph 1 above.

THE CATHEDRALS FABRIC COMMISSION FOR ENGLAND AND FABRIC ADVISORY COMMITTEES

10. The Care of Cathedrals Measure set up both the Cathedrals Fabric Commission for England (CFCE) and Fabric Advisory Committees (FACs) as both advisory and authorising bodies, for different classes of work; the CFCE has issued guidelines in order to clarify the roles of each body. Many chapters use FACs for advice on all matters, whether they will be the authorising body when a formal application is made or not. This is generally commended as good practice, since FACs will be able to be more effective when they are properly informed on all fabric matters. The CFCE does, however, have statutory responsibility for determining certain classes of application as defined in the Measure (section 6(1)), and for setting overall standards. At the same time, it is considered important that FACs should be entrusted with as high a degree of decision making as is compatible with the terms of the Measure, both to avoid overloading the CFCE, and to ensure that FACs possess a real sense of responsibility and purpose. Nevertheless, the CFCE represents a wide body of expertise and experience, not necessarily represented on FACs, and may therefore be in a position to offer additional advice to chapters and to FACs.

11. The requirements of the Care of Cathedrals Measure lay on chapters and their professional advisers duties and tasks which they did not have before, and this has its cost, both in time and money. While sympathising with the financial implications for cathedrals, we feel that the degree of accountability and the requirements for proper documentation required by the Measure ought responsibly to be undertaken by chapters and their consultants in any case, and are fully justified. Furthermore, the CFCE and FACs are drawn from a wide range of interested people, and it is clear

that a great amount of expert knowledge is being channelled to cathedrals through these committees. Although there is a cost to cathedrals, this cost seems balanced by the quality of the advice available.

12. Most apparent difficulties with the implementation of the Measure are generally observed to be overcome by co-operation and good communication between chapters, FACs and the CFCE; and the initiative taken by the CFCE in setting up conferences in order to allow members of FACs, the CFCE and chapters to meet one another and discuss matters of common interest or concern is commended, as is the practice of the CFCE inviting members of FACs to be present when delegations are sent to cathedrals.

FABRIC ADVISORY COMMITTEES

13. The Measure requires each cathedral to set up a Fabric Advisory Committee (FAC). Although it appears to have taken some cathedrals some time to achieve this, all have now done so. In order to fulfil its formal role properly, the FAC must be seen to discharge its duties impartially. Some FACs are perceived by chapters to be too heavily weighted in favour of art history, archaeology or conservation. However, the Measure establishes equal numbers of nominees from the cathedral and the CFCE, and the latter, with its specific interest in the care and conservation of cathedrals, may be assumed to have a duty to put forward members who have a particular experience in those matters which are its principal concern; chapters should therefore take care to propose those whom they feel will represent a balanced interest.

14. Under the Care of Cathedrals Measure, deans and chapters may not be members of their FACs, but in parish church cathedrals there is no bar to members of cathedral councils being members. This anomaly will be avoided on the removal of the distinction between 'dean and chapter' and 'parish church' cathedrals recommended elsewhere in this Report (see Chapter 6, paragraphs 8-10). Under the proposed new structure members of the Greater Council could appropriately be members of the FAC, but members of the Administrative Chapter – including independent members – should not be.

15. FACs have considerable freedom within the functions ascribed to them in the Measure to establish their own methods of working. There appears to be a wide range of practice, from those committees which rarely meet (perhaps indicating lack of a requirement for work at that particular cathedral – a minimum of two meetings per annum is however prescribed in the Measure) to those which not only meet frequently, but whose individual members concern themselves closely with the execution

of work which they have approved. It would appear that the relationship of the FAC to the chapter and its professional advisers has potential for conflict if the FAC takes too active a role or if it begins to initiate projects.

16. Members of FACs carry heavy responsibilities and could be held responsible for the advice which they give. It is acknowledged that the issue of indemnity of such committees is a difficult one; but cathedrals should insure or otherwise indemnify members against possible claims.

RELATIONSHIP WITH SECULAR LEGISLATION

17. We consider that there should be no overlap between consents required under the Care of Cathedrals Measure and the secular counterparts of Listed Building Consent and Scheduled Monument Consent, and we commend the steps which it is understood are being taken to clarify this issue in the context of the proposed Ecclesiastical Exemption (Listed Buildings and Conservation Areas) Order 1994.

EFFICACY OF THE MEASURE

18. Although the Care of Cathedrals Measure enshrines some procedures which had been accepted as good practice by some cathedrals before its introduction, its mandatory and formal nature has inevitably necessitated a corresponding formalisation in the way in which chapters and their advisers plan and execute work. As the Measure has only been in operation for some three years it is perhaps too early to arrive at a definitive assessment of how well it is working. Nevertheless, the care which was taken in its formulation, and the lengthy consultation and discussions which this involved, appear to have resulted in a responsible set of provisions which have real strengths and which bring a welcome degree of accountability to this important aspect of each cathedral's affairs. In the setting up of the CFCE and FACs a framework has been established for continuing the process of refinement and discussion; and since the Care of Cathedrals (Supplementary Provisions) Measure has obtained parliamentary approval, the appropriate enforcement procedures are now in place.

19. We believe that the Care of Cathedrals Measure represents a legislative framework which is well suited to the needs of cathedrals, and provides a system of control well adapted to protect and ensure the preservation of the buildings, their fittings and furnishings, and to allow for the enhancement of the buildings' use. In particular, it is noted that the legislation provides a closer control over the contents than would be afforded under the equivalent secular legislation. However, we also noted the pressure that the proper handling of its statutory tasks places on the limited

resources of the CFCE and its staff, and we would be concerned if any reduction in funding led to a situation in which the CFCE's ability to discharge its statutory responsibilities was reduced.

20. Good practice must be for cathedrals to learn to benefit from the Measure's many positive aspects, to use the advice available from their FACs and the CFCE to the full, and to ensure that good communication and co-operation between the bodies is practised in the interests of the care and conservation of the fabric.

Management of Fabric Matters

GENERAL

21. The proper management of the care and conservation of the fabric lies in:

(a) the structure by means of which the chapter is advised on fabric matters, and through which decisions made by the chapter are transmitted to those responsible for their implementation;

(b) the quality of the cathedral's professional advisers;

(c) clear definitions of the roles and responsibilities of all those concerned;

(d) the proper compliance with legal requirements.

22. It is important that cathedrals should give particular priority to establishing such clear management structures and defining the roles of those principally concerned, following the principles set out in the Management chapter of this Report. This is particularly the case in connection with the key roles of architect, archaeologist, lay administrator, canon custos and clerk of works. Especially it is recommended that:

(a) there should be a clearly defined line of command in fabric matters;

(b) one member of the chapter should have oversight responsibility for the cathedral fabric;

(c) a member of the chapter should also have oversight responsibility for the other buildings owned by the chapter. This need not be the same person, and indeed at some of the larger cathedrals ought not to be;

(d) the cathedral architect should report at regular intervals to the whole chapter;

(e) in connection with the execution of works, communications between the chapter and architect should be through the administrator;

(f) where there is a clerk of works (especially if there is a works department), he or she should perform their responsibilities relating to the fabric under the overall professional direction of the architect, but should be accountable to the administrator for the proper management of the department;

(g) where there is a clerk of works, the architect should advise the chapter on which tasks may appropriately be executed by the clerk of works on the direct instruction of the administrator.

23. A number of submissions which we received contained detailed and helpful comments on many specific aspects of this important side of cathedrals' work; and the preparation of a code of practice at least on the role and duties of the cathedral architect and of the cathedral's archaeological consultant is recommended. The preparation of such a code of practice would require specialist evaluation and consultation; but in the interim the paper *The Role and Duties of the Cathedral Architect*, prepared by the Cathedral Architects' Association, is commended, and the issuing of comparable guidance on 'The Role and Duties of the Cathedral Archaeologist' would provide similar guidance for the role of archaeologist.

PLANNING WORK

24. The Care of Cathedrals Measure requires the cathedral architect to report at least every five years on the work required to the fabric; and we consider that this report must be based on a proper inspection of the fabric. This will provide the basis for planning repair and maintenance work. In addition, it is considered good practice for the chapter to address its projected plans of a developmental nature also at five-yearly intervals, in association with the report on the fabric. This should cover plans for alterations and improvements within the cathedral, and also external projects such as visitor centres, education bases, works to Close properties, choir school and so on. This comprehensive 'audit of objectives' will enable the chapter, in consultation with its professional advisers, to order all works in a planned sequence.

25. In planning for major projects of any kind, the necessity for proper planned maintenance must never be overlooked. Regular and appropriate maintenance of the fabric is unglamorous and tends not to attract grant aid nor to be easy to raise money for, but it is fundamental in the care and conservation of the fabric. With good maintenance and properly planned forward repair programmes, the fabric of cathedrals should be able to be

brought step by step to a condition where crises can be eliminated and major works, when required, can be foreseen and properly planned in advance.

WORKS DEPARTMENTS

26. A number of cathedrals have works departments or specialist conservation workshops, and there is a great deal of sense in at least the larger cathedrals maintaining their own workforces for ongoing major repairs as well as for the maintenance and service tasks which constantly arise. They can provide the continuity and familiarity which are important ingredients to successful historic building repairs. However, such organisations can consume considerable resources and they should be constantly reviewed; their control has already received comment in the chapter on Management (see Chapter 7, paragraph 36).

27. Any cathedral employing a works department should be prepared to put repairs out to tender, especially when the demands of the fabric outstrip the capabilities of the in-house workforce.

28. Although works departments may have a clear role at the larger cathedrals, even the smallest cathedral would probably benefit from a single dedicated full-time maintenance person.

29. We have considered the view that works departments might be able to play a role in the diocese by providing specialist expertise to churches throughout the diocese. This may particularly be the case with specialist conservation workshops. If this is to be achieved, the management objectives must be clearly stated, and the financial viability reviewed regularly.

30. Some works departments and conservation workshops have an important role in the training of craftsmen, and in this way have a national contribution to make to the care and conservation of historic buildings.

ARCHAEOLOGY

31. Cathedral archaeology relates to the complete historical study of the fabric and material remains of a cathedral church, above and below ground, together with its site, contents, and historic setting. It thus extends not only to the cathedral church and its directly related buildings, but to the whole of the precinct as defined by the Care of Cathedrals Measure. Among the principal requirements of the Measure are the appointment by each cathedral of a consultant archaeologist (unless the CFCE agrees otherwise), and the adequate provision for the archaeological dimension of any programme of work. These are important considerations,

and should be seen as the proper acceptance, by a religion which is rooted in history, of its responsibilities to the historical evidence of Christian development. In particular, the choice of consultant archaeologist is an important one, and provisions for appropriate training are required in order to enlarge the field of potential candidates.

32. Given the great archaeological value of the above-ground fabric and below-ground remains of cathedrals and their precincts, this lays a heavy responsibility on chapters, with a corresponding implication for costs, which can be considerable. However, English Heritage makes financial aid available for some archaeological works, and the CFCE is seeking to reach a clear understanding between the interested parties as to the requirements for archaeological projects and sources of funding for them. It is understood that guidelines are in production the purpose of which is to clarify the issues involved, and this is commended.

33. A requirement of the Care of Cathedrals Measure is that the preparation of the architect's quinquennial report must be carried out in consultation with the cathedral archaeologist. In this way any archaeological dimension of a proposed item of work should be registered at the outset, and form part of the advanced planning for any programme of work.

34. The security and proper curation of archaeological finds is noted to be a growing issue given the greater extent of archaeological investigation as an integral part of any project. Finds are very vulnerable without proper professional curation, and it is the duty of chapters to make appropriate arrangements for this.

RECORDS

35. The Care of Cathedrals Measure lays on chapters the responsibility for recording work executed to the fabric. The importance of this requirement has been emphasised by English Heritage's report on cathedrals, which found that the availability of records of past work to cathedrals was generally very poor. English Heritage has made resources available to trace, index and copy documents and drawings, and this is commended.

36. The provision of proper records, far from being an unnecessary expense, enables work to the fabric to be handled efficiently, provides the basis for future planning, and may also have potential for educational use. A guidance note on records has been prepared by a joint working party of the CFCE and English Heritage. This document, which covers this important topic in detail, is commended.

FINANCE

37. The cost of repairing and maintaining the fabric of both cathedral and cathedral-owned property is generally the heaviest draw on a cathedral's funds, as demonstrated in Chapter 13. Major projects such as reorderings, visitor centres, educational facilities and choir schools add to this burden.

38. The necessity for proper forward planning is essential in order to ensure that funding both for projects and for repair and maintenance works will be available to suit anticipated programmes. The quinquennial reports on both cathedral and Close properties, together with the 'audit of objectives' already recommended (see paragraph 24 above), should be the essential basis for this.

39. The aim of fabric care and conservation programmes should be to bring the condition of the fabric to a state where major interventions are reduced to a minimum, or even avoided entirely; consequently, suitable fund-raising methods need to be evolved. The continuous fund-raising procedures established by some cathedrals (e.g. Lincoln, York) is commended.

GOVERNMENT GRANT AID

40. The adoption by the Church of the framework of legislation set out in the Care of Cathedrals Measure has enabled the government to make grant aid available to cathedrals. In 1991 £11.5 million was promised over the three years 1991-1994, and in March 1993 a further £8 million was promised for 1994-1996. This grant aid is handled by English Heritage, which has set up a Cathedrals Team to deal with the assessment of needs and the apportionment of the grant on an annual basis. As the official agency responsible for advising the government on the preservation and enhancement of historic buildings, English Heritage has a natural interest in cathedrals: under the provisions of the Care of Cathedrals Measure it has the right to be consulted on the appointment of one member of the CFCE, and a right to comment on applications for consent made to the CFCE under the Measure. In addition, by virtue of its responsibility to handle grant aid to cathedrals, English Heritage has a right to comment on all applications made for grant aid.

41. English Heritage produced a set of guidelines to the cathedral grant scheme at its initiation in 1991. These guidelines record an agreement to review the scheme in spring 1994, and it is understood that there is an intention to produce a revised set of guidelines following this review. A particularly noteworthy element of the cathedral grant scheme is the

absence of a requirement, as a condition of grant, that cathedrals must consult English Heritage about any other work proposed. The absence of such a requirement is warmly commended as being appropriate in the context of cathedrals.

42. English Heritage has used some of the funding of the cathedral grants' budget to establish, in consultation with the CFCE and the Cathedral Architects' Association, a research programme into certain issues of particular concern to cathedrals. This, together with other joint initiatives between English Heritage and the CFCE (such as the joint guidance note on records), has helped to build up a valuable working relationship between the two bodies. Concern has been expressed by a number of cathedrals at the possibility that English Heritage might gradually seek to take over the control of fabric matters. Although we see no evidence of an intention to do so, the greater resources available to English Heritage could tend to eclipse the CFCE, with consequent loss of credibility to the CFCE; so initiatives which provide opportunities for successful partnership between the two bodies are commended as emphasising the distinct roles played by each body.

43. We also commend the responsible way in which English Heritage has so far approached its involvement with cathedrals, and the positive way in which grant aid is being channelled to them. At the same time, English Heritage needs to continue to have confidence in the working of the Care of Cathedrals Measure as a basis for the distribution of grants from public funds.

DISASTER PLANNING

44. The fires at York Minster and other historic buildings within the past few years have led to an increased awareness of the need for improvements in the standards of fire safety in historic public buildings. The recommendation made in the Bailey report *Fire Protection for the Royal Palaces*, that each historic palace should carry out a fire safety audit on a regular basis and develop a 'fire safety policy statement', is also recommended for cathedrals. The purpose of this is to ensure that all matters of fire security for people, fabric and objects is regularly reviewed and updated. At the same time, proposals that cathedrals should be covered by a certificate under the Fire Precautions Act do not seem appropriate.

45. The insurance of the fabric of cathedrals is noted to be an increasingly heavy financial burden on fabric funds. Consultation with insurance companies in the context of plans for proper disaster management is commended as a way to approach this problem constructively.

PROVISION FOR THE DISABLED

46. Many cathedrals have taken responsible steps to arrange access and make other provisions for the disabled, often in difficult situations; and such initiatives as 'Cathedrals through Touch and Hearing' are particularly to be commended. But the impression gained during our visits to cathedrals was that much remains to be done in this difficult but important area.

Precinct and Close

47. Most cathedrals are set in Closes, many containing buildings and groups of buildings of the greatest historic interest and value. They have developed alongside the cathedral which they surround and should receive the same degree of care in their repair and maintenance. This may have particular implications for the management of Close properties, in some instances requiring separate arrangements for management responsibility. Provision for inspection and repair of cathedral property is addressed in the Cathedrals Measure 1963 (section 27), and proposals should be reviewed on a quinquennial basis in conjunction with other fabric plans.

48. Patterns of ownership in Closes are often complex, with corresponding implications for responsibilities. Disposal of properties for financial reasons are very often regretted by later generations, and a number of cathedrals have found it necessary or desirable to repurchase properties previously disposed of.

49. The definitions of 'precinct' and 'buildings in ecclesiastical use' undertaken by the CFCE in conjunction with the Department of National Heritage have been helpful in clarifying the application of statutory requirements.

Contents

50. The requirement laid on cathedrals by the Care of Cathedrals Measure for the preparation of inventories has not been popular with some chapters; yet proper inventories are of very great importance and, in our view, ought in any case to be prepared and kept up to date as a matter of proper accountability. The five-year period stipulated in the Measure does seem to be too short and could appropriately be extended; but a specific date for completion should still be set.

51. The disposal of historic treasures is also controlled by the Care of Cathedrals Measure but, where disposal is by sale in order to raise funds,

the CFCE or FAC (as appropriate) should take the views of the cathedral's Finance and Investment Advisory Committee into account in reaching their decision (see Chapter 7, paragraph 27).

Links with the Diocese

52. At various points in this chapter comment has been made on areas where cathedrals could or perhaps should help churches in the diocese by advising and by setting standards. These include the fields of maintenance and repair, of liturgical reorderings, and of commissioning new works of art and craftsmanship. The Diocesan Advisory Committee will normally be the appropriate body through which this help may be channelled.

Recommendations

1. FACs should be entrusted with as high a degree of decision making as is compatible with the terms of the Care of Cathedrals Measure (paragraph 10).

2. All interested bodies should collaborate to ensure that there is no unnecessary duality of legislation in fabric and archaeological matters (paragraph 17).

3. Cathedrals should as a matter of priority establish clear management structures and define the roles of those principally concerned in the care and conservation of the fabric (paragraph 22).

4. In particular, the role and duties of cathedral architect should be defined on the lines proposed in the paper *The Role and Duties of a Cathedral Architect* prepared by the Cathedral Architects' Association, and the role and duties of cathedral archaeologist should be defined on similar lines (paragraph 23).

5. The CFCE must not be under-resourced – it performs a national statutory role which is the key to confidence in the operation of the Care of Cathedrals Measure, and of funding via English Heritage (paragraphs 19 and 43).

6. An 'audit of objectives' covering plans of a developmental nature and a fabric report for both cathedral and Close properties should be prepared on a quinquennial basis so that all works can be properly planned and ordered (paragraphs 24, 33 and 47).

7. Cathedrals should prepare 'fire safety policy statements' and hold regular fire safety audits (paragraph 44).

11

Trading

Introduction

1. The presence of trade within the precincts of a cathedral may seem incongruous: there are some who, with New Testament sequences in mind, question the appropriateness of making money in a context which is religious and therefore set apart from the world's values. And there are those who, with minds concentrated on the financial realities of running a cathedral, see such things not only as justifiable necessities, but also as part of the ministry of service which a cathedral must offer if it is to speak to the world.

2. In Christian tradition, trading has rarely been understood as in principle incompatible with spiritual things, although the Church has often sought to set out broad principles upon which honest and reasonable transactions should take place. If cathedrals are to respond to their calling to service the needs of all sorts and conditions of people who enter their space as tourists as well as pilgrims, then trading must be seen as an honourable and important part of that whole ministry of service for which they stand, although it will always be subordinate to and supportive of their worshipping life.

3. However, there are sensitivities to be considered and it is important that in defending the policy of trading in cathedrals those involved should exercise care in the extent to which these activities, in meeting the requirements of visitors, are allowed to intrude upon 'holy space', the environment of worship, prayer and architectural splendour. Often these things are not just related to intrusions on space; they can be matters of taste and aesthetics.

4. A cathedral shop or refectory, then, is not an end in itself, justified solely on the grounds of needing to supplement the income of the cathedral. It is part of the overall ministry of welcome and hospitality, and a response to the fact that in these present days most tourists and visitors expect to return home with some tangible memory of their visit. Moreover, some of the material on sale in a cathedral shop, for example, can directly assist the process of welcome to, and the interpretation of, the building and its life. Cathedrals, like other places of public interest, are

partly in the business of helping to feed and sustain the memory of those who visit, and a souvenir or a welcome received from a guide, a shop assistant or a member of the refectory staff can be a powerful aid to this end.

5.   From a financial point of view, shops, catering, and other forms of trading make a substantial and vitally needed contribution to the income of all the cathedrals studied. Figures on net profits are difficult to compare because individual cathedrals vary in the way they charge rent and overheads, and because their activities are often heavily dependent on volunteers. For example, Worcester makes some 65% profit on a catering turnover of £23,000 which is wholly dependent upon volunteer staff, whilst Liverpool, on the other hand, with a catering turnover of nearly £300,000 and only paid staff, makes a net profit of 13%. In retail trading, Canterbury, with a turnover of nearly £750,000 and only paid staff, makes a net profit of some 17%, whilst Carlisle, with a turnover of £42,000 and only volunteer staff, makes a net profit of just over 38%. However, in net terms, the aggregate income in this area is approximately £1.8 million – 4% of total income made up as shown in the following table:

Details of Trading

			Staff Numbers			
	Turnover	Net Profit	Paid		Volunteers	
	£m	£m	Full-time	Part-time	Full-time	Part-time
Retail	6.5	1.2	66	123	1	1,150
Catering	3.1	0.5	71	196	6	355
Other trading	0.9	0.1	26	27	–	24
Total	10.5	1.8	163	346	7	1,529

6.   However, while the dangers of comparison are recognised, figures show that the level of net profits from trading differs considerably from cathedral to cathedral. Seven cathedrals – Canterbury, Durham, Liverpool, St Paul's, St Albans, Salisbury and York – earn a net profit from all forms of trading of more than £100,000 each. Eighteen, however, make a net profit of less than £20,000. Although it might have been expected that the highest shop and catering net income would be earned by those cathedrals with the highest visitor income, this is not uniformly

the case. There seems to be a wide variation in the effectiveness with which cathedrals take advantage of the opportunities to earn income from these sources. There is evidence that in some places retail and catering sales are seen as having a relatively low priority. But, as the economics of running a cathedral become increasingly difficult, so it will become essential for all cathedrals to realise the potential of their trading activities, and to increase the quality of management.

7.   A point of concern has been raised about whether cathedral trading activities are in conflict with the charitable status of cathedrals or other bodies in whose name the trading takes place. A number of cathedrals avoid this possible problem by using a wholly-owned limited company which covenants its income to the cathedral.

Cathedral shops

8.   Of the 41 cathedrals which have some form of retailing outlet (Christ Church, Oxford is excluded because of the particular relationship with its college), three have a turnover in excess of £500,000, another ten over £200,000 and another eight over £100,000 with five more (twenty-six in total) in excess of £50,000. Fifteen have a turnover of less than £50,000.

9.   In aggregate, the turnover from cathedral shops is just under £6.5 million, and such a figure indicates the scope for cathedrals making more use of their purchasing power to obtain preferential terms from suppliers. The experience of other organisations suggests that the benefits of collaborative purchasing can be very considerable, and need not mean that each cathedral shop is like all others. Not only can terms, and thus margins, be improved, but quality items can be developed jointly and sales/market research information shared.

10.   Considerable benefits accrue from being able to make inter-cathedral comparisons, and we recommend that initiatives be taken to provide more detailed analysis of trading activities, and that information be exchanged in the following areas:

(a)   turnover, stock turn, gross and net profit margins;

(b)   terms negotiated on concessions and franchises;

(c)   decision making about the siting of shops;

(d)   employment terms and training, and the importance of prior experience.

11. Cathedral shops and other activities within the building depend on a mixture of paid and volunteer staff. The contribution of the volunteers is acknowledged elsewhere in this Report (see Chapter 9), but it is essential that they are professionally managed by staff who have skills in retailing, organisation, instruction and collaboration, and who are able to promote the work of the cathedral with patience and sensitivity. To this end, a programme of training for those involved in the various forms of trading in a cathedral is vitally important. The number of people involved well justifies the sponsorship of specific training schemes involving such things as:

(a)　customer advice and service;

(b)　merchandising and stock control;

(c)　display and space allocation;

(d)　the management of volunteers.

12. The Church Shops Association (CSA) meets annually to provide a forum for the exchange of best practices and ideas. This exchange is as yet informal, but we now recommend formal collaboration between the Association of English Cathedrals (AEC) and other bodies, such as the CSA and the Association of Ecclesiastical Catering, so that a central mechanism is provided for collaborative purchasing, the pooling of trading information, the development of professional training and best practices, and for making best use of the economies of scale.

Catering

13. Catering is provided at 26 cathedrals. Five cathedral restaurants have a turnover in excess of £200,000, a further eight in excess of £100,000 and six more in excess of £50,000. In general, although with some notable exceptions, less reliance is placed on volunteers than in cathedral shops, but this is largely due to the increasing stringency of health and safety regulations. The turnover of restaurants in aggregate is just under half that of the shops and their net profit amounts to just over one-third of that from shops. The advantages of greater collaboration to which we have already referred apply also to catering, although to a lesser extent since there is less opportunity for collaborative purchasing. Nevertheless, there are benefits to be gained from the sharing of information about the siting of restaurants, the preparation and display of food, best practice on seating plans and furnishings, and the management of customer flow. The Association of Ecclesiastical Catering is already considering means of improving this exchange of information.

14. Although there is evidence that a number of cathedrals have been successful in running their restaurants on a franchise basis, we believe that where possible it is good practice for cathedrals to attempt to manage their own catering operations as being an appropriate and cost-effective way of providing hospitality for visitors, and maximising income. Such a domestic arrangement can also help to signal the fact that those who work in catering are of equal value in the wider cathedral family. Again, however, it is very much dependent upon the availability of sound professional managers, as the danger of an incompetent manager making losses is very real.

Other trading

15. We note the contribution made by those cathedrals which have set up stonemasons' yards and other craft workshops as a means of meeting the permanent needs of the building, whilst providing an opportunity both for generating income and for developing appropriate training schemes. However, there are real dangers involved in entering into such arrangements without the benefit of properly researched business plans and professional management (see Chapter 7, paragraph 36 and Chapter 10, paragraph 26). Substantial losses can easily be made when forecasts of the potential market for such services prove unrealistic or if the management is lax. We commend other trading activities such as brass rubbing centres.

Trading in the future

16. The increasingly large contribution which is being made, and could be made, by trading of all kinds to the finances of cathedrals argues for a co-ordinated policy of education, training and planning that will transform their management and effectiveness. Much of the information and many of the ideas to make this possible are already available in some form. What is now needed is a commitment from cathedrals to move away from what historically has quite reasonably been seen as their individual concern towards a more collaborative approach. Such an approach makes both theological and commercial sense. We believe that the best way to make this happen is for the AEC to explore further all aspects of cathedral trading with the aim of co-ordinating a substantial improvement in the management and performance of shops and restaurants.

Recommendations

1. Cathedrals should seek to increase professionalism in the management of their trading activities (paragraphs 6 and 11).

2. Cathedrals should reappraise their trading opportunities and arrangements in the light of information available from other cathedrals (paragraphs 6, 10 and 11).

3. Cathedrals should devise a suitable policy for collaborative purchasing for their cathedral shops to improve trading margins in general, and to encourage those whose turnover is less than £100,000 (paragraphs 9 and 10).

4. Cathedrals should take every opportunity to share information about finance, marketing/sales, training and management (paragraphs 10 and 12).

5. Cathedrals should collaborate in the sponsorship of training for staff (paragraph 11).

6. In order to facilitate 1-5, the AEC should provide increased resources for those organisations such as the Church Shops Association and the Association of Ecclesiastical Catering which have already begun the task of addressing the issues raised above (paragraph 12 and also Chapter 7, paragraphs 39-41).

7. The AEC should explore further the trading and catering activities of cathedrals with a view to co-ordinating a substantial improvement in the performance of shops and restaurants (paragraph 16).

12

Tourism

Introduction

1.   Tourism is of great significance to cathedrals – in terms of their mission of teaching, evangelism and welcome, and as an important source of income. Cathedrals also play a major part in the nation's tourism. In Chapters 2 and 3, we have looked at tourism in the context of the cathedrals' purpose, role and mission. In this chapter, we look first at the importance of cathedrals to tourism as a whole, and then at the importance of tourism to cathedrals. We go on to consider the characteristics of those who visit cathedrals as tourists and conclude with a section on the management of tourism in cathedrals.

2.   This chapter draws heavily upon a paper (*Anglican Cathedrals and Tourism – The Way Forward*) produced by Max Hanna of Sightseeing Research, until recently the Resources Research Manager at the English Tourist Board (ETB), and financed by a grant from the Department of National Heritage. That report is published separately and is available from Church House Bookshop, priced £2.95; its tables are reproduced in Appendix 4. Max Hanna's paper draws upon a number of sources, including a report produced by the Church Study Unit (CSU), which was in turn financed by the Dulverton Trust. Max Hanna was responsible for the seminal ETB report on *English Cathedrals and Tourism* published in 1979, which is in large part superseded by his current paper.

The Importance of Cathedrals to Tourism

3.   The great significance of cathedrals to the country's tourism can be demonstrated in three ways:

(a)   the number of visitors attracted to cathedrals;

(b)   the wider economic benefits generated;

(c)   the contribution which cathedrals make to the sense of British heritage offered to tourists.

VISITOR NUMBERS

4.   The ETB estimated that 68.7 million visits were made in 1992 to historic properties in England, as compared with 66.2 million visits to museums and galleries, which was the next largest category. Cathedrals and churches accounted for about 32.4 million visits, which was nearly half of the total for historic properties, and of which 14.6 million visits were to Anglican cathedrals.

5.   St Paul's Cathedral is the fifth most visited tourist attraction for which a charge is made and Canterbury Cathedral, York Minster and Westminster Abbey are only exceeded by the British Museum, the National Gallery, Blackpool Pleasure Beach and the Palace Pier, Brighton among the free attractions. As many as half of the Anglican cathedrals (21) attracted over 200,000 visitors in 1992, a feat equalled by only 7% of the 5,500 tourist attractions in the UK. The annual numbers of visitors to each cathedral are given in Tables 1 and 2 in Appendix 4.

6.   Cathedrals have a particular appeal to foreign tourists who contribute far more per head to the economy than domestic tourists. At least 33 cathedrals have attempted to estimate the proportion of their visitors who come from overseas and the weighted average of overseas visitors at those cathedrals is 31% of all visitors. The highest estimated proportions have been for St Paul's (70%), Salisbury (50%), Exeter (50%), Winchester (39%), Canterbury (35%), Ely (35%) and Chester (33%).

7.   In order to get a more accurate assessment of visitor numbers, we requested all 42 Anglican cathedrals to undertake a count of visitors and their expenditure in the two weeks between 31 July and 13 August 1993. Some of the results of that survey with comparative figures for 1978 are set out in Tables 3, 4 and 5 in Appendix 4. Detailed information of this nature is important both to demonstrate the contribution of each cathedral to local tourism and to enable each cathedral to manage its visitor facilities effectively and efficiently. That this information needs to be regularly updated is shown by the significant differences between the 1978 and 1993 figures.

ECONOMIC IMPACT

8.   Apart from the direct benefit that the cathedral derives from tourism, the impact on sales and employment in the local economy of a cathedral which welcomes visitors is considerable. In employment terms, many cathedrals now employ tourism or visitor staff who are responsible for co-ordinating and handling the visitor facilities, and the shop and catering activities employ many full- or part-time staff. Some employment on

136

maintenance work is also related to the tourism activities of the cathedrals.

9.   Thirty-five cathedrals have given information on the number of staff involved in tourism-related work in 1992 (Table 6 in Appendix 4). 454 jobs were identified, of which 196 were full-time permanent, 205 part-time permanent and 53 part-time seasonal. A further 3,147 volunteers were employed for a variety of tourism-related tasks. Ten cathedrals employed 200 or more volunteers, including 350 at Canterbury and 400 at Norwich.

10.   Research at tourist attractions indicates that there is a considerable financial contribution to the local economy as visitors use local transport, stay in local accommodation and spend money in shops and restaurants. For example, in 1985, the ETB commissioned a study covering 40 attractions which found that, for every £1 spent at a specific attraction, around £5.50 was also spent by tourists on accommodation, eating out and shopping in the local area.

UK HERITAGE

11.   In addition to the quantifiable benefits which cathedrals bring to the tourism industry, they also play an equally important, but less tangible, role as part of the UK heritage. A cathedral is often the focus for a mediaeval town centre and is the most prominent expression of the UK's complex cultural and social history. Heritage is still the most important reason why overseas tourists visit the UK. The British Tourist Authority's Survey of Overseas Visitors found that 81% of foreign tourists in 1992 cited 'heritage, countryside, or sightseeing' as being important or very important in their decision to visit Britain. The same survey reported that 72% of overseas tourists in 1984 had visited cathedrals, churches and other religious sites, which was a higher proportion than for any other attraction. A survey of cultural visits in March 1993 found that 24% of the adult population had visited a cathedral in the previous 12 months as compared with 32% visiting a stately home, 26% a castle, and 23% some other building of historic or architectural interest.

The Importance of Tourism to Cathedrals

12.   Tourism is important to cathedrals for two principal reasons – first, as part of its mission of teaching, evangelism and witness and, second, as a source of income. The first set of considerations has already been discussed in Chapter 3. The second is discussed briefly in the following paragraphs.

INCOME GENERATION

13. Cathedrals derive income from tourists in the form of donations, admission charges to all or specific areas of the cathedral, retailing and catering.

14. The total net annual income received by cathedrals from those sources (excluding Christ Church, Oxford) amounted to £6.3 million, made up as follows:

Donations and admission charges	£4.6 million
Retailing and catering	£1.7 million

The two week visitor survey (see paragraph 7 above) was used to obtain a better understanding of where and how this money was earned. In particular, it was possible to prepare a detailed analysis of the relationship between visitor numbers and expenditure at each cathedral. It was also possible to make a comparison with the expenditure per head in 1978.

15. Details of that analysis are given in Tables 7 to 14 in Appendix 4 but the key findings are as follows:

(a) the average expenditure per head at the 26 cathedrals giving full information was £1.09. This is five times as great as the average of 22p recorded at 17 cathedrals in 1978, and it is a large increase in real terms as retail price inflation rose by less than three times between 1978 and 1993;

(b) within the five categories of expenditure making up average total expenditure, retail accounted for 46p (a four-fold increase on 1978), catering accounted for 29p (again, a four-fold increase), donations 26p (a near seven-fold increase), admissions 25p and 'others' 4p;

(c) the number of items sold per 100 visitors rose by 28% from 39 in 1978 to 50 in 1993;

(d) the experience of Ely shows that an all-inclusive admission charge can be combined with a substantial income from catering and retail sales. Even the average donation at Ely was higher than at nearly a fifth of the cathedrals. However, Ely is unique in a number of ways, and it is not at all certain that Ely's experience can be replicated elsewhere.

Visitor Characteristics

16. For cathedrals to be fully effective in their mission of welcome to visitors and to meet their needs, an understanding of visitor characteristics

and their motivation is important. Two surveys conducted in 1993 are of particular interest. One was by Mintel on cultural visits among a nationally representative sample of 1,040 adults, and a second, organised for us by the CSU,[1] interviewed a sample of visitors to four cathedrals. 814 interviews were completed at Coventry, Ely, Lichfield, and Wells. The results of this second survey were compared with 3,182 interviews completed at 11 cathedrals for the ETB undertaken in 1978. The comparison was particularly significant since the questions of the 1978 survey formed the basis of the 1993 survey together with additional information on the religious aspects of cathedral visiting. Surveys from 16 other cathedrals taken during the past decade were also studied.

MINTEL

17. Mintel observed that almost a quarter of those questioned had visited a cathedral in the previous 12 months (see paragraph 11 above) and of these a significantly greater proportion were women. Over 50% were between 45 and 54 years of age and about 20% over 65. Looking at the socio-economic grouping, there appeared to be a steady increase in numbers across the social groupings from C to A and there were regional variations too, showing twice the number of visitors coming from the Midlands compared with the North West. Of all visitors, 19% came with children.

CHURCH STUDY UNIT SURVEY

18. Although this was a small sample, it is of particular interest because, for the first time, questions were asked about religious allegiance and the perceptions of visitors. In continuing to develop facilities to receive visitors, cathedrals will not only be interested to learn that a majority of those questioned had made a special journey to see the cathedral, but that around a quarter were casual visitors who 'happened to be in the area'. Significantly, too, over half were making a return visit and this may be a measure of the attractiveness of a cathedral visit, although it should be noted that other surveys have shown a lower proportion of return visitors. Canterbury (45%) and Derby (28%) are among the examples. The findings will give considerable encouragement to those responsible for the visitor ministry. There is no doubt that cathedrals can learn much from one another in the management of visitors, and we give warm encouragement to those organisations which bring together those responsible for this work.

---

[1] The full report (*A Survey of Visitors to Four English Cathedrals*) by Dr Ruth Gasson and Dr Michael Winter is available from Dr Winter, Countryside and Community Research Unit, Cheltenham and Gloucester College of Higher Education, Francis Close Hall, Swindon Road, Cheltenham GL50 4AZ.

19. Not unexpectedly the time spent varied with the size of the building, and the amount to be seen. Ely had by far the greatest number (40%) staying for more than an hour. This may reflect positive and negative aspects of charging which may deter the casual visitor but encourage others to obtain 'value for money'. The 'value for money' factor will need to be borne in mind by all cathedrals that wish to encourage higher levels of donation or to institute charges. The time spent by visitors is a significant indicator in devising policy, and emphasises the need to continue obtaining accurate data from which to assist the formulation of policy.

20. Facilities most appreciated and required were gift and book shops followed by restaurants, lavatories and car parks. The survey records that visits to the shop varied from 45% at Wells to 70% at Ely, and noted that much greater use was made of restaurants in real terms in 1993 compared with the ETB survey of 1978. Up to a fifth of visitors joined guided tours or sought help from cathedral staff, and there was much evidence from our cathedral visits which suggests, as we mention elsewhere (see Chapter 9, paragraphs 32-34), that attention must be given to the training of all volunteers and the contractual nature of their 'gift of time' to their cathedral. At Coventry 30% of visitors went to the information desk and at Lichfield just 17%. A marked improvement in information facilities since 1978 suggests an increasing demand by visitors which is being well matched by a desire on the part of cathedrals to provide a better service. This view was confirmed in 1993 when 70% of visitors felt welcome in all four cathedrals involved.

21. At all four cathedrals in the CSU survey visitors were asked how they would react to an admission charge. At Coventry, Lichfield and Wells those strongly against a charge were about half. Significantly, at Ely, which does charge, only a quarter expressed opposition. These had already paid and therefore had presumably accepted the case for charging and, indeed, felt that they were getting value for money. In 1987 at Worcester, objection, approval, and undecided were of about equal measure among those asked about charging.

22. Only a very small percentage of the sample (2-3%) criticised the way the cathedral was presented. Suggestions for improvement included the use of background music or the opening of closed parts of the building. More information about the cathedral, with improved labelling, slides, or video, as well as better access, were all mentioned. Other cathedral surveys voiced criticisms about the crowds, modern works of art, pressure to give, and trading. Noise was generally a common complaint.

23. For the first time in a cathedral survey, the CSU questions asked about religious belief and affiliation. Table 1 gives the results of the survey:

Table 1   Cathedral Visitor Beliefs and Affiliation

Denomination	Number of Interviews	% of total
Church of England	333	41
Roman Catholic	104	13
Methodist	41	5
Baptist	20	3
Other Denominations	88	11
Not Church Member	219	27
Total	805	100

24. The evidence which we received shows that cathedrals are alert to the opportunities presented to them to interpret the Christian faith in today's world. Of those visitors attending worship Table 2 below indicates the scale of that opportunity and this Report points the way forward in role, mission and responsibility:

Table 2   Visitor Church Attendance

Frequency of attendance at worship	%
At least once a week	34
At least once a month	13
At least three times a year	10
At least once a year	7
Does not attend	36
Total	100

25. Those questioned were asked to reflect on six statements about belief. Not unexpectedly, there were marked differences of perception between church members and non-members. We recognise the wide variety of motives which lead people to visit cathedrals. This fact will lead those

whose ministry is within the historic tradition and is located in cathedrals sensitively to present the claims of Christ and his Church, a Church committed to evangelism and mission. We are conscious of the dramatic interface between the Church and society that takes place at cathedrals, and we affirm the need to see them and use them as strong places of mission.

26. We recognise the value in gathering information about the religious affiliation and attitudes of visitors to cathedrals. The way information is interpreted has far-reaching implications for the methods used by a cathedral as it welcomes its visitors and what it does with them. From our visits it is also clear that more attention needs to be given to the style in which the Christian message is presented in an exciting and dynamic way to those who, of their own choice, find their way inside these testimonies of past and present faith. The Church can no longer make assumptions that those it meets in these circumstances know anything about Christ or the Christian faith. Cathedrals have a real opportunity not only to interpret for their visitors the signs and symbols of that faith but also, in the quality of the interaction of the cathedral with its visitors, to demonstrate the living of the Christian life as well.

Tourism Management

INTRODUCTION

27. It has already been observed that tourism provides two opportunities for cathedrals: a means to enhance their income and a chance to evangelise. A glance at paragraph 14 above shows that cathedrals already earn £6.3 million annually from their visitors and Tables 1 and 2 in Appendix 4 show that over 14 million people visit the English Anglican cathedrals each year.

28. The magnitude of those figures requires that cathedrals should exercise effective management of their tourism activities. In that context, major improvements have been made in recent years, but the pressure and demands of both tourist numbers and cathedral economics are relentless and call for continuing management decisions and initiatives by the cathedrals. Those decisions and initiatives are discussed in the following paragraphs.

RESEARCH

29. Knowledge of visitor numbers and their characteristics, motivation, expectations and behaviour is vital to the effective management of the tourism and trading activities in and around the cathedral so that both the visitors and the cathedral itself achieve the greatest benefits.

30. The first requirement is to know visitor numbers, ideally by time of day and day of week for the different parts of the year. More accurate numbers will facilitate the handling of tourism arrangements and the testing of new initiatives. For example, flow patterns can be used in deciding what staff are required at different times of the day, week and year.

31. That information can be obtained either from continuous (census) counts or by some form of extrapolation from sample counts. Table 1 (in Appendix 4) shows that most cathedrals use some form of extrapolation from either sample counts or proxy measures (e.g. the number of purchases in a shop) to estimate their total numbers. It is essential that the basis on which such extrapolation is made is checked regularly and at least every third year. However, we believe that continuous counts using electronic devices should be introduced wherever possible (and all the evidence shows that vertical beam electronic counters are more accurate than the horizontal variety).

32. In addition to continuous electronic counting and extrapolation, two week physical counts at all cathedrals such as that undertaken for us (see paragraph 7 above) have considerable advantages in validating the continuous counting and extrapolation methods and providing important corresponding data on expenditure patterns (see paragraph 15 above). Therefore, there seems to be considerable merit in all the cathedrals collaborating in repeating a simultaneous count every three to five years.

33. In addition to the quantitative data, qualitative data on visitor characteristics, motivation, expectations and behaviour is also important in taking decisions about how to attract and manage tourists and what should be provided. The survey undertaken by the CSU (see paragraphs 18 to 26 above) shows how revealing such surveys can be, and we recommend that the cathedrals agree a standard format of questions using the CSU questionnaire as a base so that comparisons can be made over time and between different cathedrals. We believe that the Association of English Cathedrals (AEC) should seek academic support to carry out such surveys periodically at all cathedrals.

MARKETING

34. Few cathedrals actively market themselves and seemingly have little motivation to do so since other bodies include cathedrals in their literature and the more popular cathedrals sometimes wish that they had fewer visitors. Indeed, 'marketing' is a term alien to most chapters with respect to their cathedral.

35. However, marketing is an important tool for managing visitors in order to:

(a)   encourage visitor numbers in the face of increased competition and, if so desired, increase the number of visitors;

(b)   encourage visits at off-peak periods;

(c)   manage visitor expectations by explaining to visitors what they will see, what guides and facilities are available, how long it will take and why donations are requested.

In that context, cathedrals will find it helpful to chapters, paid staff and volunteers to issue a statement of their objectives in relation to visitors. Such a statement sets their marketing into context and could cover such matters as the cathedral's mission to visitors in terms of witness, evangelism, education and welcome; and its aims in terms of facilities, quality of experience and income generation.

36. The marketing means employed need to incorporate the full spectrum, including:

(a)   developing closer relations with national and regional tourist boards, local authority tourism and leisure officers, and local associations of tourist attractions. At the local level, this is clearly best undertaken by the individual cathedrals – at the national level, the AEC has a part to play with the British Tourist Authority, particularly in the context of the overseas tourist;

(b)   the production and distribution of promotional and inform-ational leaflets and other material by the individual cathedral.

VISITOR FACILITIES

37. It is very clear that many improvements in facilities for visitors have been made over recent years. Imaginative and informative literature is important, and virtually all cathedrals now provide leaflets and guide-books for their visitors, often in several languages. Exhibitions have been provided, refectories opened and walk-around guides and audio-visual presentations introduced to augment the personal guides. Improved interpretation of the spiritual aspects of cathedrals is also very apparent. Perhaps the biggest advances have occurred in the educational facilities offered by cathedrals. These now often include excellent literature for children and opportunities for schools to bring parties for an educational experience which forms part of the National Curriculum. Tactile models and audio guides for the blind have also been provided in many cathedrals.

38. However, although the improvements are considerable and impressive, there are few cathedrals where further progress, sometimes considerable, could not with advantage be made. Often the improvements needed are in mundane areas. The provision of lavatories, clear and simple signs, road directions to cathedrals and the availability of parking, are all examples of visitor facilities to which cathedrals should give attention. Some much needed facilities will not be within the gift of cathedrals, but close liaison and co-operation with local authorities and tourist organisations will help.

39. In almost all cathedrals, there is scope for some improvement in less mundane areas – for example, in their catering and retail outlets, guides and guided tours and, importantly, in the spiritual interpretation of the cathedral as a whole and its various parts in furtherance of its mission of witness, education and evangelism.

40. In summary, it is clear that the best practices are very good and, indeed, most cathedrals show excellence in one or more areas. However, where for any area they were deficient, most could usefully learn from others. Exchange of ideas in such cathedral forums as the Pilgrims' Association, the group of four largest cathedrals, regional groupings (e.g. the southern cathedrals) and with local tourist boards is bound to be beneficial.

MANAGEMENT OF STAFF AND VOLUNTEERS

41. Making effective use of visitor facilities and providing an experience to visitors, which not only meets their expectations but also gives a spiritual dimension to their visit, require careful management by professional and well-trained staff. Ideally, both paid staff and volunteers should be managed by a permanent member of the cathedral's staff, clerical or lay. Eleven of the larger cathedrals have a visitor officer and we strongly support such an appointment wherever possible. It is difficult to over-emphasise the benefits which flow from such an appointment which can give the necessary focused attention to visitor management, such as the organisation of volunteers who serve the visitors as welcomers and guides, the flow of visitors, the provision of literature and other facilities, and helping tour and coach operators.

42. We have commented in Chapter 9 on the use, training, care and control of volunteers. Nowhere is that more important than with those volunteers dealing with visitors. Such management is of even greater importance for permanent staff. Instructions in first aid, security, health and safety and fire precautions should be arranged through appropriate agencies and, for those in direct contact with visitors, training in 'people

skills' is vital. The Industrial Society runs many courses of relevance to cathedral staffs and we commend that institution to deans and chapters.

43. The training of guides, stewards and welcomers is of the utmost importance. Again, the cathedrals with the best practice in this area were very impressive; others were almost amateur in their approach. The need for each cathedral to have training material is very clear and there is a strong argument for cathedrals to collaborate in providing a 'Train the Trainers' course.

VISITOR MANAGEMENT

44. The impact which large numbers of visitors have on the fabric and precincts of cathedrals cannot be ignored. ICOMOS surveys have high-lighted the damage which can be done to floors, brasses, decorative tiles and tombs. Some cathedrals have installed devices to measure the extent of wear and damage. Information of such potential hazards should be used in planning routes to minimise damage. However, action needs to be taken with discretion and judgement; we would not wish to see large areas of cathedrals excluded from visitors if that can be avoided. Cathedrals are there to be seen and used.

45. However, it is very clear that the number of visitors cannot, in the most popular cathedrals, continue to grow unchecked, particularly in peak periods. Not only has the question of damage to be considered, but the very numbers themselves destroy the quality of experience and, inevitably, tranquillity and spirituality are lost and the building is seen only for its architectural and historical merits.

46. Although routing visitors around the cathedral can help, eventually some way of limiting numbers may be required. This could come about by a number of means – for example, programming coach arrivals, timed tickets, limiting the rate of entry, and by charging. Such actions, particularly the last, raise issues of principle.

47. A specific aspect of visitor management that merits particular attention is that of tour party management. It was clear that some cathedrals were markedly more successfully active than others in their control of both the number and timing of tour parties to the benefit of both the visitors and the cathedral.

48. In the context of a training programme for all those who work in the cathedral, both paid staff and volunteers, we recommend that the AEC should arrange specialised courses which make use of secular expertise in the management of people who come as guests. The Pilgrims' Association

has already provided opportunities for those who work closely with tourists and pilgrims to understand how staff can be trained to 'manage' people with a professional care. Not everyone possesses an intuitive ability to welcome and deal with people who come with a variety of expectations and needs, but much can be done to teach staff those skills of care and attention which are vital if an appropriate quality of hospitality is to be maintained.

Admission Charges

49. At the start of the nineteenth century cathedrals normally levied a charge on visitors: Britain, at that time, was used to an enormous number of internal tolls and customs charges on goods and persons in transit and the arrangement would have seemed quite unexceptional. It was a dimension of Victorian educational idealism, however, to suppose that the people should be supplied with free access to cultural and historical information. The nineteenth century, therefore, became the century of the free public library, the municipal reading-room, the art gallery and free primary education. Pew-renting in churches was mostly swept away; access was allowed to public buildings which had before been reserved to the privileged. It was in this context that cathedrals ended charging for admission. In our own day, it could be argued, people once again expect to pay for cultural facilities – the heritage centres and themed museums of the later years of the twentieth century usually make charges. The question is whether the experience of a century of free admission to cathedrals has itself created different public expectations because they are sacred places; whether, unlike commercial enterprises or municipal public services, the essential purposes of cathedrals are best fulfilled when the public senses that it may freely enter them – whether the public, that is to say, now associates the sacred character of the building with open access. People are conscious that cathedrals have to be maintained, and that the costs involved must be high; do they regard the levy of a charge to enter all or part of the building as incompatible with the sense, simultaneously experienced, that they are in God's house?

50. We have been very conscious during the course of our work of the issue of charging for admission. The financial information gathered has shown the high cost of running and maintaining cathedrals and brought into sharp focus the stringent circumstances in which many find themselves. A number see some form of charging for admission as the only solution to their financial difficulties, particularly when faced with a reduction, or possibly withdrawal, of the Church Commissioners' grants. Furthermore, the existing guidelines for English Heritage grant aid state that EH 'take into account potential visitor income in assessing a particular cathedral's ability to raise funds'.

51. There are various options available to cathedrals in introducing charging. They can:

(a) charge for entry to the close or precincts;

(b) charge for entry to the whole cathedral;

(c) charge for entry to parts of the cathedral.

Any of the above methods can be applied during particular times and on specified days.

52. Although around a third of cathedrals charge for 'extras' or entry to specific parts of the cathedral (for example, the roof or the treasury) (see Table 13 in Appendix 4), only Ely and St Paul's have introduced compulsory admission charges. (At Salisbury, the charge is not compulsory.) At both Ely and St Paul's, however, it is possible for a visitor to enter free to a limited part of the cathedral for prayer and meditation, and charges are not made on Sundays or at the time of services.

53. The arguments in favour of and against charging have been extensively rehearsed, but they can be usefully summarised as follows. Those in favour of charging say that:

(a) it would, in many cases, solve the financial problems which many cathedrals face. A charge of only £1 would probably multiply the income received from visitors by a factor of from 3 to 5;

(b) visitor flow could be more easily controlled by peak hour pricing or timed tickets;

(c) fewer visitors would enter, reducing wear and tear on the fabric and enabling the quality of welcome and experience to be enhanced. The 'atmosphere' in the cathedral would improve;

(d) more money would be available to finance improved facilities and interpretation;

(e) more accurate visitor statistics would be available;

(f) those who impose costs but gain benefits from a visit should pay;

(g) it is a myth that all those who visit a cathedral do so on a 'spiritual quest'; the majority who visit are coming to a tourist site and would expect to pay. Further, those who are on a 'spiritual quest' are more likely to understand the reason why money has to be charged. Most people thus expect to pay but will not do so unless it is mandatory;

148

(h)   early indications from those few cathedrals which have introduced charging are that resistance to an admission charge declines once it has been introduced, that people stay longer and that retail and catering income remains at a high level;

(i)   the funds generated could be used for the cathedral's other activities, or used to release moneys for other cathedrals which do not have the same opportunities or for the Church elsewhere.

54. The arguments against charging are as follows:

(a)   God's love and grace are free and should be seen to be free;

(b)   the opportunities for evangelism and to communicate the Christian faith will diminish;

(c)   the relationship between cathedral and visitor will change from one of giving to receiving, from faith to commercialism;

(d)   with many parish churches now locked and not freely accessible for security reasons, cathedrals are among the few remaining places where free access to the rich symbolism of living Christianity may still be gained; to curtail or remove that free access would be sad;

(e)   the poorer members of society will stay away; only the wealthier or culturally minded will continue to visit;

(f)   those seeking pastoral advice will be too frightened or too poor to enter;

(g)   there would undoubtedly be expenditure involved in introducing charges in respect of the means of collection, extra staff, insurance and security costs;

(h)   visitors who pay will have even greater expectations and more will have to be provided for them.

There is certainly some evidence from those cathedrals which do charge to support (e) and (f) above.

55. There are also tax and VAT implications of charging for admission. On balance, cathedrals which charge are able to recover increased amounts of VAT, but the position is somewhat fluid and each cathedral would have to establish its own position.

56. We have become fully aware of the arguments for and against some form of charging – and the passion with which they are sometimes put forward and held. We believe that it would be inappropriate to make any general recommendation either in favour of or against charging; each

cathedral has to reach its own decision. However, we are very clear about the principles which should be followed by a cathedral when considering (as it should) whether or not to introduce some form of charging:

(a)   each cathedral should go through the exercise of examining the issues of charging in detail in the light of all the arguments and factors and their own circumstances, priorities and location (but bearing in mind that the additional resources which they generate could benefit other cathedrals and parts of the Church which do not have the same opportunities);

(b)   any decision may change with time and as circumstances and priorities change;

(c)   there should be wide consultation and the experience of others should be taken into account.

57.   If a decision to implement some form of charging is taken, then again certain principles are clear:

(a)   there should always be free access to some part of the cathedral for prayer and meditation and for those seeking pastoral and spiritual solace and support;

(b)   again, the wisdom and experience of others should be taken into account in how best to implement the decision;

(c)   all the options and the full implications need to be thought through and implementation carefully planned and executed;

(d)   the decision and new arrangements should be well communicated to all those affected.

Recommendations

1.   Cathedrals should introduce continuous counts of visitors using electronic devices since knowledge of visitor numbers is vital to the effective management of tourism. This information should be supplemented by regular (three to five year) physical counts and questionnaire surveys (paragraphs 29-33).

2.   Cathedrals should seek to improve their tourism marketing (paragraphs 34-36).

3.   Cathedrals should review their visitor facilities and exchange ideas in such forums as the Pilgrims' Association (paragraphs 37-40).

4.   A visitor officer should be appointed whenever possible (paragraph 41).

5.   Visitor management should be given high priority, and the AEC should arrange specialised courses which offer secular expertise in the management of visitors and help cathedral staff to improve their skills in welcoming and caring for tourists (paragraphs 44-48).

6.   Each cathedral should examine the issues of charging in detail in the light of its own circumstances and location (paragraphs 49-57).

13

Finance

Introduction

1.   As part of our enquiries, a survey was carried out of various aspects of the finances of cathedrals. The principal purpose of the exercise was to determine the cathedrals' overall financial health and to enable us to make suitable recommendations. The survey included both chapter funds and trust funds held for the benefit of the cathedral.

2.   Previous Commissions on cathedrals have examined their financial position, notably those in 1885, 1927 and 1961. All three reported on the parlous financial state of individual cathedrals but, as far as is known, this exercise is the most comprehensive review of cathedral finances under-taken this century and, probably for the first time, brings together the figures for both capitular and trust funds. The resulting analysis and interpretation are described in the rest of this chapter; more detail is provided in Appendix 5 together with the definitions used in collecting the underlying data. The data provided by the cathedrals was for the latest accounting year that each cathedral could supply; of those, 3 related to periods ending in 1993, 32 to those ending in 1992 and 6 in 1991.

Overall results

3.   A summary of the overall financial analysis is shown in Table 1 for all 41 cathedrals for which data has been received, that is for the 42 Church of England cathedrals, less Christ Church, Oxford whose finances are closely intertwined with those of its college activities. The overall figures have been further analysed for:

(a)   the dean and chapter cathedrals (D&CC), sub-divided as follows:

   (i)   the 4 largest D&CC (Canterbury, St Paul's, Salisbury and York) whose income figures outstrip all other ('The Top 4') (Table 1 in Appendix 5);

   (ii)   the 9 next largest D&CC with income of around £1 million and more (Chichester, Durham, Ely, Gloucester, Hereford, Lincoln, Wells, Winchester and Worcester) ('The 9 next largest D&CC') (Table 2 in Appendix 5);

Table 1   Analysis of All Cathedrals

Balance Sheet:

	Chapter		Trust Funds	
	Cost	Market Value	Cost	Market Value
Property Investments	44.293	124.100	1,324	1,395
Other Investments	30.833	38.527	23.362	25.060
Other Assets	27.926	29.409	10.088	9.851
Liabilities	103.052	192.037	34.774	36.306
Net Assets	9.110	9.110	385	385
Maintenance Overhang	93.943	182.927	34.389	35.921
Net Chapter Assets after Overhang	38.400	38.400		
	55.542	144.526		

Income Analysis:

	Chapter	Trust	Total	Percentage
Other Investment Income	3.768	5.242	9.009	21%
Investment Property Income	5.720	53	5.773	14%
Direct Tourist Income	5.943	48	5.991	14%
Net Shop, Refectory & Other Trading Income	1,841	0	1,841	4%
Church Commissioners' Stipends & Grants	5.423	0	5.423	13%
HBMC & Other Grants	1.962	135	2.097	5%
Diocesan Stipends & Grants	792	1	793	2%
Collections/Almsgiving	2.317	1	2.318	5%
Appeals	1.679	2.580	4.259	10%
Friends	969	54	1.023	2%
Legacies	1.058	506	1.564	4%
Transfers from Trusts	6.201	(6.201)	0	0%
Other Income	2.044	169	2.213	5%
Total Income	**39.716**	**2.589**	**42.304**	**100%**

Expenditure Analysis:

	Total	Percentage
Upkeep of Fabric	10.554	27%
Chapter Costs	4.769	12%
Administration Costs	4.948	12%
Services/Music/Choir School	4.605	12%
Vergers/Upkeep of Interior	3.900	10%
Upkeep of Precinct/Gardens	2.077	5%
Long-term Maintenance Charge	1.405	4%
Visitors/Tourists/Education	1.364	3%
Library/Archives	402	1%
Special Projects	1.730	4%
Outward Giving	640	2%
Payments to Diocese	291	1%
Other Expenditure	3.086	8%
Total Expenditure	**39.770**	**100%**

	Chapter	Trust	Total
Surplus/(Deficit)	**(55)**	**2.589**	**2.534**

All figures in £'000

Other Income

Library/Archives	108
Fees	472
Sundry Operating Income	323
Profit on Sale of Property/Investments	837
Other Non-Operating Income	472
Total	**2.213**

Other Expenditure

Insurance for Cathedral	912
Loss on Sale of Property/Investments	219
Interest Paid	132
Other Long-term Charges	377
Other Operating Expenditure	1.446
Total	**3.086**

		Sensitivity (% change in Income Type to Break Even)
Surplus/(Deficit) Excluding Profit/Loss on Sale of Property/Investments	1,916	410%
Surplus/(Deficit) Excluding Investment Income	(12,248)	17%
Surplus/(Deficit) Excluding Net Tourism	(2,093)	55%
Surplus/(Deficit) Excluding Church Commissioners' Grants & Stipends	(2,889)	47%
Surplus/(Deficit) Excluding All Grants & Stipends	(5,779)	30%
Surplus/(Deficit) Excluding Appeals & Legacies	(3,289)	44%
Net Tourist/Visitor/Pilgrim Profit Margin	4,627	77%
Total Return on Investments	8%	
Net Return on Investment Property	5%	
Net Return on Other Investments	14%	
Administration as a percentage of Income	12%	
Restoration Expenditure (in last 10 years)	57,898	1,412 per Cathedral

Balance Sheet Analysis:

Maintenance Overhang as percentage of Net Assets	18%
Expenditure Cover: Net Assets (Chapter)/Expenditure	4.6
Expenditure Cover: Net Assets (Total)/Expenditure	5.5
Years to Clear Overhang at Current Year's Expenditure Rate	3.6
Years to Clear Overhang at 10 Year Average Expenditure Rate	6.6

Projections: Surplus/(Deficit)

	Budget (no Restoration)	Restoration	Budget (after Restoration)
One Year Ahead	6,609	7,959	(1,350)
Two Years Ahead	5,476	7,585	(2,109)
Three Years Ahead	3,523	5,349	(1,826)
Four Years Ahead	2,897	4,359	(1,462)
Five Years Ahead	2,990	4,290	(1,300)
	21,495	**29,542**	**(8,047)**

Note: Figures in this and other tables are subject to rounding errors.

(iii)   the 7 remaining D&CC which are of pre-19th century establishment in their present form (Carlisle, Chester, Exeter, Lichfield, Norwich, Peterborough and Rochester) ('The next 7 D&CC') (Table 3 in Appendix 5);

(iv)   the 7 D&CC whose current dioceses are fundamentally of 19th and 20th century establishment (Bristol, Guildford, Liverpool, Manchester, Ripon, St Albans and Truro) ('The 19th and 20th century D&CC') (Table 4 in Appendix 5);

(b)   the parish church cathedrals (PCC), sub-divided as follows:

(i)   the 5 PCC with tourist income of £10,000 or more (Birmingham, Coventry, St Edmundsbury, Southwark, and Southwell) ('Hi-tourist PCC') (Table 5 in Appendix 5);

(ii)   the 9 PCC with tourist income of less than £10,000 (Blackburn, Bradford, Chelmsford, Derby, Leicester, Newcastle, Portsmouth, Sheffield and Wakefield) ('Lo-tourist PCC') (Table 6 in Appendix 5).

4.   Table 1 to this chapter (and Tables 1 to 6 in Appendix 5) are set out in the same format and contain the same headings as those prepared for each individual cathedral. The information given is grouped under the following headings:

(a)   the balance sheet (assets and liabilities) data for chapter and trust funds separately at cost and market values. Cathedrals were asked to estimate the 'maintenance overhang' (the estimated cost of major restoration work still outstanding), but not all cathedrals could give figures for this item ('restoration' was the term used when collecting financial information from cathedrals to distinguish major conservation/restoration work from routine repairs and maintenance). Various statistics based on the balance sheet figures are also shown, for example, the cover which the net assets provide for the annual expenditure;

(b)   income analysis – again showing chapter and trust fund figures separately, with a total of the two. The transfer from trust funds to the chapter includes both actual transfers and any expenditure on cathedral activities directly from trust funds;

(c)   expenditure analysis – only shown in total, including any expenditure by trusts on their cathedral ((b) above);

(d) surplus or deficit – separately for chapter, trust funds and in total. The trust surplus or deficit indicates the amount by which trusts have underspent or overspent their inflows. Sensitivity analyses show the impact on the total surplus or deficit of various items of income, for example, if investment income is excluded. Various other figures and analyses are also shown, including past restoration expenditure;

(e) projected future surplus or deficit – for each of the next five years, with the major restoration estimates shown separately.

5. In interpreting the information in this chapter, and in Appendix 5, it is vital to ensure that the definitions used (and attached at the end of Appendix 5) are fully understood.

Balance Sheet

6. The overall wealth of the 41 cathedrals can be gauged from the following figures (Table 2) for average chapter and trust net assets at market value and percentages of the total. The assets include both property and investments of all kinds, but the property values do not include a figure for the greatest asset of all – the cathedral itself – whose value cannot be practically measured:

Table 2   Cathedral Net Assets at Market Value – Averages and % of Total

	No of Cathedrals	Chapter Average £'000	Trust Average £'000	Total Average £'000	% of Total	Average Property Assets £'000	Average Other Net Assets £'000	% Other Net Assets £'000
Top 4	4	18,265	4,882	23,147	42	15,168	7,979	34
9 next largest D&CC	9	4,384	751	5,135	21	2,457	2,678	52
Next 7 D&CC	7	4,946	803	5,749	19	3,356	2,393	42
19th & 20th century D&CC	7	2,433	370	2,803	9	1,486	1,317	47
Hi-tourist PCC	5	2,220	111	2,331	5	1,181	1,150	49
Lo-tourist PCC	9	851	97	948	4	324	624	66
All	41	4,462 (84%)	876 (16%)	5,338 (100%)	100	3,061	2,277	43

7.   The table shows the very skewed distribution of net assets across the cathedrals with the 14 PCC owning only 9% of the total with the 7 Lo-tourist PCC having average net assets of less than £1 million. The relative lack of wealth of the 7 19th and 20th century D&CC shows clearly compared with the older D&CC; their capital is not very different from the Hi-tourist PCC. The table also shows the split between property and other net assets. As a considerable doubt attaches to the validity of property valuations in these changeable times, we have separated the figures between property assets and other net assets. This shows a rather more favourable distribution to the PCC; in other words, the older cathedrals have a bigger proportion of their assets tied up in property which is probably not so readily available to meet financial strains.

8.   Maintenance overhang figures were provided by 28 cathedrals, totalling £38 million. That represents 18% of total net assets for all cathedrals, but 28% of the total net assets for the 28 cathedrals, with 5 cathedrals having an overhang greater than their net assets.

9.   In terms of coverage of expenditure, the total net assets before overhang would provide for just over 5.5 years expenditure for all cathedrals. If trust funds are excluded, then the cover is just over 4.5 years expenditure. Within that, the Top 4 had the best cover at 8 years, the other D&CC had over 5 years cover and the PCC had just over 3 years in total (chapter and trust fund) net asset terms. However, these aggregates disguise significant variations within each group as shown by the following Table 3. From that, it will be seen that just over a quarter of all cathedrals have less than 2 years cover and just over a half have less than 4 years cover:

Table 3   Number of Years Expenditure Cover from Total Net Assets

	Number of Years Cover					
	0-2	2-4	4-6	6-8	8-10	>10
Top 4	–	1	–	1	–	2
9 next largest D&CC	3	3	1	–	1	1
Next 7 D&CC	1	2	1	–	–	3
19th & 20th century D&CC	1	2	2	2	–	–
Hi-tourist PCC	1	2	–	1	–	1
Lo-tourist PCC	5	1	3	–	–	–
All	11	11	7	4	1	7

Income and Expenditure

10. The overall average income for the 41 cathedrals was made up as follows (Table 4):

Table 4   Overall Average Cathedral Income

	No of Cathedrals	Chapter Average £'000	Trust Average £'000	Total Average £'000	% of Total
Top 4	4	2,469	710	3,179	30
9 next largest D&CC	9	968	387	1,355	29
Next 7 D&CC	7	614	104	718	12
19th & 20th century D&CC	7	556	164	720	12
Hi-tourist PCC	5	671	15	686	8
Lo-tourist PCC	9	376	57	433	9
All	41	818	214	1,032	100

Note: The chapter and trust (but not the total) figures in the above table differ from the total income figure in Table 1 as a result of excluding the transfers from trust to chapter funds.

11. Total income is less skewed than net assets. However, the inclusion of trust income still means that 59% of income is earned by 13 D&CC cathedrals. If trust income is excluded, then those same 13 cathedrals earn 55% of total chapter income. The average total income per cathedral drops steadily as one goes across the groups with only the middle two groups being similar.

12. The significance of the key components of income in terms of the percentages of total income is shown in Table 5 on the following page.

13. From that table:

(a)   the importance of investment income to all the older established D&CC is clear;

(b)   the importance of tourism income, especially to the Top 4, stands out;

(c)   shop, refectory and other trading income is an important contributor. It is interesting to note how very much more the 19th and 20th century D&CC earn from this source compared with the Hi-tourist PCC whose tourist income (in absolute and percentage terms) is similar;

(d)   the dependence upon the Church Commissioners by the PCC and the 19th and 20th century D&CC is stark.

Table 5   Sources of Income

	Top 4		9 next largest D&CC		Next 7 D&CC		19th & 20th century D&CC		Hi-tourist PCC		Lo-tourist PCC		All	
Number of Cathedrals	4		9		7		7		5		9		41	
	%	%	%	%	%	%	%	%	%	%	%	%	%	%
Investment Income		36		46		38		32		18		13		35
Church Commissioners'														
Stipends and Grants	4		8		15		20		22		38		13	
HBMC and other Grants	2		7		7		3		1		15		5	
Diocesan Stipends and Grants	–		2		3		3		2		5		2	
		6		17		25		26		25		58		20
Tourism (gross)	30		11		9		4		5		–		14	
Shop, refectory and other trading (net)	5		5		5		7		2		1		4	
		35		16		14		11		7		1		18
Collections/Almsgiving	3		4		7		8		8		12		5	
Appeals	10		6		9		7		32		8		10	
Friends	2		4		2		2		1		1		2	
Legacies	4		4		2		5		3		2		4	
Other	5		4		3		10		6		5		5	
		24		22		23		32		50		28		27

Note: 'Other' income is primarily fees, profits on sale of investments and, for two cathedrals, income from funds of a discretionary nature.

160

14. On the expenditure side, the overall figures are as follows (Table 6):

Table 6   Overall Average Cathedral Expenditure

	No of Cathedrals	Total Average £'000	% of Total
Top 4	4	2,815	29
9 next largest D&CC	9	1,262	29
Next 7 D&CC	7	785	14
19th & 20th century D&CC	7	764	13
Hi-tourist PCC	5	511	6
Lo-tourist PCC	9	417	9
All	41	970	100

15. The significance of the key components of expenditure as a percentage of total expenditure is shown in Table 7 on the following page.

16. Points arising include:

(a)   the proportion of expenditure on servicing the building in over-all terms is a massive 46% overall, with the Top 4 spending 41%, the 9 next largest D&CC spending 57% and the next 7 D&CC 44%, with the figures falling thereafter with all PCC spending 37% of their total expenditure;

(b)   the spend on services, music and the choir school is remarkably uniform at around 12% of total spend, except for the next 7 D&CC at 15% and the Lo-tourist PCC at 8%;

(c)   similarly, the spend on administration is also very similar across the six groups at around 12% overall, except for 18% for the Hi-tourist PCC;

(d)   chapter costs rise as a percentage as total expenditure falls, and therefore the PCC come out with the highest percentage spend under that heading;

(e)   outward giving at around 2% is similar across all groups;

(f)   'other' is a miscellany of items, including insurance, losses on sale of investments and miscellaneous expenditure.

Table 7   Make-Up of Cathedral Expenditure (% of total expenditure)

	Top 4	9 next largest D&CC	Next 7 D&CC	19th & 20th century D&CC	Hi-tourist PCC	Lo-tourist PCC	Total
Number of Cathedrals	4	9	7	7	5	9	41
	%	%	%	%	%	%	%
Fabric	25	35	26	22	8	23	27
Vergers/Interior upkeep	9	9	10	11	16	10	10
Precinct upkeep	5	8	7	1	1	3	5
Long-term maintenance	2	5	1	4	6	5	4
Building maintenance upkeep	41	57	44	38	31	41	46
Chapter costs	8	9	13	15	16	24	12
Administration	13	11	12	11	18	12	12
Services/Music/Choir							
School	12	11	15	12	12	8	12
Library	2	1	–	–	–	–	1
Operations	35	32	40	38	46	44	37
Tourism/Education	8	2	2	2	2	1	3
Outward giving	1	2	2	1	1	2	2
Payments to Diocese	–	–	–	–	2	4	1
Outreach	9	4	4	3	5	7	6
Special projects	5	2	3	7	9	3	4
Other	8	5	9	13	9	5	8
	13	7	12	20	18	8	12

162

17. Included in 'other income' and 'other expenditure' are profits (£837,000) and losses (£219,000) on the sale of property and investments. The net gain was thus £618,000 across all cathedrals for both chapter and trust funds, made up as follows (Table 8):

Table 8   Net Gains on the Sale of Property and Investments

	£'000
Top 4	394
9 next largest D&CC	63
Next 7 D&CC	(108)
19th & 20th century D&CC	125
Hi-tourist PCC	70
Lo-tourist PCC	74
Total	618

Surplus/Deficit

18. The 41 cathedrals had an aggregate overall surplus of £2.53 million (taking chapter and trust funds together) with the groups in aggregate being in the black, except for the smaller, older established and the 19th and 20th century D&CC. The numbers in surplus or deficit in each group are shown in Table 9:

Table 9   Number of Cathedrals in Overall Surplus or Deficit

	No in Surplus	No in Deficit
Top 4	4	0
9 next largest D&CC	6	3
Next 7 D&CC	2	5
19th & 20th century D&CC	4	3
Hi-tourist PCC	2	3
Lo-tourist PCC	4	5
All	22	19

19. The aggregate figures hide significant variations with 19 cathedrals in deficit, of which 8 were PCC. The biggest single deficit was £486,000 (a 'next 7 D&CC' cathedral), with 7 cathedrals (only one of which is a PCC and the others being spread evenly between the D&CC sub-groups below the Top 4) having deficits of more than £100,000. At the other end of the scale, the largest surplus was £959,000 (a D&CC), with a further 12 cathedrals having surpluses of £100,000 or more. Those 13 comprise 3

from the Top 4, 5 from the 9 next largest D&CC, 2 from the 19th and 20th century D&CC, and 3 PCC.

20. If we look below the level of the overall (chapter and trust) surplus or deficit and have regard to chapter and trust funds separately, then we have the following very different picture (Table 10):

Table 10   Average Overall Surpluses and Deficits

	Overall Surplus/(Deficit)		
	Chapter Average £'000	Trust Average £'000	Overall Average £'000
Top 4	57	307	364
9 next largest D&CC	(23)	116	93
Next 7 D&CC	(10)	(59)	(67)
19th & 20th century D&CC	(122)	78	44
Hi-tourist PCC	173	2	175
Lo-tourist PCC	(2)	18	16
Total	(1)	63	62

21. From this table we can see that, in aggregate, chapter funds are marginally in deficit with nearly all the surplus being accumulated in the trust funds which are in surplus for all groups except for the next 7 D&CC.

22. The dependence of cathedrals upon legacies and appeals (amounting in aggregate to £1.56 million and £4.26 million) can be seen from the fact that the overall surplus of £2.53 million is reduced to an overall deficit of £3.29 million if legacies and appeals are excluded, with the number of individual cathedrals in deficit increasing from 19 to 30. The breakdown by average for each group of cathedrals is as follows (Table 11):

Table 11   Importance of Legacies and Appeals on Overall Surpluses and Deficits

	Overall Average Surplus/(Deficit)		No in Overall Surplus/(Deficit)	
	Including legacies and appeals £'000	Excluding legacies and appeals £'000	Including legacies and appeals	Excluding legacies and appeals
Top 4	364	(88)	4 (0)	2 (2)
9 next largest D&CC	93	(47)	6 (3)	3 (6)
Next 7 D&CC	(67)	(145)	2 (5)	1 (6)
19th & 20th century D&CC	(44)	(131)	4 (3)	3 (4)
Hi-tourist PCC	175	(66)	2 (3)	– (5)
Lo-tourist PCC	16	(27)	4 (5)	2 (7)
All	62	(80)	22 (19)	11 (30)

23. Apart from legacies and appeals, the dependence of the various groups upon key income elements is indicated by the sensitivity analysis shown on the summary sheets, from which:

(a)   for the Top 4, the key income factors are investment income and tourism;

(b)   for all the other D&CC, they are even more sensitive to variations in the same two factors plus the Church Commissioners' grants;

(c)   for the PCC, their key exposure is to the Church Commissioners' grants; tourism is far less a risk and falls in investment income have a proportionally smaller impact than for the D&CC.

24. The overall returns on the market value of investments were 5% on property and 14% on other investments, with some small variations between types of cathedral.

Past Restoration Expenditure

25. Restoration expenditure over the last ten years was a massive £58 million, made up as shown in Table 12. The enormous burden carried by the older D&CC shows clearly. The table also shows the number of years current income which this expenditure represents:

Table 12   Past Restoration Expenditure

	No of Cathedrals	Average 10 year Restoration Expenditure £'000	% of Total	No of Years Income
Top 4	4	5,043	35	1.6
9 next largest D&CC	9	2,349	37	1.7
Next 7 D&CC	7	1,197	15	1.8
19th & 20th century D&CC	7	451	5	0.6
Hi-tourist PCC	5	398	3	0.6
Lo-tourist PCC	9	340	5	0.8
All	41	1,412	100	1.4

Forward Projections

26. Forward projections of anticipated surpluses and deficits were received from 33 cathedrals. The horizon of cathedral financial planning can be gauged from Table 13, but this is flattering as 5 of the 33 projected a break-even position simply in terms of expecting 'expenditure to balance income':

Table 13   Cathedrals providing Forward Projections

	No of Cathedrals
Providing no projections	8
Providing 1 years projections	5
Providing 2 years projections	2
Providing 3 years projections	1
Providing 4 years projections	Nil
Providing 5 years projections	25
All	41

27. The overall figures for those responding are shown in Table 14 on the following page.

Table 14   Forward Projections

	No of Cathedrals	Nos Responding	Average Projected Overall Surplus/(Deficit) before Restoration			Average Projected Restoration	Average Projected Overall Surplus/(Deficit) after Restoration		
			£'000	No in surplus	No in (deficit) or break-even	£'000	£'000	No in surplus	No in (deficit) or break-even
Top 4	4	4	535	3	1	1,870	1,335	–	4
9 next largest D&CC	9	8	1,946	8	–	1,923	23	4	4
Next 7 D&CC	7	6	306	6	–	469	(163)	3	3
19th & 20th century D&CC	7	5	133	3	2	157	(24)	2	3
Hi-tourist PCC	5	4	188	4	–	530	(342)	–	4
Lo-tourist PCC	9	6	89	5	1	160	(71)	1	5
All	41	33	651	29	4	895	(244)	10	23

28. From that table, all groups are projecting surpluses before restoration expenditure. Within those aggregates, 29 cathedrals are projecting surpluses and 4 deficits – only one of which is large. After restoration expenditure, 23 cathedrals project deficits and 10 surpluses. The majority of cathedrals have not yet formulated plans to handle this problem.

29. The scale of the projected restoration work is daunting, particularly in the Top 4 and the 9 next largest D&CC, and amounts in aggregate for all the 33 cathedrals to £29.5 million. In total, this restoration expenditure over the next five years is projected to be just under 50% of the expenditure over the last ten years and rather less than in the last five years.

Balance of Payments with Dioceses

30. A point, frequently encountered in our visits, concerned the clear differences of view between many cathedrals and their dioceses over the 'balance of payments' between the two. To clarify the position, we asked each cathedral and its Diocesan Board of Finance to agree figures. All but one produced such agreed figures – the remaining difference was not material.

31. The balance of payments comprises the three elements shown in Table 15 – contributions made directly by parishes to cathedrals were not included:

Table 15   Diocese/Cathedral Balance of Payments

	£'000
The net cost to cathedrals (after taking account of amounts paid by their dioceses) of the time spent by cathedral clergy on diocesan duties such as archdeacon, director of education and director of ordinands. This in aggregate amounted to	864
The aggregate cost of other facilities provided by cathedrals which were not reimbursed	233
The aggregate of the cash payments made by cathedrals to their dioceses, either specifically in lieu of quota or for other reasons	291
Total	1,388

32. Thus, from the figures provided by cathedrals in agreement (except for one cathedral) with their Diocesan Boards of Finance, cathedrals are net contributors to the extent of £1.4 million in aggregate to their dioceses. At the level of the individual cathedrals, all but 4 cathedrals are net contributors to their dioceses; 2 of those 4 are in balance and 2 in deficit.

Friends' Accounts

33. The overall summary for the Friends at all cathedrals is shown in Table 16. Net assets amount to just under £5 million, yielding an investment income of £444,000. Total income was £1,474,000 with subscriptions and donations producing £603,000 and legacies £269,000. Grants and donations amount to just over £1 million (some 70% of total income) and administration costs were £279,000 – some 19% of total income and 27% of what was given to cathedrals:

Table 16   Analysis of Friends' Accounts (total for all cathedrals)

	£'000	%
Balance Sheet		
Net assets	4,958	
Income		
Investments	444	30.1
Subscriptions/donations	603	40.9
Legacies	269	18.3
Other income	159	10.8
Total Income	**1,475**	**100**
Expenditure		
Grants/donations to cathedral	1,039	74.2
Administration costs	279	19.9
Cost of member benefits	22	1.6
Other costs	62	4.4
Total Expenditure	**1,402**	**100**
Surplus/(Deficit)	**73**	
Analysis		
Administration costs as percentage of total income		18.9
Administration costs as percentage of grants/donations to cathedrals		26.8
Administration costs as percentage of net assets		5.6
Grants to cathedrals as percentage of total income		71
Number of Friends		53,713
Subscriptions/donations per member		£11.22
Cost of member benefits per member		£0.41

Findings

34. In general, the overall state of cathedral finances is not at all comfortable. Although, at the aggregate level, cathedrals have just about been breaking even, that hides the fact that, individually, they divide almost equally between those in surplus and those in deficit. However, if the benefits of legacies and appeals are excluded, then the overall deficit is nearly £3 million, with only about a quarter of cathedrals in surplus and the rest in deficit. The single largest item of expenditure is building maintenance and upkeep which accounts for 46% across all cathedrals – a considerable £18 million out of a total expenditure of £40 million.

35. Looking to the future, only 10 out of the 33 cathedrals providing projections anticipate a surplus after restoration expenditure although that figure improves to 29 if restoration expenditure is excluded. The level of projected restoration expenditure in these 33 cathedrals is a daunting £29.5 million which, although high, is less than that spent in the last five years.

36. Given the recent fall in investment income yields and the certain reduction in the Church Commissioners' grants, the majority of cathedrals are therefore facing continuing deficits. The fact that only 33 were able to give any projections and, of these, 5 were merely hoping that income would keep up with expenditure indicates a dangerously low level of forward thinking and planning in too many cathedrals. We therefore recommend strongly that each cathedral should put time and effort into projecting forward its future financial position and into drawing up appropriate plans to ensure that income and expenditure are balanced.

37. It is also our recommendation that cathedrals should exercise, and be seen to exercise, the highest standards of financial management – both in terms of their own housekeeping and of investment management. In the context of the former, recommendations have already been made in Chapter 7 on employing a suitably qualified and experienced head of finance, proper budgeting, regular management accounts and an effective management structure. In the context of investment management, the same chapter contains recommendations on the creation of a Finance and Investment Advisory Committee and the use of an executive Finance and Property Committee to ensure that the dean and chapter have available, and use, the best possible securities and properties investment advice to safeguard both capital and income in the longer term.

38. It is to be expected that improved planning and financial management should produce significant tangible benefits. The critical urgency of those actions is underscored by the very low asset cover for expenditure

with just over half the cathedrals having less than 4 years cover and a quarter less than 2 years. Of those, the groups most at risk are the lower income pre-19th century D&CC and the PCC.

39. The finely balanced nature of cathedral accounts also emphasises the critical importance of making the best possible use of the visitor and trading opportunities. On the latter front, Chapter 11 of this Report on trading shows clearly how some cathedrals (including some with relatively low visitor numbers) are much more effective than others in their retailing, catering and other trading activities. On the visitor front, we are very well aware of the arguments in connection with charging or otherwise encouraging fair contributions from visitors (see Chapter 12). However these arguments may be decided, there are opportunities to increase net revenue from visitors for use elsewhere, even if admission charges are not levied.

40. In the latter context, some (but not all) opportunities best exist for those cathedrals which are not immediately in need themselves of raising additional funds. It must be asked, therefore, given the likely ever-tightening financial circumstances, whether those with the opportunity to increase revenue (but with no immediate need) should do so in order either to release Church Commissioners' funds for those that do not have the opportunity and do have the need, or to provide funding for collaborative work for the benefit of all cathedrals.

41. There was wide variation of individual cathedral financial results about the overall and group averages and between the figures for individual cathedrals. Those differences support the recommendation that cathedrals should share detailed information in order to help each in its drive to improve efficiency, effectiveness and economy. Already that suggestion has been taken up by the Association of English Cathedrals (AEC) which has circulated the detailed results of this survey, cathedral by cathedral, among its numbers. Comparisons of individual items of expenditure and income (either in absolute or percentage terms) with either the averages or other cathedrals do not of themselves mean that those at the top or bottom of the list are necessarily better or worse than others. However, such comparisons can put cathedrals on legitimate enquiry in their search to achieve best value for money and other benefits.

42. Our visits to cathedrals showed how ingenious many have been in finding ways to save money, to tap new sources and to increase income from existing sources. There are, however, too few opportunities to share that information on a continuing and systematic basis so that other cathedrals can consider making use of best practices elsewhere. We believe that the AEC should actively encourage the continual exchange of

best practice information through the Cathedrals' Finance Conference and other similar forums.

43. The outcome of the 'balance of payments' exercise (showing an overall net contribution by cathedrals of £1.4 million to their dioceses) was a surprise to many and certainly contradicts the views expressed by some lay diocesan staff during our cathedral visits. Many of those saw the cathedral as being a net absorber of diocesan resources whilst, at the same time, not contributing a quota or quota equivalent. We believe, therefore, that it is important that each cathedral and its diocese should each year prepare and agree a 'balance of payments' statement. Moreover, on the basis of that, the cathedral's finances and the diocese's needs, a decision should then be taken on what, if any, further contribution by the cathedral to the diocese in lieu of quota should be made.

44. The aggregate scale of the Friends' finances and giving to cathedrals was also something of a surprise to some. The variation between cathedrals was in some cases large. The Friends are clearly a source of support which each cathedral should encourage to the full and each cathedral should explore how it can attain the performance of the best in comparable circumstances. In this, again, inter-cathedral comparisons will be helpful.

Recommendations

1. Each cathedral should forecast its future financial position and draw up appropriate plans to ensure that income and expenditure are balanced (paragraph 36).

2. Cathedrals should exercise the highest standards of financial management both in terms of their own housekeeping and of investment management (paragraph 37).

3. The AEC should encourage cathedrals to exchange financial information to assist in the improvement of efficiency, effectiveness and economy (paragraphs 41 and 42).

4. Each cathedral and the rest of the diocese should prepare and agree each year a 'balance of payments' statement and, in the light of that, a decision should be taken on what contribution in lieu of quota should be made (paragraph 43).

14

Conclusions and Recommendations

1.   The adaptability and openness to change of the cathedrals of the Church of England are illustrated by the fact that we were appointed following an approach to the Archbishops of Canterbury and York by the deans and provosts of all the cathedrals and that our work has been funded substantially by them. On our visits to all 42 cathedrals, we have found majestic buildings better maintained than many may imagine, and in which many examples of the best worship and pastoral service can be experienced. In Appendix 6 we have listed just a few of the good things which we encountered.

2.   The cathedrals of the Church of England are not institutions in crisis. There have of course in recent years been particular examples of difficulty, some of which played their part in the inception of our review. The cathedrals themselves feel the need of a contemporary restatement of their purpose. There is scope for considerable reform and improvement of the way they are governed, staffed and manage their affairs. The overall state of their finances is not at all comfortable. All these challenges are perfectly capable, however, of being resolved within the evolving tradition which has marked the development of the Anglican cathedrals of England over the last 450 years. In Chapter 2 of this Report, we have attempted a contemporary restatement of the role and relationships which characterise the life of the cathedrals.

3.   At the heart of cathedral life is the daily offering of worship and praise to God. Without the warming fire of worship, these elegant buildings would be ancient monuments rather than living temples capable of inspiring the souls of men and women with glimpses of the divine. The variety of worship found in cathedrals reflects their engagement with many different aspects of the community, of which their role in national or local civic life is simply one part. So we envisage a creative approach to worship in cathedrals, in which the communication of the Christian faith has a high priority. We urge a musical and liturgical rapprochement between the cathedral and the rest of the diocese. And we recommend regular evaluation of the pattern and content of the cathedral's worship, with particular reference to the overall mission of the cathedral.

4.   In all their ministry and mission cathedrals are called upon to look outward rather than inward. It is when they fail to engage, when the cathedral Close becomes closed, that many tensions and difficulties arise. As centres of mission as well as worship, cathedrals must give attention to their ministries of teaching, of service, of evangelism and of witness. In Chapter 3 of this Report, we have posed a number of questions designed to encourage cathedrals to see all they do in terms of the total mission of the Church. We wish to encourage cathedrals in using their resources to help meet immediate human need in their own city or diocese, or in forging links with the world Church. We want them to see evangelism as an explicit and vital part of their purpose, and for all cathedral staff to embrace this vision. We believe it essential that the beauty and the space of the cathedral and its furnishings are used to evoke questions of meaning and faith in the mind of even the most casual visitor.

5.   For cathedrals do not exist independently of the rest of the Church but only as part of its general mission and ministry. The cathedral is the seat of the bishop and he must have an important voice in its overall policy, so that the cathedral is an integral part of the local strategy of the diocese. At the same time, cathedrals are more than a rather grand parish church with the bishop as a kind of superior vicar. Their ministry will certainly be of regional and may be of national or even international importance. The dean and chapter need space in which to develop that ministry, while being accountable for the way in which they do it. Interdependence rather than independence is the key concept, not least because it reflects that mutuality of support and responsibility which should underlie all Christian relationships.

6.   We have sought to propose a set of arrangements for the governance and management of cathedrals which embody that interdependence between cathedral and diocese as part of the whole Church. Within a new framework of accountability, we propose that the dean and chapter should continue to have clear responsibility for the direction and management of the cathedral, in a context of policy proposed by the chapter and discussed in the Greater Council with the bishop and representatives of the wider diocese and community of which the cathedral is part. We seek to encourage the application of the best in modern management practice to the running of cathedrals, while avoiding a slavish adoption of business techniques which are not suited to the cathedral context.

7.   Our aim is to encourage cathedrals to make the very best use of their considerable resources of people, buildings and finance in the service of their fundamental goals of ministry and mission. So, for example, we suggest that appointment to cathedral posts should not be seen as a

reward to clergy for their past service but as a means of deploying the best talents and skills available in this vital aspect of the Church's work. We suggest that limited term cathedral appointments might be seen as a means of enabling younger and older clergy to gain an insight into cathedral ministry before returning to a parochial appointment. We call for improvements in the way the considerable number of lay paid staff and even larger number of volunteers on whom the cathedrals depend are trained, managed and cared for. We urge an improvement in the effectiveness of cathedral trading operations, operations which already account for a turnover of some £10.5 million a year. We point out not only the economic significance of tourism for cathedrals and their surrounding communities but the educational and evangelistic opportunity it presents. We make various detailed proposals for the better management of the fabric and heritage responsibilities of the cathedrals. And, in conjunction with the Association of English Cathedrals (AEC), we have already instituted various steps to improve financial accounting, management and planning practices in cathedrals.

8.   In some of these areas – notably in relation to the unified and simplified system of governance which we propose for cathedrals – legislation will be necessary before our recommendations can be implemented. If the Church is minded to accept our proposals, we hope that the Archbishops of Canterbury and York will rapidly set up a small team to steer through the General Synod the necessary changes. In respect of many of our recommendations, however, all that is needed is the application of an energetic and imaginative approach by cathedrals themselves to the running of their own affairs, an energy and imagination which we know from our visits to cathedrals will not be lacking. There is also a need for cathedrals to be open to each other's experience and willing to learn from best practice elsewhere. We hope that the cathedrals will be willing to give their own Association broader terms of reference in encouraging just such collaboration, mutual problem solving, advice and information exchange. In this as in other aspects of their life, cathedrals need to learn to value their mutual interdependence, as well as their independence of action.

9.   We offer this Report to the cathedrals of the Church in admiration and respect. In the course of our review, we have seen a number of things to criticise but also much to praise. We have been struck by the continuing capacity of cathedrals, in a world which is often depicted as secular and materialistic, to stir the hearts and minds of men and women of all types and conditions. It is in the firm belief that our recommendations will enhance the service provided by cathedrals to God and humanity within the wider service performed by the whole Church that we offer those recommendations to the cathedrals themselves and to all who are concerned with them.

175

Recommendations

Chapter 3: Mission

We recommend that in their strategic planning of their mission cathedrals address the questions in the following paragraphs.

WORSHIP

1. In what respect is the cathedral developing an imaginative and creative approach to its worship? (paragraph 8)

2. Is the cathedral bridging the perceived gaps, musical or liturgical, between cathedral and diocese? (paragraph 10)

3. In what ways is the cathedral taking ecumenical initiatives in its worship? (paragraph 12)

4. Does the cathedral affirm its congregations both liturgically and pastorally? (paragraph 14)

5. Are the dean and chapter satisfied that the resources for worship and music are of the right order for their cathedral? (paragraphs 15 ff)

6. Is the cathedral encouraging the composition of new liturgical and musical material? (paragraph 21)

7. When did the cathedral last review its policy about preaching and reading the scriptures and to what effect? (paragraphs 22 ff)

8. Is the cathedral seeking to include a wide spectrum of Christian worship? (paragraph 26)

TEACHING

1. Is the preaching ministry of the cathedral capable of being extended through public lectures or other methods of presentation? (paragraph 34)

2. Are those who work in the cathedral trained and able to respond to the expectation that they will be mediators of the essential purpose of the building? (paragraphs 35 and 36)

3. Are all the opportunities for teaching, especially to the young, and using new forms of media being fully exploited? (paragraphs 37 and 38)

SERVICE

1. Is the cathedral so planning its resources as to include the meeting of immediate human need locally and regionally? (paragraph 41)

2. Is the cathedral developing partnerships with other churches and caring agencies to meet human need? (paragraph 42)

3. In what ways does the cathedral carry out a prophetic role in the context of a needy world? (paragraph 43)

4. How is the cathedral forging links with the world Church? (paragraph 44)

EVANGELISM

1. Is evangelism explicit in the cathedral's strategy? (paragraph 48)

2. Is the evangelistic purpose of the cathedral known by all staff and volunteers and included in their training programmes? (paragraph 48)

3. Should consideration be given to the establishment of an enquiry centre in the cathedral? (paragraph 49)

4. Does the job description of at least one full-time member of staff include the development of the ministry of evangelism in preaching and teaching? (paragraph 50)

WITNESS

1. Are the beauty, the space, and the furnishings of the cathedral explicitly used to evoke questions of meaning and faith? (paragraph 55)

2. Is it explicit that the cathedral as a building is a witness to the Resurrection which has been lived out in history? (paragraph 55)

3. Are all cathedral staff and volunteers taught and inspired to a corporate witness? (paragraph 57)

4. Is the theology and practice of hospitality in the cathedral capable of further development? (paragraphs 58 ff)

5. Are the cathedral's partnerships with other churches and statutory and voluntary agencies showing signs of growth and development? (paragraph 67)

EVALUATION

Are there, built into the cathedral's life, mechanisms by which regular evaluation of the cathedral's mission can take place?

Chapter 4:   Education

1.   Cathedrals should be active in contributing to Christian reflection about the whole process and direction of education (paragraph 4).

2.   Work carried out in developing links with schools and in relating other areas of education to the Christian faith is of great value and could be enhanced (paragraph 9).

3.   The resources available for education should be increased by the continued exchange of material and ideas between cathedrals (paragraph 10).

4.   Attention should always be given to a creative relationship between the cathedral and its choir school (paragraph 12).

5.   The future governance of choir schools needs to be carefully explored, and any potential conflicts of interest between chapter and school, particularly in the areas of finance and property, need to be resolved (paragraphs 14 and 15).

6.   Involvement between cathedrals and theological colleges can be most fruitful (paragraph 26).

7.   Cathedral administrative chapters should give collective thought to education with a view to creating educational priorities in liaison with diocesan resources (paragraphs 27-29).

Chapter 5:   Music

1.   Cathedrals should seek to provide chorister education for girls as well as boys (paragraphs 7-9).

2.   Where possible, a system of choral scholarships for altos, tenors and basses should be established (paragraph 15).

3.   One member of the chapter should be the liturgist, in charge of worship (paragraph 16).

4.   Careful consideration should be given both to the role of director of music and to the musical and management expertise needed to perform the role (paragraphs 19 and 20).

5.   Cathedral musicians should be adequately and appropriately remunerated (paragraph 20).

6.   The musical resources of the cathedral should be seen as a resource also for the rest of the diocese (paragraph 21).

7.   There should be regular appraisal of members of the music department and in-service training should be encouraged (paragraph 22).

Chapter 6: The Governance of Cathedrals

1. The distinction between 'dean and chapter' and 'parish church' cathedrals should be ended and a single broad system of governance for all cathedrals introduced, capable of flexible adaptation to suit local circumstances (paragraphs 8-9).

2. The senior clergy member of all Administrative Chapters should in future be known as the 'dean' (paragraph 10).

3. Each cathedral should have a Greater Council. This would be the body to which the dean and chapter would account for their stewardship of the cathedral. Its membership would embrace the various interests touched on by the cathedral (paragraphs 11-15).

4. The present Greater Chapter should become a College of Canons, residentiary and non-residentiary, lay as well as ordained (paragraph 16).

5. The Administrative Chapter would be legally responsible for the administration of the cathedral and its properties (paragraph 12). In addition to the dean and residentiary canons its membership should include an administrator and up to three independent members (of whom at least one should be lay) (paragraphs 17-19).

6. The dean should be executive chairman of the Administrative Chapter (paragraphs 20-21).

7. Precisely how a cathedral is staffed is for local decision but two is the minimum number of full-time residentiary canons or their equivalent required to work with the dean and suitable lay or other ordained staff in running a cathedral (paragraph 22).

8. The cathedral community should meet annually to elect up to four representatives to the Greater Council, as well as the members of a Cathedral Community Committee which would be involved in the purely domestic activities of the cathedral (paragraphs 23-25).

9. Where the parish is no longer central to a cathedral's work, the formal parochial status of the cathedral should be ended. All cathedrals should be given a recognised place in the structure of synodical government (paragraph 27).

10. Other than in exceptional circumstances, the diocesan bishop should chair the Greater Council. He should be prepared to advise on matters affecting the cathedral. The bishop's right of visitation should be retained but may be delegated (paragraphs 28-30).

11. A Cathedrals Commission of modest size should subsume the functions of the Cathedral Statutes Commission, to which should be added certain other advisory duties (paragraph 34).

12. There should be a simplified and streamlined system for approving and amending the constitutions and statutes of cathedrals, embodied in a revised Cathedrals Measure. The Privy Council's role in the present procedure should cease (paragraphs 35-44).

13. The Dioceses Measure 1978 should be amended to allow a more gradual evolution of cathedral establishments in the event of the creation of new dioceses (paragraphs 45-48).

Chapter 7: Management Structure and Process

1. The management arrangements of a cathedral should be precise and clear, and the responsibility and accountability for each function known (paragraph 6).

2. The dean, as 'executive chairman', should exercise effective leadership, should always occupy the chair of the Administrative Chapter, and should have an additional casting vote (paragraph 10).

3. Residentiary canons should have oversight responsibility, executive line management responsibility or be totally free of executive responsibility depending on their talents and the particular local circumstances (paragraphs 14-18).

4. A senior lay administrator should be appointed in all cathedrals and he or she should be a full participating and voting member of the Chapter (paragraphs 19 and 20).

5. Each head of department and professional adviser should be responsible to a specified member of the Chapter (paragraphs 21 and 22).

6. The head of finance should be a qualified accountant (paragraph 25).

7. A Finance and Property Committee and a Finance and Investment Advisory Committee should be appointed in every cathedral (paragraphs 26 and 27).

8. Clear-cut management structures should be established, fully explained to all staff and kept under constant review (paragraphs 29-31).

9.   Cathedral accounts should show a true and fair view, be prepared and audited in accordance with best current practice, incorporate (in an appropriate manner) non-capitular trust and other funds held for the benefit of the cathedral, and be published (paragraphs 32-34).

10. Annual budgets, annual long-term financial projections and monthly management accounts should be produced (paragraph 35).

11. The AEC should extend its role and formally foster greater collaboration and exchange of information between cathedrals (paragraphs 39-42).

Chapter 8:   Cathedral Clergy: Appointment and Terms of Service

1.   The Church should seek to open discussions with the Crown about the prospects for the introduction of a single system of appointment to cathedral posts. The processes of appointment should be characterised by openness and a structured approach to consultation (paragraphs 2-10).

2.   Issues of advertising and interviewing are best left to be decided in relation to the particular post in question (paragraph 11).

3.   A proportion of cathedral posts should be used to stretch and develop clergy who then move to more senior posts or into particularly demanding posts in the parochial ministry. A system of secondment could help in this respect (paragraphs 12-15).

4.   The freehold of cathedral posts should be abolished. Within cathedrals there should be a mix of appointments, some open-ended, some for a term of years. All appointments should be capable of termination after a period of notice (paragraphs 16-18).

5.   Stipend rates for all deans and canons should be set nationally. Expenses should be reimbursed by the cathedral, on a basis to be set by the Finance and Investment Advisory Committee. Other additional payments to deans and canons in certain cathedrals should be abolished in respect of future appointments (paragraphs 19-23).

6.   Appraisal or ministry development review of cathedral clergy should be introduced in all cathedrals (paragraphs 24-25).

7.   The Archbishops' adviser on bishops' ministry should work closely with the AEC in developing an induction and training package for deans and provosts and other cathedral clergy (paragraph 27).

8. The present arrangements for ending the appointment of a dean or canon because of a misdemeanour or unsuitability for the post in question should be reviewed (paragraphs 28-31).

9. Cathedrals should do proper honour to area and other suffragan bishops, who should each have their own separately designated seat in the quire (paragraph 32).

Chapter 9:   Lay Paid Staff, Volunteers and Cathedral Friends

1. Job descriptions and person specifications defining the requirements for each job should be prepared for all heads of department and senior staff posts (paragraph 6).

2. Procedures for the appointment and personnel management of lay staff should be improved in many cathedrals, with all such staff having contracts of employment and being appraised annually (paragraphs 9-12, 16 and 18-20).

3. Training in specific skills and induction into the ways of the cathedral should be provided for all employees and the AEC should sponsor the development of appropriate courses (paragraphs 14-15).

4. There should be regular (at least monthly) meetings of all staff to ensure good communication (paragraph 17).

5. The role of volunteers in performing their various tasks and the spiritual dimension of these must be carefully established and explained (paragraph 26).

6. Guides should be clear that the historic story of the cathedral must be set in a Christian context (paragraph 27).

7. Specific task-orientated training should be introduced for all areas of volunteer activity (paragraph 32).

8. Volunteers must know to whom they are accountable and each volunteer activity should have a volunteer co-ordinator (paragraphs 36 and 37).

9. The contribution of cathedral Friends should be acknowledged, encouraged and affirmed, and opportunities provided for recruitment by a 'presence' in the cathedral (paragraphs 40-42).

Chapter 10: Fabric

1. FACs should be entrusted with as high a degree of decision making as is compatible with the terms of the Care of Cathedrals Measure (paragraph 10).

2. All interested bodies should collaborate to ensure that there is no unnecessary duality of legislation in fabric and archaeological matters (paragraph 17).

3. Cathedrals should as a matter of priority establish clear management structures and define the roles of those principally concerned in the care and conservation of the fabric (paragraph 22).

4. In particular, the role and duties of cathedral architect should be defined on the lines proposed in the paper *The Role and Duties of a Cathedral Architect* prepared by the Cathedral Architects' Association, and the role and duties of cathedral archaeologist should be defined on similar lines (paragraph 23).

5. The CFCE must not be under-resourced – it performs a national statutory role which is the key to confidence in the operation of the Care of Cathedrals Measure, and of funding via English Heritage (paragraphs 19 and 43).

6. An 'audit of objectives' covering plans of a developmental nature and a fabric report for both cathedral and Close properties should be prepared on a quinquennial basis so that all works can be properly planned and ordered (paragraphs 24, 33 and 47).

7. Cathedrals should prepare 'fire safety policy statements' and hold regular fire safety audits (paragraph 44).

Chapter 11: Trading

1. Cathedrals should seek to increase professionalism in the management of their trading activities (paragraphs 6 and 11).

2. Cathedrals should reappraise their trading opportunities and arrangements in the light of information available from other cathedrals (paragraphs 6, 10 and 11).

3. Cathedrals should devise a suitable policy for collaborative purchasing for their cathedral shops to improve trading margins in general, and to encourage those whose turnover is less than £100,000 (paragraphs 9 and 10).

183

4.   Cathedrals should take every opportunity to share information about finance, marketing/sales, training and management (paragraphs 10 and 12).

5.   Cathedrals should collaborate in the sponsorship of training for staff (paragraph 11).

6.   In order to facilitate 1-5, the AEC should provide increased resources for those organisations such as the Church Shops Association and the Association of Ecclesiastical Catering which have already begun the task of addressing the issues raised above (paragraph 12 and also Chapter 7, paragraphs 39-41).

7.   The AEC should explore further the trading and catering activities of cathedrals with a view to co-ordinating a substantial improvement in the performance of shops and restaurants (paragraph 16).

Chapter 12:   Tourism

1.   Cathedrals should introduce continuous counts of visitors using electronic devices since knowledge of visitor numbers is vital to the effective management of tourism. This information should be supplemented by regular (three to five year) physical counts and questionnaire surveys (paragraphs 29-33).

2.   Cathedrals should seek to improve their tourism marketing (paragraphs 34-36).

3.   Cathedrals should review their visitor facilities and exchange ideas in such forums as the Pilgrims' Association (paragraphs 37-40).

4.   A visitor officer should be appointed whenever possible (paragraph 41).

5.   Visitor management should be given high priority, and the AEC should arrange specialised courses which offer secular expertise in the management of visitors and help cathedral staff to improve their skills in welcoming and caring for tourists (paragraphs 44-48).

6.   Each cathedral should examine the issues of charging in detail in the light of its own circumstances and location (paragraphs 49-57).

Chapter 13:   Finance

1.   Each cathedral should forecast its future financial position and draw up appropriate plans to ensure that income and expenditure are balanced (paragraph 36).

2. Cathedrals should exercise the highest standards of financial management both in terms of their own housekeeping and of investment management (paragraph 37).

3. The AEC should encourage cathedrals to exchange financial information to assist in the improvement of efficiency, effectiveness and economy (paragraphs 41 and 42).

4. Each cathedral and the rest of the diocese should prepare and agree each year a 'balance of payments' statement and, in the light of that, a decision should be taken on what contribution in lieu of quota should be made (paragraph 43).

Note on the Historical Background

1.   Despite the venerable atmosphere of English cathedrals very many of their most characteristic functions are quite modern. Anyone seeking splendid liturgical music in early nineteenth-century London, for example, would have attended the services held in the two major Roman Catholic chapels: the great Anglican tradition of Choral Evensong had not yet begun – it was a Victorian invention; it was only then that the old choral services received the formality and professionalism which later generations have come to take for granted. The long association between the cathedrals and education was fairly residual until the Endowed Schools Act of 1869 obliged the chapters or the trustees of the ancient schoolrooms to turn them into proper educational institutions. Even the cathedral fabrics are so indebted to the restorers of the last century that in many cases few real traces of authentic mediaeval stonework have survived. It is also commonly supposed that there was once a time when cathedrals were untroubled by fundamental uncertainties as to their purpose. Such a time may indeed have existed, but it must have preceded the last couple of centuries. When he arrived in Hereford as its new bishop, in 1918, Hensley Henson thought it of immediate prudence to enquire of the learned men who at the time constituted the chapter exactly how they saw the purpose of their cathedral. In the end Henson derived more information, as he supposed, from the episcopal butler; yet the exercise indicated a permanent difficulty. 'The right use to be made of the cathedral foundation,' Henson observed, 'has long perplexed the bishops, and constitutes a problem which none has yet succeeded in solving'.

2.   There is not much doubt, however, about the original purpose of cathedrals. They were the place where the bishop maintained his household, his familia, and where there was, among other buildings, a church which contained his teaching-chair or cathedra. What is unclear, though, is how many of those original cathedrals were also intended to achieve monumental scale – to be the Christian equivalent of the great structures which people in all civilised societies have raised in honour of the majesty of God. The Temple of Jerusalem itself offered the principal example, and one which the first Christians could remember; built by Herod and destroyed by the Romans in AD 70, the Temple was Greek in architectural style. Those early Christians, who were often Hellenised Jews, were familiar with the splendour of the religious buildings of the Greek gods –

some of which, like the fifth century BC Doric temple at Syracuse, were actually turned into Christian cathedrals. The more usual form for the first cathedrals, after the Edict of Milan in 313, was the Roman basilica: a meeting hall, a place for worshippers, not a house for the god as in classical paganism. These early structures were superseded, in the eastern empire, by cathedrals in the Byzantine style; emulations of the great cathedral of Constantinople itself, Hagia Sophia, completed in 537. These were ideological buildings, representations of heaven upon earth; sacred spaces, beneath a central dome from which a mosaic Christ in judgement, as supreme disposer of the universe, presided over the Christian world. The functional Roman basilicas, too, began to incorporate ideological features: the small apse at the east end, where the altar was placed, became a great triumphal arch, and the columns which flanked the nave assumed the monumental proportion of a sacred way or stoa. Symbolical importance became attached to the various architectural features, although here there must be caution, because not much is known about early liturgical uses, and because rather too much reliance has been placed upon the symbolism of the cathedral built by Bishop Paulinus at Tyre simply due to the chance that there is a description of it by Eusebius. It may have been quite untypical. The cruciform shape of great church buildings was not a symbolical representation of the cross of Christ: it developed out of the porticus (or small chambers, for the priest and for the bones of the dead) which were added to the Roman basilica churches of the later period.

3.   At an early stage cathedrals and shrines became linked. It is hard, at this distance of time and culture, to recapture the importance of the cult of the relics of saints for Christian believers. The authority of a bishop was perceived to be enormously enhanced if his cathedra was set up in a church which housed the relics of a particularly venerated saint; sometimes remains were translated from their first shrines to receive the place of honour in an existing cathedral. The archetypal shrine was the Church of the Holy Sepulchre in Jerusalem, begun in 335 in the rotunda form of a Roman martyrium – like the mausoleum of Constantine's daughter in Rome (St Constanza), or the first Church of St Peter, built over the tomb of the Apostle in 333. It was a style derived from the Pantheon, which itself became a Christian church. The great Romanesque and Gothic cathedrals of mediaeval Christendom were deeply influenced by these early developments. Their baptisteries were constructed as rotundas, signifying baptism into Christ's death; the ambulatories around shrine-tombs echoed the same idea. Entrusting the sacred building to monastic orders, to guard the shrine and to supplicate for the faithful in the presence of the sanctified, soon began to obscure the actual purpose of the building – the meeting place where the bishop could teach from his chair. Saxon

cathedrals in England had been small structures; the increasing grandeur of the mediaeval cathedrals derived in part from the need to provide space for pilgrims visiting shrines. Cathedrals were centres of tourism from a very early date.

4.   Greek and Roman civilisation had been urban, and cathedrals were first established in towns. In England too, cathedrals tended to be sited in towns or within the walls of surviving Roman forts. Synods in 1070 and 1075 further required that the seats of bishops should be located in centres of population. There were some exceptions. In Ireland, which had not experienced Roman occupation, the Church was rural and almost exclusively monastic; the pattern of cathedrals which emerged looked very like the English, however, because of the towns built by the Christianised Viking settlers, and because of the assimilation of the Celtic to the Anglo-Norman Church in the eleventh century. Throughout Europe the early spread of Christianity to the countryside resulted in a distinction between the rural clergy, whose churches were later organised into parishes, and those left in the town some of whom were of the bishop's household. The latter began to adopt the custom of living a common life defined by disciplined rules or canons. By the fourth century the pattern of canons in charge of the administration of the bishop's church already existed, therefore, in embryo form. By the ninth century donations of land and other property to the Church, and especially to the cathedral churches, allowed some of the canons to live separately from the rest of the community. These 'secular' canons were not always favoured by a Christian spiritual culture which was increasingly coming to regard the monastic life as the religious life in its most authentic expression, and reforming bishops tended to hand cathedrals over to the orders. This was a policy particularly promoted during the primacy of Lanfranc. As a result nine English cathedrals eventually remained in the charge of secular canons, while nine others were administered by the Benedictines, and one (Carlisle) by Austin canons. Reinforced by the custody of the major shrines, the monastic domination of cathedral life – which was much more important in England than in other countries – operated to the disadvantage of the episcopal presence, even where the bishop was himself a regular. The attachment of secular administrative functions to the episcopal office, and the need for senior bishops to reside at court (itself not in a fixed location, since government was still peripatetic), laid further foundations to the practice of cathedral independence. Instead of exercising pastoral functions in his cathedral the mediaeval bishop became possessed, in practice, of largely judicial powers. In his place the cathedrals and their property were administered by the deans and chapters. The central monastic orders came to enjoy considerable freedom from episcopal jurisdiction – which in some places was almost complete – and this privilege,

when practised in relation to cathedral churches, resulted in the apparent paradox that bishops had few rights in their own cathedrals. The secular canons soon took advantage of this situation and followed the practice. The cathedrals which existed at the time of the Reformation, whether monastic or secular in character, were small corporations providing for regular worship (conducted for the members of their own community), for the administration of their estates, and having custody of any shrine which might exist within their walls.

5.   Apart from their attendance to these duties, the functions of mediaeval cathedrals are not clear – perhaps they were not extensive. The mediaeval past is hedged with romantic inventions, mostly of nineteenth-century origin (or of the 'Gothick' imaginings of the eighteenth), and it is through the screen of interpretation still provided by this largely fictional understanding that cathedrals of the time are assessed. The Victorians believed that they saw the naves filled with earthy folk whose happy and rude religiosity was etched forever in the very decorative devices of the stonework. The reality was a fairly enclosed small community administering a church for their own use. Mediaeval cathedrals were in fact built and decorated by professional contractors operating under instructions from their clients. They were largely financed, as contemporaneous merchant enterprises were, by primitive joint-stock arrangements which, like their later equivalents, often failed. That is why most cathedrals are a hotch-potch of styles, their building phased over time, not according to changed liturgical or social use, but according to the dictates of unstable financial resources. The scale and monumental quality of the building did not go unquestioned either. The criticism of worldly splendour, which lay at the heart of the Cistercian ideal, led some to ask whether the glory of the mediaeval cathedrals was really the most authentic representation of the religion of fishermen gathered from the lakeside of Galilee. The Victorians also liked to suppose that the world came into the mediaeval cathedral: that the great buildings were used for 'secular' purposes, like community assembly, feasting, the holding of markets, and so forth. They certainly were used for such purposes, but the evidence for this use is largely derived from the records of complaints about it. There is no way of knowing what was normal and acceptable; as so often the historical record may preserve only what is unusual or untypical. The division into 'sacred' and 'secular' functions, anyway, which is appropriate for modern analysis of social fact, is hardly applicable to mediaeval society.

6.   The English Reformation left the cathedrals more or less untouched. There were some necessary administrative changes. Cathedrals in the custody of the monastic orders were secularised, and were thereafter known as cathedrals of the New Foundation. Those already administered

by secular canons continued (the Old Foundation cathedrals). The dismantling of the major shrines ended one of the most important perceived functions of the mediaeval cathedral, and spiritual tourism, accordingly, largely disappeared. A few attempts were made to encourage the use of cathedrals to propagate Protestant learning: at Canterbury a College of Six Preachers was added to the foundation for this purpose. But no one took the occasion of the general upheaval of religion to ask what the cathedrals were actually for. Cathedral reform, which was anyway conceived in extremely modest terms, envisaged a return to some purified past use, a removal of corrupt accretions rather than a radical restructuring. The Cathedrals Commission of 1559 was not the vehicle of any large idea: cathedrals were to attend to their duties, and to make provision for sound theology. There was no suggestion that bishops should recover an immediate role in them, or that cathedrals might be regarded as centres of diocesan life. A few residual traces of pastoral care for surrounding populations remained undisrupted – no one, again, suggested that cathedrals should annexe parochial functions – and the traces were, anyway, very residual. Not since before the eleventh century, when parochial organisation became universal, had the cathedrals felt any pastoral responsibility for the city populations which surrounded them. The fate of the English cathedrals was to remain unreformed.

7. In the ensuing two centuries there were periodic adjustments of cathedral statutes, especially as an adjunct of the Laudian attempts to transform English institutions and the English Church. Later alterations did not reflect any profound – or even any superficial – changes in the functions of cathedrals either. They corresponded to legislative changes to the terms of property-holding. When in 1840 Archbishop William Howley spoke in favour of revising the statutes of Canterbury Cathedral – against the dean and chapter's insistence on the integrity of their ancient rights – he was able to point out that the statutes were not ancient at all, but dated from the time of Charles I. What was true was that, by the nineteenth century, the piecemeal adaptation of statutes had produced a very diverse set of arrangements for cathedral governance. The Cathedrals Commission of 1852 suggested a common framework for all the foundations, but this simplicity has never been able to find acceptance. So generalisations made about cathedrals in modern times all need to be regarded with some reserve, when there are so many exceptions. The canons of the Council of Trent imposed a reasonable and uniform structure for the regulation of cathedral chapters in the Roman Catholic Church. The genius of Anglicanism has flourished without that measure of centralised authority; it may sometimes be discerned, in consequence, only with a certain historical imprecision.

8.   That the cathedrals have survived to the present in the form they have – as corporations with rights and property independent of the rest of the Church – is actually a consequence, not of the long neglect of reform, but of early reform in the nineteenth century. The cathedral chapters were included among the other unreformed institutions to which government turned its attention in the 1830s. They were lumped together with the municipal corporations, the ancient parish administrations, the parliamentary representative system itself, and all the rest, and subjected to tests of efficiency and accountability which were largely pragmatic and utilitarian. Their real function was not an issue: reform was about the stewardship of their supposed wealth, not what cathedrals were for. The excited hopes of some radicals to turn them into 'Libraries of Useful Knowledge' were unfulfilled: the cathedrals survived because they were reformed at an early date, when their friends and opinion in general were unprepared for anything like secularisation. Their property rights were defined and circumscribed, but they were not abolished. They continued as corporations aggregate. Sir Robert Peel's temporary Ecclesiastical Commission of 1835 was in 1836 made permanent, thus creating effective machinery for the redistribution of Church wealth. Its second Report, in 1836, produced a scheme to use cathedral resources to provide parish clergy for the great urban areas of spiritual destitution. The Ecclesiastical Duties and Revenues Act of 1840 abolished all the non-resident prebends and sinecure rectories annexed to cathedrals, and restricted the number of residentiary canonries to four in each cathedral – with exceptions (six each) at Westminster Abbey, Christ Church Oxford, Canterbury, Durham and Ely, and (five each) at Winchester and Exeter. Conservative opponents of the reform argued without success in Parliament that the doomed offices were necessary as a reward for learning and pastoral excellence in the Church. In the event the Act of 1840 only produced its effects extremely slowly, since vested life-interests were respected; but in due course it secured the abolition of 382 cathedral offices and impoverished many chapters. Yet it left their ancient rights intact. (Many of these ancient rights, like the statutes in which they were encased, were anyway yet another example of the Victorian weakness for representing every kind of recent anomaly as a quaint mediaeval survival.) The reforms, that is to say, were about property and not about function. It also came as a surprise to the reformers to discover that the cathedrals' wealth had been greatly exaggerated both by themselves and by defenders. When the accounting had been done and the 'ancient' leases examined it was found that no huge surplus existed to redistribute. The same revelation accompanied the disestablishment and disendowment of the Irish Church in 1869.

9.   Defenders of ancient institutions in the 1830s stood on firm ground, at least as it seemed to their contemporaries: opposition to the notion that the State had the legitimate power to violate property rights. Their weakness was that unreformed corporations of all sorts appeared incapable of their own reform. In the resulting compromise a very characteristically English emphasis on the funding of institutions, rather than on the functions which they existed to sustain, allowed most of the structures to continue. The symbols of the old order often went; the form endured. The cathedral chapters had argued that their corporate status and privileges were necessary to protect their independence. The unreformed munici-palities and the universities did the same, but in their case independence could be seen to have recognised advantages as bulwarks against centralised authority – and everyone was opposed to centralisation on the assumption (backed up by foreign examples) that it was full of threats to individual liberty. The gentle inconsequence of the cathedrals was rather different, especially as they did not seem to have a clear purpose. Their independence, like that of the Church of England in general, was anyway tempered because both the religious and the political culture assumed an erastian polity in which the accountability of the clergy to the laity assem-bled in Parliament was perceived as an essential ingredient of liberty. One unexpected fruit of the parliamentary reform of the Church in the 1830s was the revival of ideals of Christian spiritual autonomy whose first (but not the only) appearance was on the high tables of Oxford. In the cathedrals themselves some saw their need for independence in another very English offshoot of erastianism. Some supposed that they required their independence, not against the political interference of government, but against their own bishop. The idea that cathedrals were a kind of no-go area for the episcopate was to be revived by dignitaries outraged over the acquiescence of the bishops in their reform. Until the middle years of the nineteenth century political power was directly linked to the possession of property, and the sense that corporate privilege also gave 'a stake in the country' was strong. Now that has all passed away, and the political culture no longer envisages, not even residually, that society is a nexus of property. Yet the cathedral chapters survive as corporations.

10. The pragmatism of English change proceeded beyond the first impulses, as the Ecclesiastical Commission established its stewardship of the national religious endowments. Suggestions for further change were, however, broadly within the limits originally set. A Commission appointed in 1852 to look into the state of English cathedrals reported first in 1854, and twice in 1855, with modest amendments. The Commissioners saw the primary purpose of cathedrals in the provision of worship; they recommended more attention to educational work and theological training. They also favoured placing the populations who lived immediately

adjacent to the cathedrals under the pastoral care of the chapters. But these recommendations lay mostly unfulfilled, and it can scarcely be said that the reports, anyway, had done much to help define the actual purpose for which cathedrals exist within the general ministry of the Church of England. A meeting of cathedral deans held at Lambeth Palace in 1869 had comparatively limited vision, and so did the publication by J.S. Howson, in 1872, of *Essays on Cathedrals*. It was clear that pragmatic reform of cathedral finance and property was to be a main feature of the century, and that redefining the role of cathedrals in the general ministry was not. The Cathedrals Commission of 1879-85 wanted a standing committee empowered to alter statutes: that was not achieved until the Measure of 1976.

11. Yet there were some for whom the atmosphere of reform cultivated further questionings about the purpose of cathedrals. Isolated thinkers produced a continuing stream – which never became anything like a torrent – of commentary upon aspects of cathedral function. Surprisingly, they were hardly ever articulated in relation to the new foundations, begun at Ripon in 1836. For the new cathedrals of modern times, the 'parish church' foundations, were a response to population shifts and administrative rationale; although each showed differences of constitution they were not expressions of any particularly modern insights into the function of cathedrals. It is true that at Truro the will and force of Edward White Benson managed to combine the offices of bishop and dean, a novelty in English experience – but there the taste for novelties expended itself to the full. No other experiments were tried. As no one could agree about what cathedrals were for, it was scarcely to be expected that the new ones would be the embodiments of ideological revisionism. When in 1950 it was decided to launch a competition for the architectural design of the new cathedral at Coventry, Bishop Neville Gordon and Provost R.T. Howard asked 'In terms of function what should such a cathedral express?' They added: 'It stands as witness to the central dogmatic truths of the Christian faith.' Sir Basil Spence's marvellous design doubtless witnesses to those truths, but what of the 'function' to which the bishop and the provost had directed attention? Coventry Cathedral has impressed by the inventiveness and splendour of its witness. Its organisation and structure, however, are largely those of a conventional cathedral.

12. Some in the nineteenth century were glad that the cathedrals were left without ministerial transformation. These were the returning visitors. After two centuries of comparative neglect a kind of sacred tourism revived. People were drawn to them out of antiquarian interest. It was hardly possible to move in the nave of Westminster Abbey in the nineteenth century because of the press of visitors. As a boy Thomas Arnold

filled many sketchbooks with his notes and drawings of English cathedrals, which he seems to have visited with the enthusiasm expended by most boys on the healthy sports with which his name is conventionally associated. When Dean Bennett later began, at Chester, what Bishop Wand of London once described as 'the spiritualisation of the tourist traffic '(he put up notices inside the cathedral telling people what they were looking at), he was merely updating a very traditional service of the cathedrals: the provision of 'history in stone.' Before the mid-century cathedrals had been kept locked most of the time and were only opened for divine service. That now changed, and the practice of charging for admission at the specified times when visitors could enter was also abandoned – in correspondence with the general cessation of pew-renting throughout the English churches.

13. If it was surprising that the establishment of the parish church cathedrals did not stimulate thought about the functions of cathedrals generally, it was equally surprising that the setting up of cathedral churches in overseas colonies did not provide any particularly fresh insights. The great Anglican diaspora of the nineteenth century shared the national confidence that English institutions were universally beneficial, without the need for extensive local adaptation. Native peoples who were astonished to be handed Prayer Books in which they were invited to pray for the descendants of the House of Saxe-Coburg-Gotha were doubtless equally puzzled by the intact transference of cathedral institutions to their shores, their functions as vaguely understood beneath the tropic sun as they were upon the rain-soaked lawns of the English cloisters and precincts. The colonial cathedrals resembled the English parish church models, and showed as many local variations of practice as they did – but with no new concepts about how they fitted into the general ministry of the Church.

14. If the older cathedrals were not to be regarded as large-sized parish churches, what then was their function? The question was asked by a few men of the nineteenth century with worrying persistence – and with a worrying lack of resonance in the thought of those who conducted the affairs of the Church. In 1838, aghast at some of the proposals then being made for the 'confiscation' of chapter property, George Augustus Selwyn exclaimed that 'they had all taken it for granted that the cathedral canon is a less useful minister of Christ than the parish priest'. His words anticipated an important development. One of the most significant features of nineteenth-century society was the growth of professionalism. Related to educational reform, inspired in some measure by the emergence of collectivist practices in government, and associated with the new confidence and expectations of the bourgeoisie, the growing professionalism of public life made its mark upon the clergy as well. It was only as professionalism

195

spread everywhere else that cathedral dignitaries began to relate their own existence to the performance of clearly defined functions. They found that they did not, in all truth, have much to do. Together with the preceding reforms of cathedral establishments this made for a crisis of identity which, in subdued sequences, has continued to this day. It has probably been this sustained unease, rather than particular scandals over internal conflicts, which has made a body of institutions which are actually notable for a splendid record of service to the Church in modern times still liable to ponder their existence. Scandals and dissensions are distributed across the history of cathedrals, as of other institutions, and are not to be taken as the surface indications of any particular rottenness beneath. Recent well-publicised exchanges at one or two cathedrals, for example, have to be set against the 1940 letter of the canons of Canterbury to *The Times* explaining why they were boycotting the sermons of their dean. Their dispute with Hewlett Johnson was not, it has to be said, entirely political in complexion: there had been some preceding divergence of view about his proposal to paint the cathedral green as a measure of wartime camouflage. Fears of bishops wishing to extend their jurisdiction into cathedrals seem, upon historical examination, to exist more in the telling than in the reality. There is, in that context, the interesting legal opinion of Sir Robert Phillimore, one of the greatest ecclesiastical experts of the nineteenth century, that the bishop is as much the ordinary of a cathedral as he is of any church in the diocese. In 1865 the Earl of Harrowby proposed that deans and chapters be abolished, and the cathedrals run by chaplains responsible to the bishop. It did not seem at the time to be the right thing to do.

15. The truth was that, while the cathedrals were fruitlessly wondering what they were for, the dioceses themselves scarcely had a coherent strategic existence. The notion of the cathedral as a focus of diocesan activity could hardly occur in a world in which the diocese itself had little activity to focus. The dioceses were just, in the mid-nineteenth century, beginning the first steps towards the creation of professional administration. It was necessary to win against the visible erastianism of the patronage system, and progress rested upon the more faithful attendance of the bishops in their dioceses. One sign of this was that the bishops encountered opposition from the parishes – urging their local rights – which paralleled sentiments hostile to episcopal interference within the cathedrals. Yet there were, again, isolated prophetic voices which from an early stage expostulated about a diocesan role for the cathedrals. Selwyn again, in 1838: he saw, he said, the cathedrals as 'supplementary to the parochial system.' They could be 'a sort of bank of supply upon which the great body of the clergy might draw for almost any kind of clerical assistance'. He outlined a scheme (later put into effect when he was bishop in New Zealand), whereby

the canons divided the diocese into districts and undertook preaching and assistance to the clergy in each.

16. Although not perceived at the time, and unnoticed by subsequent commentary, there was here the germ of the idea of suffragan bishops; the diocesan problems were eventually solved, as it happened, by other means. Realists, anyway, had some doubts about releasing the canons upon the innocent population. Some conservative reformers, including Selwyn, also wanted the cathedrals to become 'divinity schools' for the training of ordinands. Manning, then still an Anglican, favoured such a use of cathedral resources; so did Bishop Phillpotts of Exeter; and Pusey – whose *Letter to Archdeacon Hoare* (1836) unfolded the most noble of several contemporaneous schemes to convert the cathedrals into centres of intellectual excellence. But the need was not really apparent: the colleges of Oxford and Cambridge were under clerical control, and were thought to be the places where young men could encounter intellectual excellence in at least one or two particulars. And when the theological colleges were eventually set up, from the 1850s, it was at the initiative of the bishops, and the cathedrals in the cities where they were founded had very little if anything to do with them – an experience in some ways echoed in the middle years of the twentieth century when new Church Voluntary Colleges were created.

17. The modern educational responsibilities of the cathedrals do not really derive from a traditional function: schools attached to chapters had survived because as charitable trusts they were almost impossible to get rid of. Modern involvement with education stems from the provisions of the Endowed Schools Act of 1869, which led to the resuscitation and reform of the ancient cathedral schools, and from the late Victorian penchant for musical entertainment, preferably of the high-minded variety, which breathed new life into the choir schools. At about the same time the cathedrals underwent a considerable transformation. They were cleaned and restored, often to the dismay of later architectural purists; surviving secular uses of the naves and side-chapels were swept out; music became professionalised; and the services were in many places subject to those innovations and experiment which, by the end of the century, had produced what are today thought of as timeless cathedral use. It was, in its way, an astonishing set of changes, brought about by some remarkable men. At their head, perhaps, was that gifted band of canons (Liddon, Lightfoot, and Dean Church) who converted St Paul's, in the 1870s, into a major centre of liturgical and preaching splendour. There, and at Westminster Abbey, and then at Ely, the first nave services began, and the cathedrals started to recover something of that popular numinous atmosphere, now taken for granted, which once attached to the great shrines of the middle ages.

18. During the middle years of the twentieth century some of the ideas mooted in the nineteenth were again brought forward. But the basic question of what cathedrals are for, and how they should integrate with the general ministry of the Church, remained unanswered. The Commission appointed by the Church Assembly in 1924 was required to consider property and revenues, in the nineteenth-century tradition, 'and also to make a full and independent inquiry as to the ways in which the Cathedral and Collegiate Churches might most adequately fulfil their great functions in the life of the Church and people.' The Commissioners duly visited each of the then 39 cathedrals, but their Report, in 1927, made few recommendations which had not been around for years and which, anyway, scarcely amounted to a transformation of understanding about cathedral functions. They wanted to encourage closer links with diocesan work yet rejected the proposal that residentiary canonries should be annexed to diocesan offices. They saw the cathedrals as 'centres of religious learning' and contended that their resources should be exploited for diocesan educational enterprises. It could all have been written by Pusey a century before. They further suggested a permanent Cathedrals Commission, of seven members. This idea came to nothing. On the rather crucial issue of defining the authority of the bishop as ordinary in a cathedral the Commission had no recommendation.

19. Also very much in the nineteenth-century tradition of attending to the temporalities, but leaving the spiritualities to the determination of private initiative, was the Measure of 1931. Although superseded in 1963 the provisions made in this legislation for the general winding up of cathedral ownership of land laid the effective foundations of all modern cathedral finance. The Church Commissioners, who compensated each foundation for the land ceded, also began the practice of block grants to meet the expenses of maintaining the cathedral dignitaries. The 1961 Report of another Cathedrals Commission set up by the Church Assembly, *Cathedrals in Modern Life*, was in the familiar genre, dominated by questions of finance. 'It was felt by the Commission,' they wrote, 'and particularly strongly by the representatives of the Church Commissioners, that it was useless to prescribe all manner of requirements for cathedrals by Statutes, if there was no possibility that the necessary financial provision would be available.' The result of their labours was accordingly modest and actually rather trite – 'The Commission has come to the conclusion that the cathedrals of England cannot sufficiently discharge their duties unless in some way or other their income is made to cover their work more adequately.' It was, nevertheless, a true assessment.

20.   When legislation followed, however, it somewhat exceeded the vision of the Commissioners. The Measure of 1963 has provided the legal framework for cathedral development in the second half of this century. Guidelines were established for the revision of statutes, with a requirement that certain core provisions were made, leaving each cathedral to produce additions compatible with local or historical uses. But no really uniform arrangements were made for the authority of chapters, or for how they were to conduct themselves. The Measure also broadly subjected property and financial transactions made by chapters to the scrutiny and approval of the Church Commissioners. Section 38 required each cathedral to transmit their audited accounts to the Church Commissioners annually, and to see that their accounts were published.

21.   In 1976 a new Measure systematised the process for the revision of statutes, and a permanent body known as the Cathedral Statutes Commission came into existence. The growth of tourism, and the general inclination to give an enhanced priority to the preservation of national cultural treasures, has led to another development whose importance to the English cathedrals is enormous: grants of money made for specified and approved works to cathedral fabrics by the State (and administered by English Heritage). These arrangements succeeded many years of accumulating concern about the professionalism appropriate for the care of cathedrals. In 1949 a Cathedrals Advisory Committee had been instituted by the Council for the Care of Churches; in 1981 the General Synod had created a Cathedrals Advisory Commission. The Care of Cathedrals Measure of 1990 derived from prolonged exchanges between Church and State about the benefits and disadvantages of the exemption of ecclesiastical structures from 'listed building' control. A central body, the Cathedrals Fabric Commission for England, came into existence in 1991, charged with authorising proposals for 'significant works' coming from chapters. It was also explicitly required to respect the religious purpose of the cathedral as 'the seat of the bishop and a centre of worship and mission'. An ancient definition of the function of cathedrals had at last emerged, again.

22.   'It is not within the scope or purpose of this Report to describe their past history,' the Cathedral Commissioners of 1927 observed; 'such an attempt would demand a long historical treatise.' True words indeed: but the present Commission offers this brief essay in the hope that it will do justice to some of the historical resonances that hang around the cathedrals of England, and which make them an integral part of the popular spirituality of the English nation. The guardianship of these great resources, inherited from the past, is a recognised duty of the present. 'They are monuments on a vast scale, very well preserved, rather austere, with huge fantastic

spaces, full of history, mystery and piety, veritable ships of the spirit where matter has not only a use but a meaning' – the words are those of Giovanni Battista Montini, the future Paul VI, as he visited nine of the English cathedrals in 1934 – 'where glorious and sorrowful memories of the past are brought into living contact with the present.'

Acknowledgements

As will be clear from the scope of this Report, we could not have carried out our work without the assistance and goodwill of a very large number of people. Mention must first of all be made of the deans and provosts and their colleagues, both ordained and lay, who not only responded by way of written evidence and detailed information about cathedral finances but also prepared a warm welcome and extensive programme for each of our cathedral visits. We are also most grateful to the following:

the Church Commissioners, who financed the full-time staffing of the Commission and also made their facilities available for eight of our meetings;

Messrs Coopers and Lybrand, who seconded five of their staff to help with the financial and other analyses – Miss Katharine Ogilvie, Mr Charles Peters, Mr Philip Doel, Mr Andrew Miller and Miss Clair-Marie Slater;

the Association of English Cathedrals, which met the expenditure incurred by us on travel and accommodation;

Mr John Newton, the former Administrative Secretary of the Advisory Board of Ministry, who undertook a detailed analysis of all the evidence submitted to us;

Mr Max Hanna, the former Resources Research Manager at the English Tourist Board, who with the financial support of the Department of National Heritage oversaw the cathedral visitor count and provided valuable background information on cathedral tourism;

Dr Michael Winter, the former Director of the Centre for Rural Studies at the Royal Agricultural College, Cirencester, who, with the financial support of the Dulverton Trust, formulated and analysed the visitor survey which was carried out at four cathedrals by volunteers from Cathedral Camps;

St George's House, Windsor, and the Dean, the Very Reverend Patrick Mitchell, who provided a welcoming base for our two residential meetings;

Mr Robert Young and Mr John Macgregor, British Embassy in Paris, who arranged for Lady Howe and the Very Reverend

Raymond Furnell to meet representatives of the Ministry of Culture and the Centre National de Pastorale Liturgique;

the 14 members of staff of the Church Commissioners and the General Synod Office who acted as recorders on the cathedral visits – Mr Robert Banfield, Mr Alastair Callcutt, Mrs Dawn Christmas, Mrs Alison Harding, Mr Peter Hopkins, Mr Paul Howlett, Mr Philip James, Mr Andrew Male, Mrs Michèle Manders, Mr Jamie Milford, Miss Andrea Mulkeen, Mr Michael Patrick, Miss Carol Pym, Mrs Maggie Rodger.

The Commission

2.1 Terms of Reference

To examine the future role in Church and nation of the Cathedrals of the Church of England and to make recommendations as to how best that role could be fulfilled, including proposals for their government and support.

2.2 Membership

Chairman: The Lady Howe of Aberavon

Members: The Right Reverend Michael Turnbull, Bishop of Durham (and previously Bishop of Rochester)

The Right Reverend Ronald Gordon, Sub-Dean of Christ Church, Oxford

The Very Reverend Raymond Furnell, Dean of York (and previously Provost of St Edmundsbury)

The Very Reverend Richard Lewis, Dean of Wells

The Very Reverend Kenneth Riley, Dean of Manchester (and previously Canon Precentor of Liverpool Cathedral)

The Reverend Dr Edward Norman, Dean of Chapel, Christ Church College, Canterbury

Mrs Elaine Storkey, Director, London Institute for Contemporary Christianity

Mr Robert Aagaard OBE JP, Trustee and Chairman, Cathedral Camps

Mr Peter Burnham, Former Partner, Messrs Coopers and Lybrand

Mr Ian Hay Davison, Chairman, Storehouse plc

Mr Richard Shephard, Headmaster of the Minster School, York

Mr Martin Stancliffe, Architect and member of the Cathedrals Fabric Commission for England

Assessors:	Mr Patrick Locke, Secretary to the Church Commissioners
	Professor David McClean CBE, Chairman, Cathedral Statutes Commission
	Rear Admiral David Macey CB, Receiver General, Canterbury Cathedral
	Mr Philip Mawer, Secretary-General of the General Synod
Secretary:	Mr Nigel Waring
Secretariat:	Miss Trish Hetherington
	Mrs Sandy Meggs

2.3 Number of Meetings

We met 11 times between July 1992 and June 1994. Of these, nine were meetings for the greater part of a day and two were residential at St George's House, Windsor (13/14 September 1993 and 21/22 March 1994).

2.4 Method of Working

At our inaugural meeting on 1 July 1992 we agreed that written evidence should be invited from a wide range of interested parties and that all cathedrals should be visited (see Appendix 3.6). We also agreed to set up a small Sub-Group (comprising the Chairman, the Provost of St Edmundsbury, Mr Burnham and Mr Mawer) to take forward the detailed procedures and timetable for our meetings. At our second meeting on 17 November 1992 we set up Working Parties on Tourism (comprising the Dean of Wells, Mrs Storkey, Mr Aagaard, Mr Burnham and Admiral Macey) and on Finance and Administration (comprising the Dean of Wells, Mr Burnham, Mr Davison and Admiral Macey). While the visit programme was taking place during the first half of 1993, we gave preliminary consideration to the major issues which were arising from the evidence and other sources. We put in hand a detailed analysis of the many written submissions to ensure that all the issues raised were fully taken into account. Also, the Working Party on Tourism decided, with the help of Mr Max Hanna and Dr Michael Winter, to carry out a visitor count of all cathedrals in August 1993 and a visitor survey at four cathedrals.

At the first residential meeting in September 1993 initial draft papers were prepared and the outline of our eventual Report was agreed. Further work by individual members and by the two Working Parties was considered at subsequent meetings until a first draft Report was ready for the second residential meeting in March 1994. Redrafting and editing of the Report continued to the end of July.

2.5 Finance

The main work of the Commission was completed in just over two years. The Church Commissioners agreed to the full-time secondment of a Principal and Personal Secretary, for the duration of that period, to undertake the servicing of the Commission. Messrs Coopers and Lybrand also made available five members of staff, each for a period of two/three months, to help with the analysis of cathedrals' finances and other matters. The costs incurred in respect of travel and accommodation for the cathedral visits and Commission meetings were met by the Association of English Cathedrals and totalled £51,000. In addition, grants of £1,500 and £7,500 were received respectively from the Department of National Heritage and the Dulverton Trust to meet the costs of the visitor count and survey.

To all of these bodies we would like to express our great gratitude for enabling us to undertake our work.

Notes on Christ Church, Oxford and Royal Peculiars

Christ Church is, uniquely, both the cathedral of its diocese (Oxford) and a college chapel. It is exempt from the Care of Cathedrals Measure 1990 and also, except for a few specified provisions, from the Cathedrals Measures 1963 and 1976.

Because the governance and finances of the cathedral and the college are so closely intertwined, Christ Church has been excluded from consideration in those chapters of the Report dealing with organisation, management and resources but, as far as a cathedral's role and mission are concerned, it is like the other 41 Anglican cathedrals in England.

Royal Peculiars did not come within the Commission's terms of reference but helpful discussions were held informally with the Deans of Westminster and Windsor.

The Evidence

3.1   Publications

A letter inviting comments on a range of issues relevant to cathedrals (copy attached – see Annex I) was sent on 21 August 1992 to the following:-

Deans and Provosts	42
Chapter Clerks/Administrators	42
Diocesan Bishops	42
DBF Secretaries	42
Local Authorities (City/District 43, County 29)	72
Local Authority Associations	6
Other Public Bodies	33
TOTAL	279

The Chairman of the Commission also wrote to the Church and national press.

3.2   Correspondence from Individuals

As a result of the general knowledge and publicity about the Commission's work written submissions were received from the 182 individuals listed in Annex II.

3.3   Submissions from Dioceses, Deaneries and Parishes

108 submissions were received as listed in Annex III.

3.4 Submissions from Local Authorities and other Public Bodies

87 submissions were received as listed in Annex IV.

3.5 Oral evidence

The following gave evidence in person at meetings of the Commission:-

6 July 1993	The Right Reverend Eric Kemp, Bishop of Chichester
	The Reverend Canon Rex Davis, Subdean of Lincoln Cathedral
14 September 1993	Mr Hector McLean, the Archbishops' Secretary for Appointments
5 October 1993	Mr John Holroyd CB, the Prime Minister's Secretary for Appointments
21 March 1994	Sir Bernard Feilden CBE) the Cathedrals The Reverend Canon) Fabric Richard Hanford) Commission Dr Richard Gem (Secretary)) for England
	Mr Oliver Pearcey) the Historic Buildings Mr Richard Halsey) and Monuments Mrs Corinne Bennett) Commission (English Heritage)

In addition, on 16 April 1993, the Chairman and the Provost of St Edmundsbury travelled to Paris and met the following to discuss the role of French cathedrals:-

M. Christian Dupavillon, Directeur du Patrimoine) M. Philippe Geffré, Administrateur Civile)	Ministry of Culture
Père Jean-Louis Angué) Mlle Renée Moineau)	Centre National de Pastorale Liturgique

On 11 January 1994, the Chairman, the Provost of St Edmundsbury and the Dean of Manchester attended the meeting of the House of Bishops in Manchester for a discussion, in particular, of the bishop's ministry as reflected by the cathedral and the relationship between bishop, cathedral, diocese and parishes.

3.6 Cathedral Submissions and Visits

In addition to written evidence submitted by 32 cathedrals we gained a valuable insight into the daily working of cathedrals from the individual cathedral visits. We divided into five teams, each of which comprised two or three members accompanied by a recorder. Each visit took place over the weekend (Friday afternoon to Sunday morning).

After two 'pilot' visits were made to Sheffield and Lichfield Cathedrals in October 1992, the remaining 40 visits took place between January and September 1993. On each occasion our team met not only the diocesan bishop and members of the cathedral chapter but also a large number of those involved in cathedral life, for example, members of the congregation, volunteers and paid staff, representatives of diocesan bodies, the local authorities and other organisations. In total, some 1,600 people were interviewed during the 42 visits.

The Archbishops' Commission on Cathedrals

Chairman: Lady Howe   Secretary: N M Waring
                                                 1 Millbank
                                                 London SW1P 3JZ

                                        Tel: 071-222 7010 Ext. 4330

Copy of letter sent to all Deans and Provosts etc.

21 August 1992

Dear

As you know, the Archbishops of Canterbury and York have recently set up a Commission whose terms of reference are

'To examine the future role in Church and nation of the Cathedrals of the Church of England and to make recommendations as to how best that role could be fulfilled, including proposals for their government and support.'

The Commission wishes to consult as widely as possible and, to aid the process of consultation, the enclosed schedule sets out some of the issues which the Commission considers to be of particular importance. It invites comments and views from all interested parties on these issues and indeed on any other relevant matter within the Commission's terms of reference. I should be very grateful if all responses could be sent to me *by the end of January 1993* (or earlier if possible).

Yours sincerely

N M Waring

ENC

The Archbishops' Commission on Cathedrals

SOME ISSUES

1. **The Cathedral's role**
    -   as a centre of worship, ministry and mission
    -   as a centre of pilgrimage and tourism
    -   as an educational and cultural resource

2. **The Cathedral's relationships**
    -   to the Bishop
    -   to the cathedral congregation and laity
    -   to the diocese, the parishes and the synodical structure
    -   to the local community
    -   to other Christian churches
    -   to the nation and beyond

3. **The Cathedral's government**
    -   the existing legislation
    -   the Statutes

4. **The Cathedral's stipendiary staff (ordained and lay)**
    -   the members of staff
    -   *the methods and criteria of appointment
    -   the conditions of service
    -   the assignment of authority
    -   the question of appraisal and accountability

5. **The Cathedral's management**
    -   the management structure and formal as well as informal systems of management
    -   the supervision of staff
    -   the involvement of lay people
    -   the use and maintenance of the building for its various roles

6. **The Cathedral's finances**
    -   the system of financial administration
    -   the sources of finance
    -   future financial requirements

* In examining this aspect the Commission will have regard to the forthcoming report of the General Synod's Working Party on Senior Church Appointments.

List of Submissions from Individuals

The Right Reverend Michael Adie, Bishop of Guildford

Mr George Allery, Salisbury

Mr Michael Anyar, Gainsborough

The Reverend Canon John Armson, Rochester Cathedral

The Reverend Prebendary Richard Askew, Bath

Miss Barbara Aspell, Coventry

Mr Geoffrey Atkinson, Brighton

The Very Reverend Peter Baelz, formerly Dean of Durham

Mr Jack Barker, Hythe

The Reverend Peter Barnett, Bristol

The Reverend Philip Barrett, Winchester

The Right Reverend Michael Baughen, Bishop of Chester

Mrs Jean Beattie and Mr Christopher Timbrell, Birmingham Cathedral Churchwardens

Mr S R Beet, Ascot

The Very Reverend Peter Berry, Provost of Birmingham

The Reverend Canon Colin Beswick, Norwich Cathedral

Mr Brian Beves, Ledbury

Mr Richard Bickmore and 4 others, Lincoln Cathedral Community Association

Mr W Bigland, Northampton

Mr James Black, Lincoln

Mr Colin Bodkin and 5 others, Norwich

Miss Gwen Box, Burton on Trent

Ms Jayne Boys, Canterbury

Mrs Elisabeth Bragg, Cambridge

Mrs Susan Brazier, March, Cambs.

Major General Keith Burch CB, CBE, Chapter Clerk, York

Miss Anne Burkett, Coventry

Mr Peter Burman, York

The Reverend Canon Maurice Burrell, Norwich Diocesan Director of Training

Mr D W Butcher, Newbury

Mr Ronald Carless, Totnes

The Reverend Terence Carter, Portsmouth

Mrs Dulcie Chrismas, Chichester

The Reverend Canon Thomas Christie, Chairman, Cathedrals' Finance Conference

Miss Rosemary Clarke, Leamington Spa

Mr Philip Clayton, Oxford

Mr George Collard, Chester

The Reverend Canon Owen Conway, Chester Cathedral

The Reverend Canon Edward Cook, Greater Chapter's Working Party, Lincoln Cathedral

Commander Roger Corbet-Milward RN, Worcester

The Reverend R W Cotton, Herne Bay

Mr Frank Cranmer, Twickenham

Mr W R Cullimore, Chapter Clerk, Chester

Mr Eric Dare, Truro

Mr David Davies, Canterbury

The Reverend Canon Rex Davis, Lincoln Cathedral

The Right Reverend Peter Dawes, Bishop of Derby

The Reverend Robert de Berry, London W9

Mr Peter Dexter, Truro

Mr Larry Dickens, Lincoln

Mr H E Dobles, Farnborough

Mr A J Donaldson, Malton, N Yorkshire

Mrs Constance Downes MBE, Coventry

Mr A T Dudley, Hassocks, W Sussex

Mr Thomas Dunne, Leominster

The Reverend Canon David Durston, Salisbury Cathedral

Mr M K Elkington, Longfield, Kent

The Reverend Canon Michael Fisher, St Ives, Cornwall

Mr David Flood, Organist, Canterbury Cathedral

The Very Reverend Graham Forbes, Provost of St Mary's Cathedral, Edinburgh

Mr J W G Frith, Hon Secretary, Wells Cathedral Council

Miss L M Gabriel, Lincoln

Mr David Gibson, Nottingham

Miss Joan Goodrich, Lincoln

Mr Christopher Gower, Master of the Music, Peterborough Cathedral

The Right Reverend Alec Graham, Bishop of Newcastle

Miss Caroline Graham-Brown, London WC2

Mr Trevor Griffin, Rugby

The Reverend Canon Terence Grigg, Cottingham, Hull

The Reverend Canon John Grimwade, Cirencester

Mr Paul Hale, Rector Chori, Southwell Minster

Miss Jean Hall, York

Mr F Hands, Canterbury

The Reverend Canon P C and Mrs P D Hawker, Lincoln

Professor G R and Dr M S Hervey, Wells

Mr Richard Hill, York

The Very Reverend Robert Holtby, formerly Dean of Chichester

Mr Timothy Hone, Master of the Music, Newcastle Cathedral

Miss Joan Hough, Edinburgh

Mr Gordon Jackson, Lincoln

The Reverend Canon Dr William Jacob, Warden, Lincoln Theological College

Mr Colin Jeffries MBE, Sevenoaks

Mrs Cherry Johnstone, Canterbury

Mr John Jordan, Chester

Mrs Margaret Jowett, Faversham

The Right Reverend Eric Kemp, Bishop of Chichester

Mrs Sheila Kirkland, Dean's Secretary, Guildford Cathedral

The Reverend Canon David Knight, Chelmsford Cathedral

Mr James Lancelot, Organist, Durham Cathedral

The Very Reverend John Lang, formerly Dean of Lichfield

Mr R G Lawrence, Headmaster, The Chorister School, Durham

Mr S C Lawrence, Ely

Mrs Janet Lawson, Bookshop Manager, Guildford Cathedral

Miss Margaret Leigh, Canterbury

Mr Adrian Lucas, Organist, Portsmouth Cathedral

Mrs Rosalind Lucas, Lincoln

Ms Elaine Macaulay, Castle Cary

The Venerable Jeffrey Maples, formerly Archdeacon of Swindon

The Reverend Margaret Mascall, Herne Bay

Miss Barbara May, Faversham

The Reverend Jean Mayland, previously Minster Deacon, York Minster

The Right Reverend Malcolm Menin, Suffragan Bishop of Knaresborough

Mr J Meyrick, Truro

Mr Terry Miller, Lincoln Diocesan Countryside Officer

Colonel Douglas Millington OBE, on behalf of York Minster Fund

The Very Reverend Patrick Mitchell, Dean of Windsor

Mr Philip Moore, Organist, York Minster

Mrs Heather Morgan, Exeter

The Reverend Canon Edwin Morris, Bristol

Dr John Morris, Winchester

Mr Michael Nash, Canterbury

Mr Patrick Nield, Cockermouth

Mrs M V Nicholson, Peterborough

The Reverend Canon E G Orland, Peterborough

The Reverend Michael Parker, Bedford

Miss J E Park, Truro

Mr Roger Parsons, Executive Director, Lincoln Cathedral Preservation Council

The Reverend Richard Paten, Peterborough

Mr Bruce Patterson, Manchester

Mr Stephen Petter, London E3

Mr William Pettit, Canterbury

Mr Russell Pond, Chapter Clerk, Lincoln

Mr Paul Pumfrey, Lincoln

Mrs Pamela Pye, Wells

Lady Ralphs, Norwich

The Reverend Canon Alastair Redfern, Bristol Cathedral

Ms Juliet Reeve, Birmingham

Miss Ruby Relf, Worthing

Mrs Janet Reynolds, Holsworthy, Devon

The Reverend Canon Eric Richards, Scarborough

Mrs Joan Richards, Oxford

Mr Graeme Richardson, Southwell

Miss D Riley, Leyburn, N Yorkshire

Ripon Cathedral Parish Church Council

Miss Olive Rippengal, Westcliff on Sea

The Reverend Canon Ewan Roberts, Canterbury

Mr Miles Roberts, Hon Treasurer, Guildford Cathedral

Mr Charles Robinson, Canterbury

The Right Reverend Mark Santer, Bishop of Birmingham

The Right Reverend John Saxbee, Suffragan Bishop and Archdeacon of Ludlow

Mr Mark Shepherd, Assistant Organist, Lichfield Cathedral

Mr Robin Sherlock, Secretary, Friends of St Paul's Cathedral

Miss M N Short, Pulborough

The Very Reverend Edward Shotter, Dean of Rochester

The Reverend Canon John Simpson, Bristol Cathedral

Dr Joyce Skinner CBE, Lincoln

The Reverend David Sladden, Doncaster

Mrs Anne Smith, Swindon

The Reverend Michael Smith, Uppingham

Mr John Snell, Lincoln

The Very Reverend John Southgate, formerly Dean of York

The Reverend Professor H F D and Mrs M J Sparks, Canterbury

The Venerable Leslie Stanbridge, formerly Archdeacon of York

The Right Reverend David Stancliffe, Bishop of Salisbury and previously Provost of Portsmouth

The Reverend Prebendary P S Stephens, on behalf of the Non-Residentiary Prebendaries of Exeter Cathedral

Mrs Betty Sterry, Hon Secretary, Wakefield Cathedral PCC

Mrs Mary Stewart, Lincoln

Mrs Jean Sturdy, Lincoln

Mr M O Tanner, Southwold

The Reverend Canon Frank Telfer, Guildford Cathedral

Mr Michael Thomas, Chairman, Fabric Advisory Committee, Worcester

The Reverend Richard Thomas, Oxford Diocesan Communications Officer

The Reverend John Thorold, Hawarden

Dr H C Tomlinson, Headmaster, The Cathedral School, Hereford

Mr Simon Tonking, on behalf of the Lichfield Cathedral Congregation

The Reverend Prebendary Christopher Tookey, Wells

The Reverend Canon John Toy, York Minster

The Venerable A H M Turner, Archdeacon of The Isle of Wight

The Reverend Canon Edward Turner, Rochester Cathedral

Mr J B R Vartan, Peterborough

The Right Reverend John Waine, Bishop of Chelmsford

Mr John Walker, Lincoln

The Reverend Canon Graham Walker, on behalf of the Greater Chapter, Bradford Cathedral

Dr Jeffrey West, London N4

The Reverend Canon Robert Western, Headmaster, The Cathedral School, Lincoln

The Right Reverend William Westwood, Bishop of Peterborough

Mrs B I Wilkinson, Longfield, Kent

The Reverend W E R Wilkinson, Beverley

Miss Joan Williams, Librarian, Hereford Cathedral

Mr James Wilson, Cathedral Administrator, Lichfield

Colonel M J Woodcock OBE, Chapter Clerk, Exeter

Mr Arthur Wyn-Davies, Verger, Ely Cathedral

List of Submissions from Dioceses, Deaneries and Parishes

Birmingham
Bishop's Council

Bradford
Ben Rhydding, St John, PCC
Bingley, All Saints, PCC
Bradford, St Clement, PCC
Burley in Wharfdale, St Mary the Blessed Virgin, PCC
Eccleshill, St Luke, PCC
Grindleton, St Ambrose, PCC
Hubberholme, St Michael and All Angels, PCC
Ingleton, St Mary, PCC
Ingrow, St John the Evangelist, PCC
Kildwick, St Andrew, PCC
Lothersdale, Christ Church, PCC
Low Moor, St Mark, PCC
Manningham, St Chad, PCC
Shelf, St Michael and All Angels, PCC
Skipton, Christ Church, PCC
Thornton, St James, PCC
Tosside, St Bartholomew, PCC
Utley, St Mark, PCC

Bristol
Diocesan Board of Finance

Knowle West, St Barnabas, PCC

Carlisle
Diocesan Board of Finance

Barrow in Furness, St George with St Luke, PCC
Carlisle, St John the Evangelist, PCC
Eskdale, St Catherine, PCC

Kells, St Peter, PCC
Kirkby Ireleth, St Cuthbert, PCC
Mirehouse, St Andrew, PCC
Natland, St Mark, PCC
Newton Reigny, St John, PCC
Sebergham, St Mary, PCC
Ulverston, St Mary with Holy Trinity, PCC
Waverton, Christ Church, PCC

Chichester
East Grinstead Deanery
Petworth Deanery

Coventry
Coventry East Deanery
Kenilworth Deanery

Alveston, St James, PCC
Bedworth, All Saints, PCC
Bilton, St Mark, PCC
Binley Woods LEP
Hunningham, St Margaret, PCC
Leamington Priors, All Saints, PCC
North Radford, St Francis, PCC
Tile Hill, St Oswald, PCC
Wolverton with Norton Lindsey and Langley PCC

Durham
Bishop's Council

Barnard Castle Deanery
Darlington Deanery
Gateshead Deanery
Lanchester Deanery

Hartlepool, St Luke, PCC
Lamesley, St Andrew, PCC

Ely
Diocesan Synod/Board of Finance

Gloucester
Diocesan Secretary

Hereford
Bishop's Council

Rural Dean and Lay Co-Chairman of
Hereford City Deanery Synod

Lichfield
Diocesan Working Party

Lincoln
Diocesan Boards/Committees and
Deaneries

Christianity Deanery (Lincoln City)

Liverpool
Bishop's Council/Diocesan Board of
Finance Executive

Bootle Deanery

London
Synodical Secretary

Manchester
Diocesan Board of Finance

Bolton Deanery
Bury Deanery
Deane Deanery
Withington Deanery

Newcastle
Bishop's Council

Humshaugh, St Peter, PCC

Oxford
Lay Chairman of Oxford Diocesan
Synod

Milton Keynes, Christ the
Cornerstone, LEP

Portsmouth
Fareham Deanery
East and West Wight Deaneries
Gosport Deanery
Petersfield Deanery

Ripon
Lay Chairmen of Diocesan/Deanery
Synods

Birkby, St Peter, PCC
Calverley, St Wilfrid, PCC
Harrogate, Low, St Mary with All
Saints, PCC
Holbeck, St Luke, PCC
Richmond Hill, Leeds, PCC

Rochester
Diocesan Board of Education

Rural Deans and Lay Co-Chairmen of
Deanery Synods/General Diocesan
Secretary

St Albans
Bedford, St Andrew, PCC
Chalgrave, All Saints, PCC
Chells, St Hugh and St John, LEP

Dunstable Team Ministry

Elstree, St Nicholas, PCC

Haynes, St Mary, PCC

Highfield, St Paul, District Church Council

Leighton Buzzard, All Saints, PCC

Lewsey, St Hugh, Parish Staff and Churchwardens

Little Heath, Christ Church, PCC

Luton, St Andrew, PCC

North Mymms, St Mary, Parishioner

Oxhey, St Matthew, PCC member

Radlett, Christ Church, PCC

Stevenage, St Nicholas, PCC

Sundon, St Mary, PCC

Ware, Christ Church, PCC

Sheffield

Bishop's Council

Sharrow, St Andrew, PCC

Southwell

Farnsfield, St Michael, PCC

Worcester

Diocesan Board of Finance

York

Archbishop's Council/Diocesan Board of Finance and Pastoral Committee

Middlesborough Deanery, Clergy Chapter

Note:

Evidence was also received on behalf of Deans' and Provosts' wives.

List of Submissions from Local Authorities and other Public Bodies

LOCAL AUTHORITIES

Avon County Council
Bradford Metropolitan District Council
Bristol City Council
Canterbury City Council
Chelmsford Borough Council
Cheshire County Council
Chichester District Council
Cornwall County Council
Coventry City Council
Cumbria County Council
Derby City Council
Derbyshire County Council
Durham County Council
Essex County Council
Exeter City Council
Gloucestershire County Council
Hampshire County Council
Hereford and Worcester County Council
Kent County Council
Leicester City Council
Lincolnshire County Council
Corporation of the City of London
Manchester City Council
Newark and Sherwood District Council
Norfolk County Council
Northamptonshire County Council
North Yorkshire County Council
Norwich City Council
Nottinghamshire County Council
Oxfordshire County Council
Portsmouth City Council
Salisbury District Council
St Edmundsbury Borough Council
Surrey County Council
Wakefield Metropolitan District Council
West Sussex County Council
Worcester City Council
York City Council

PUBLIC AND OTHER BODIES

Anglican Consultative Council
Board of Mission
Bristol Free Church Council
British Tourist Authority

Cathedral Architects' Association
Cathedral Camps
Cathedrals Fabric Commission for England
Cathedrals' Finance Conference
Cathedral Libraries and Archives Association
Cathedral Music Working Party
Cathedral Organists' Association
Cathedral Statutes Commission
Choir Schools' Association
Christian Enquiry Agency
Christianity and the Future of Europe
Church of England Guild of Vergers
Church Shops Association
Churches Together in Cheshire
Churches Together in Cumbria
Churches Together in England
Council for British Archaeology
Council for the Care of Churches
Coventry Council of Churches
Deans and Provosts' Conference
Deans and Provosts Vergers' Conference
Department of the Environment
Department of National Heritage
Dioceses Commission
Ecclesiastical Law Society
English Clergy Association
English Heritage
Friends of Cathedral Music
Governing Body of the Church in Wales
Grubb Institute
Guild of Church Musicians
Heart of England Tourist Board
House of Bishops
Insite Trust
Inter-Faith Consultative Group
Local Government Management Board
North American Deans' Conference
Partnership for World Mission
Precentors' Conference
Royal Fine Art Commission
St Albans Cathedral Ecumenical Chaplaincy
Scottish Episcopal Church
Society for the Protection of Ancient
  Buildings
Somerset and S. Avon Ecumenical Council
United Reformed Church
  (Southern Province)

Tourism

1.   This appendix contains the 14 tables included in the report *Anglican Cathedrals and Tourism – The Way Forward* prepared for us by Max Hanna of Sightseeing Research.

2.   Copies of that report are available from Church House Bookshop, priced £2.95.

3.   The tables in this appendix are referred to in Chapter 12. For a full interpretation, readers are referred to Max Hanna's report.

Table 1: Cathedral visitor estimates for 1992 (in alphabetical order)

Cathedral	Visitors		Trend from 1991 to 1992	Method of calculation	% of visitors from overseas		% of visitors who were children
Birmingham	25,000		up	visitors' book	10		20
Bradford	5,000	(1991)	-	manual	N/A		30
Bristol	30,000		same	sample count	20		50
Canterbury	2,250,000		same	sample count	35		25
Carlisle	208,655		down	electronic	N/A		N/A
Chelmsford	42,000		up	N/A	N/A		30
Chester	1,000,000		up	sample count	33	(1990)	N/A
Chichester	250,000		same	sample count	17		N/A
Coventry	350,000		same	sample count	12	(1991)	N/A
Derby	45,630		up	visitors' book	16		N/A
Durham	364,646		down	manual	23	(1978)	N/A
Ely	200,000		up	ticket sales and count	35		8
Exeter	400,000		same	electronic	50		12
Gloucester	300,000		down	leaflet count	15		10
Guildford	216,900		up	manual and ticket sales	N/A		N/A
Hereford	220,000		up	electronic and ticket sales	10		33
Leicester	20,000	(1991)	-	sample count	20		50
Lichfield	180,000		down	sample count	10		33
Lincoln	375,000		same	electronic	30		30
Liverpool	300,000		up	electronic	30		25
Manchester	75,000		same	sample count	8		25
Newcastle	33,000		down	sample count	15		25
Norwich	500,000		N/A	electronic	20	(1991)	33
Oxford	226,000		down	manual	25	(1991)	N/A
Peterborough	200,000		same	sample count	10		40
Portsmouth	10,000	(1988)	-	donations revenue	N/A		N/A
Ripon	150,000		up	sample count	5		25
Rochester	220,000		N/A	sample count	N/A		7
St Albans	400,000		N/A	sample count	N/A		N/A
St Edmundsbury	70,000		same	sample count	10		10
St Paul's	1,400,000		same	ticket sales and count	70		30
Salisbury	550,000		up	manual	50		30
Sheffield	48,000		same	sample count	N/A		40
Southwark	50,000		N/A	N/A	20		N/A
Southwell	110,000		same	sample count	3		20
Truro	300,000		same	leaflet count	5		25
Wakefield	55,000		down	sample count	2		33
Wells	391,000		same	electronic	25		35
Winchester	500,000		down	sample count	39	(1991)	12
Worcester	300,000		same	manual and ticket sales	11	(1987)	50
York	2,250,000		same	ticket sales	25		25

Source: Survey of Visits to Tourist Attractions 1992, English Tourist Board

Table 2: Cathedral visitor estimates for 1992 (in rank order)

Cathedral	Visitors		Factors influencing visitor trend in 1992
Canterbury	2,250,000		Visits similar, but large increase from USA
York	2,250,000		
St Paul's	1,400,000		
Chester	1,000,000		Many extra events to celebrate 900th anniversary
Salisbury	550,000		Advertising, publicity for Spire appeal, more groups
Norwich	500,000		
Winchester	500,000		Reduced number of overseas visitors
Exeter	400,000		
St Albans	400,000		
Wells	391,000		
Lincoln	375,000		
Durham	364,646		
Coventry	350,000		Visits similar but more from overseas
Gloucester	300,000		Three Choirs Festival preparations limited visitor access
Liverpool	300,000		
Truro	300,000		
Worcester	300,000		
Chichester	250,000		
Oxford	226,000		
Hereford	220,000		
Rochester	220,000		
Guildford	216,900		Marketing and publicity by "Valley of the Wey" group
Carlisle	208,655		
Ely	200,000		
Peterborough	200,000		
Lichfield	180,000		
Ripon	150,000		
Southwell	110,000		
Manchester	75,000		
St Edmundsbury	70,000		
Wakefield	55,000		Visits reduced by refurbishment of precincts
Southwark	50,000		
Sheffield	48,000		
Derby	45,630		National Association of Flower Arrangers 10th Anniversary festival
Chelmsford	42,000		
Newcastle	33,000		Visit down as 1991 was 9th centenary year celebration
Bristol	30,000		
Birmingham	25,000		Opening of International Convention Centre in mid-1991
Leicester	20,000	(1991)	
Portsmouth	10,000	(1988)	
Bradford	5,000	(1991)	
Total	14,620,831		

Source: Survey of Visits to Tourist Attractions 1992, English Tourist Board

Table 3: Visits to Cathedrals in a Fortnight in August 1993

Results of Count (31 July to 13 August)

| Cathedral | 9am - 6pm | | Estimate other times | Total |
	1978	1993		
York	188,269	178,800	5%	188,200
Canterbury	143,468	123,876	8%	135,076
St Paul's	208,658	127,681***	0.5%	128,323
Chester	51,416	62,986	10%	69,984
Salisbury	54,796	49,720	2%	50,787
Durham	54,217	49,726	-	49,726
Wells	N/A	37,258	3%	38,410
Lincoln	48,027	35,965	5%	37,700
Exeter	40,890	34,005	6%	36,176
Winchester	50,908	34,417*	-	34,417
Truro	N/A	33,078	0.1%	33,095
Norwich	N/A	29,500	10%	32,770
St Albans	22,582	23,940	1%	24,206
Oxford	N/A	23,480	-	23,480
Chichester	32,133	22,120	3%	22,900
Gloucester	24,750	22,378**	1%	22,604
Coventry	55,223	16,733	19%	20,658
Ely	N/A	16,226	9%	17,831
Liverpool	N/A	15,445	4%	16,089
Hereford	N/A	13,792	-	13,792
Carlisle	13,503	11,723	8%	12,742
Rochester	9,025	12,480	-	12,480
Lichfield	15,052	12,002	0.6%	12,074
Peterborough	11,249	11,292	2.5%	11,580
Worcester	29,605	10,689*	-	10,689
Ripon	N/A	9,384	-	9,384
Southwell	N/A	6,357	0.3%	6,376
Birmingham	N/A	4,649	-	4,649
St Edmundsbury	8,985	4,170	8%	4,533
Guildford	9,023	4,092	-	4,092
Sheffield	3,848	2,732	-	2,732
Wakefield	N/A	2,640	1%	2,667
Manchester	3,900	2,474	1.5%	2,512
Portsmouth	N/A	2,479	-	2,479
Derby	N/A	2,208	-	2,208
Chelmsford	N/A	1,395	-	1,395
Leicester	700	1,580	-	1,580
Blackburn	N/A	746	-	746
Total		1,054,218	4%	1,101,142

* Includes 10% estimate for Sundays when no count carried out.

** Numbers in second week assumed to be the same as in first week.

*** Estimate based on count carried out between 18 September and 1 October.

Table 4: Peak Season Weekly and Daily Visitor Flow

Results of Count (31 July to 13 August) 9am - 6pm

Cathedral	Number of visits per day - average							Weekly average	Daily average
	Mon	Tue	Wed	Thur	Fri	Sat	Sun		
Birmingham	444	413	318	385	317	345	103	2,325	332
Blackburn	52	70	54	43	79	68	9	373	53
Canterbury	10,329	9,768	9,917	9,185	7,894	11,427	3,419	61,938	8,848
Carlisle	935	867	1,163	945	647	931	375	5,862	837
Chelmsford	78	113	104	134	122	115	33	698	100
Chester	3,828	5,269	4,996	4,758	4,351	5,313	2,978	31,493	4,499
Chichester	1,712	1,820	2,094	1,568	1,499	1,563	805	11,060	1,580
Coventry	998	971	1,622	1,015	1,455	1,432	875	8,367	1,195
Derby	180	160	128	111	172	312	44	1,104	158
Durham	4,812	3,498	3,693	3,208	3,693	4,064	1,897	24,863	3,552
Ely	956	1,142	1,052	1,029	871	1,233	1,833	8,113	1,159
Exeter	3,227	2,269	3,459	2,351	1,772	2,419	1,508	17,003	2,429
Gloucester	1,550	1,784	1,556	1,472	1,730	2,129	968	11,189	1,598
Guildford	284	311	416	251	279	289	217	2,046	292
Hereford	998	1,117	1,253	1,147	1,047	1,257	79	6,896	985
Leicester	139	119	134	81	166	124	28	790	113
Lichfield	590	942	670	694	747	1,332	1,028	6,001	857
Lincoln	1,975	2,882	2,531	2,438	2,217	3,137	2,804	17,983	2,569
Liverpool	1,164	1,084	1,297	1,320	677	1,318	865	7,723	1,103
Norwich	2,412	2,171	2,740	2,255	1,630	2,028	1,515	14,750	2,107
Oxford	1,740	1,570	1,758	1,628	1,778	1,804	1,463	11,740	1,677
Peterborough	706	955	969	742	934	920	421	5,646	807
Portsmouth	148	200	136	161	237	235	123	1,240	177
Ripon	624	759	805	775	626	801	304	4,692	670
Rochester	912	1,067	1,004	825	788	907	739	6,240	891
St Albans	1,388	1,432	1,938	1,307	1,521	2,750	1,686	11,970	1,710
St Paul's*	6,006	4,332	3,448	3,975	4,015	4,920	9,205	35,899	5,128
Salisbury	2,965	4,009	3,572	3,165	2,851	3,845	4,454	24,860	3,551
Sheffield	155	239	228	198	314	188	45	1,366	198
Southwell	337	394	459	387	416	637	551	3,179	454
Truro	3,975	2,292	4,670	1,998	1,600	1,419	587	16,539	2,363
Wakefield	177	204	182	168	236	354	-	N/A	N/A
Wells	2,709	3,094	3,198	2,893	2,209	2,516	2,012	18,629	2,661
Winchester	2,481	2,465	2,569	2,740	2,138	3,096	N/A	N/A	N/A
Worcester	289	1,182	833	797	677	946	N/A	N/A	N/A
York	13,224	14,601	13,479	13,904	11,800	13,106	9,287	89,400	12,771
Total	65,496	67,382	71,411	62,373	56,439	69,964	43,055	436,119	
%	15.0	15.4	16.4	14.3	12.9	16.0	9.9	100	
% in 1978	14.1	16.0	16.1	15.1	13.1	13.9	11.8	100	
Average rank order	4.3	3.3	2.9	4.3	4.4	2.7	6.1		
Average rank order in 1978	4.3	2.8	3.0	3.6	4.9	4.0	5.4		

* Totals do not include figures for St Paul's as the count there was carried out between 18 September and 1 October.

225

Table 5: Peak Season Average Hourly Flow

Results of Count (31 July to 13 August) 9am - 6pm

Cathedral	Number of visits per hour								
	AM 9-10	10-11	11-12	PM 12-1	1-2	2-3	3-4	4-5	5-6
Birmingham	10	29	37	49	54	73	45	21	16
Blackburn	.1	6	6	13	8	9	7	3	-
Canterbury	465	911	1,260	1,278	1,266	1,246	977	970	475
Carlisle	32	63	95	116	141	151	118	81	41
Chelmsford	41	67	94	89	72	152	97	87	-
Chester	286	383	548	640	541	577	587	496	440
Chichester	34	112	195	255	239	269	228	152	95
Coventry	70	110	195	186	155	156	143	120	60
Derby	8	13	24	22	26	27	19	14	3
Durham	168	498	622	623	619	579	567	153	N/A
Ely	42	111	141	160	129	183	166	113	114
Exeter	116	215	347	340	383	386	309	198	136
Gloucester	34	136	240	234	219	275	242	198	102
Guildford	13	49	54	27	36	49	36	25	4
Hereford	29	68	157	166	154	152	137	99	22
Leicester	2	8	11	20	17	24	16	11	4
Lichfield	21	79	94	124	130	170	125	80	36
Lincoln	117	250	349	351	407	366	341	235	154
Liverpool	96	100	134	165	174	158	120	87	73
Norwich	62	174	317	303	301	329	309	211	102
Peterborough	24	57	94	115	106	155	126	79	50
Portsmouth	7	13	16	18	17	30	28	27	20
Ripon	25	81	106	90	82	109	111	66	N/A
Rochester	22	62	117	130	129	157	127	103	46
St Albans	22	131	209	254	242	269	306	191	86
St Paul's*	364	728	599	486	552	951	558	566	324
Salisbury	136	312	576	525	453	497	443	373	236
Sheffield	11	36	31	26	26	27	21	12	6
Southwell	12	33	60	53	52	70	86	54	32
Truro	54	228	397	437	379	325	298	174	70
Wells	75	144	333	363	349	442	419	340	196
Winchester	92	235	341	345	378	445	353	238	155
Worcester	24	91	97	96	111	99	131	103	35
York	450	1,010	1,443	1,775	1,902	2,062	1,868	1,443	817
Total	2,408	5,236	8,012	8,675	8,596	9,330	8,228	6,338	3,626
%	4.0	8.7	13.3	14.4	14.2	15.4	13.6	10.4	6.0
% in 1978	3.5	8.1	12.1	12.4	13.8	16.4	16.0	11.3	6.4
Average rank order	8.7	6.6	3.8	3.2	3.3	1.9	3.5	6.0	8.0
Average rank order in 1978	8.7	7.3	4.9	4.0	3.5	1.7	2.0	5.0	7.9

* Totals do not include figures for St Paul's as the count there was carried out between 18 September and 1 October.

Table 6: Tourism-related employment at cathedrals in 1992

Cathedral	Full-time permanent	Part-time permanent	Full-time seasonal	Part-time seasonal	Total paid employment	Volunteers
Birmingham	-	1	-	-	1	4
Bradford	3	1	-	-	4	88
Bristol	-	1	-	-	1	15 per day
Canterbury	2	8	-	8	18	350
Carlisle	5	-	-	-	5	170
Chelmsford	2	-	-	-	2	2
Chester	35	-	-	6	41	200
Chichester	12	-	-	-	12	N/A
Coventry	2	8	-	-	10	N/A
Derby	-	1	-	-	1	3
Ely	9	23	-	11	43	84
Exeter	2	3	-	2	7	20
Guildford	15	38	-	-	53	250
Hereford	4	10	-	-	14	200
Lichfield	3	10	-	2	15	200
Lincoln	1	18	-	-	19	200
Manchester	4	2	-	-	6	3
Newcastle	8	10	-	-	18	60
Norwich	5	-	-	-	5	400
Oxford	14	-	-	-	14	N/A
Peterborough	1	-	-	-	1	10 per day
Portsmouth	-	1	-	-	1	25
Ripon	-	-	-	-	-	5
Rochester	2	-	-	-	2	30
St Albans	3	6	-	-	9	25
St Paul's	14	8	-	-	22	15 per day
Salisbury	7	6	-	12	25	30
Sheffield	-	-	-	-	-	14
Southwark	6	-	-	-	6	200
Southwell	-	-	-	-	-	100
Truro	10	-	-	-	10	20
Wakefield	-	-	-	-	-	4
Wells	4	-	-	2	6	10
Worcester	20	-	-	-	20	210
York	3	50	-	10	63	200
Total	196	205	-	53	454	3,147

Source: Survey of Visits to Tourist Attractions 1992, English Tourist Board.

Table 7: Income from visitors to cathedrals in 1992

Cathedral	Income from donations and admission charges		Shop, refectory and other trading income	Total visitor income	% of total income	% change in visitor income 1991-1992
	Gross £'000	Net £'000	Net £'000	Net £'000		
St Paul's	2,215	1,900	152	2,052	31.7	N/A
York	957	664	143	807	12.5	N/A
Salisbury	386	257	120	377	5.8	10
Canterbury	307	196	168	364	5.6	9
Winchester	232	232	74	306	4.7	same
Durham	187	149	103	252	3.9	same
Ely	213	157	81	238	3.7	N/A
Wells	172	149	86	235	3.6	same
St Albans	98	56	129	185	2.9	N/A
Lincoln	189	166	16	182	2.8	15
Chester	90	90	67	157	2.4	N/A
Exeter	114	83	60	142	2.2	same
Hereford	62	60	68	128	2	N/A
Gloucester	54	52	75	128	2	30
Worcester	100	87	18	105	1.6	N/A
Norwich	74	51	46	97	1.5	same
Liverpool	24	-3	97	94	1.5	N/A
Guildford	19	14	80	93	1.4	9
Chichester	77	46	44	91	1.4	N/A
Lichfield	58	35	38	73	1.1	N/A
Peterborough	45	34	33	67	1	same
Southwell	43	43	21	64	1	5
Coventry	104	73	-17	56	0.9	15
Carlisle	34	24	26	50	0.8	-5
Ripon	43	37	11	48	0.7	N/A
St Edmundsbury	17	17	21	38	0.6	1
Southwark	11	0	27	28	0.4	N/A
Bristol	14	9	12	21	0.3	same
Chelmsford	0	0	12	12	0.2	10
Blackburn	1	1	5	6	0.1	N/A
Wakefield	3	2	3	5	0.1	N/A
Newcastle	0	0	1	1	0	N/A
Portsmouth	3	-7	7	0	0	N/A
Leicester	0	-1	0	-1	0	N/A
Manchester	6	-4	3	-1	0	same
Derby	7	-2	0	-1	0	5
Sheffield	0	-4	3	-1	0	N/A
Birmingham	11	-4	0	-4	0.1	N/A
Rochester	21	-9	4	-5	0.1	N/A
Bradford	1	-23	3	-20	0.3	N/A
Total	5,991	4,627	1,841	6,468	100	

Source: Archbishops' Commission on Cathedrals and the English Tourist Board

Table 8: Analysis of retail trading in 1992

Cathedral	Turnover £'000	Net Profit £'000	Profit as % turnover**	Staff numbers			
				Paid: full-time	part-time	Volunteers: full-time	part-time
Canterbury	733	124	16.9	11	20	0	0
York	552	130	23.6	4	7	0	0
St Paul's	544	140	25.7	8	4	0	0
Salisbury	372	110	29.6	2	5	0	12
Durham	369	69	18.7	4	3	0	0
Ely	297	45	15.2	4	3	0	30
Norwich	248	35	14.1	2	4	0	34
St Albans	244	64	26.2	2	4	0	94
Wells	243	35	14.4	2	13	0	0
Chester	242	68	28.1	1	1	0	72
Liverpool	237	59	24.9	4	0	0	0
Chichester	232	12	5.2	6	4	0	2
Lichfield	220	29	13.2	1	3	0	120
Coventry	189	-23	-12.2	2	10	0	0
Exeter	179	45	25.1	1	2	0	30
Guildford	171	54	31.6	0	2	1	122
Winchester	141	30	21.3	0	2	0	3
Truro	141	34	24.1	1	1	0	48
Sheffield	138	9	6.5	2	1	0	0
Worcester	127	18	14.2	0	9	0	30
Peterborough	116	17	14.7	2	0	0	40
Hereford	93	22	23.7	1	6	0	17
Derby	90	4	4.4	1	1	0	18
Gloucester	82	13	15.9	1	2	0	70
Southwell	66	21	31.8	0	2	0	70
Southwark	56	11	19.6	0	3	0	25
St Edmundsbury	49	15	30.6	0	1	0	2
Rochester	47	5	10.6	0	3	0	9
Carlisle	42	16	38.1	0	0	0	60
Ripon	42	11	26.2	0	1	0	20
Portsmouth	40	8	20.0	0	0	0	30
Lincoln	39	8	20.5	3	2	0	8
Bristol	35	13	37.1	0.3	0	0	30
Chelmsford	16	4	25.0	0	0	0	31
Blackburn	14	5	35.7	0	1	0	50
Wakefield	13	3	23.1	0	1	0	15
Birmingham	8	0	0.0	0	1	0	27
Newcastle	8	1	12.5	1	0	0	30
Bradford	7	3	42.9	0	0	0	1
Leicester	1	0	0.0	0	1	0	0
Manchester	N/A	N/A	N/A	N/A	N/A	N/A	N/A
Total	6,483	1,267	19.5	66.3	123	1	1,150

Source: Archbishops' Commission on Cathedrals

** Details of overheads were not requested. This effectively distorts the inter-cathedral comparison of the net profit/turnover ratios, due to the fact that overheads may be met in full by the trading company, or fully or partially subsidised by the cathedral.

N/A = No retail outlet at this cathedral

Table 9: Analysis of catering trading in 1992

Cathedral	Turnover £'000	Net Profit £'000	Profit as % turnover**	Staff numbers			
				Paid: full-time	part-time	Volunteers: full-time	part-time
Liverpool	283	38	13	10	5	0	0
Guildford	279	20	7	5	40	0	0
St Albans	238	65	27	5	4	0	65
Wells	234	41	18	6	42	0	5
Ely	213	36	17	6	9	0	0
Chichester	198	32	16	4	21	0	4
Durham	197	34	17	2	9	0	0
Southwark	170	17	10	*	*	*	*
Gloucester	170	17	10	7	0	0	0
Exeter	142	14	10	4	8	0	8
Salisbury	142	6	4	3	6	6	0
Chester	138	-1	-1	4	6	0	1
Truro	128	27	21	6	4	0	18
Winchester	99	38	38	1	1	0	8
Carlisle	82	10	12	1	5	0	0
Lichfield	76	9	12	1	16	0	30
Norwich	73	11	15	2	4	0	38
Peterborough	72	16	22	0	1	0	40
Coventry	58	7	12	*	*	*	*
Hereford	46	20	43	0	9	0	12
Worcester	23	15	65	0	0	0	115
Newcastle	15	6	40	1	0	0	27
Lincoln	9	0	0	2	2	0	2
St Edmundsbury	6	6	100	0	0	0	variable
Southwell	5	5	100	1	4	0	0
Bradford	2	0	0	0	0	0	variable
Leicester	N/A	N/A	N/A	N/A	N/A	N/A	N/A
Sheffield	N/A	N/A	N/A	N/A	N/A	N/A	N/A
Canterbury	N/A	N/A	N/A	N/A	N/A	N/A	N/A
Birmingham	N/A	N/A	N/A	N/A	N/A	N/A	N/A
Ripon	N/A	N/A	N/A	N/A	N/A	N/A	N/A
York	N/A	N/A	N/A	N/A	N/A	N/A	N/A
Chelmsford	N/A	N/A	N/A	N/A	N/A	N/A	N/A
Rochester	N/A	N/A	N/A	N/A	N/A	N/A	N/A
Portsmouth	N/A	N/A	N/A	N/A	N/A	N/A	N/A
Bristol	N/A	N/A	N/A	N/A	N/A	N/A	N/A
St Paul's	N/A	N/A	N/A	N/A	N/A	N/A	N/A
Blackburn	N/A	N/A	N/A	N/A	N/A	N/A	N/A
Wakefield	N/A	N/A	N/A	N/A	N/A	N/A	N/A
Derby	N/A	N/A	N/A	N/A	N/A	N/A	N/A
Manchester	N/A	N/A	N/A	N/A	N/A	N/A	N/A
Total	3,098	489	16	71	196	6	373

Source: Archbishops' Commission on Cathedrals

* Information not available

** Details of overheads were not requested. This effectively distorts the inter-cathedral comparison of the net profit/turnover ratios, due to the fact that overheads may be met in full by the trading company, or fully or partially subsidised by the cathedral.

N/A = No catering at this cathedral

Table 10: Peak Season Visitor Expenditure

31 July to 13 August 1993

Cathedral	Number of:			Value of:					
	guide books sold	all items sold	paid admissions	all items sold £	paid admissions £	donations £	catering £	other revenue £	Total gross revenue £
Birmingham	63	929	-	N/A	-	396	-	-	N/A
Blackburn	56	716	-	774	-	N/A	-	-	N/A
Canterbury	5,998	N/A	8,673	58,111	3,810	23,321	-	8,713	93,955
Carlisle	239	4,410	-	3,901	-	4,898	5,737	-	14,536
Chelmsford	114	244	-	414	-	166	-	-	580
Chester	N/A	N/A	-	19,172	-	5,237	10,853	-	35,262
Chichester	354	13,022	1,206	13,874	280	5,926	12,930	465	33,475
Coventry	1,460	N/A	-	N/A	-	5,900	N/A	N/A	N/A
Derby	49	N/A	830	215	433	455	-	-	1,103
Durham	4,336	28,445	8,058	36,903	3,660	7,443	13,830	927	62,763
Ely*	1,109	15,940	8,052	20,892	19,607	1,847	4,379	336	47,061
Exeter	843	8,658	-	14,881	-	10,319	7,985	70	33,255
Gloucester	580	4,226	1,648	6,083	722	3,638	6,710	-	17,153
Guildford	47	5,042	-	8,712	-	1,218	10,740	325	20,995
Hereford	430	N/A	5,296	7,783	5,343	3,618	4,770	-	21,514
Leicester	101	-	-	51	-	N/A	-	-	N/A
Lichfield	357	N/A	-	9,729	-	4,627	3,066	-	17,422
Lincoln	654	13,894	747	17,234	974	19,308	5,761	-	43,277
Liverpool	118	N/A	655	13,280	998	1,626	12,182	-	28,086
Manchester	61	506	-	139	-	126	-	-	265
Norwich	727	N/A	-	15,229	-	5,375	4,294	-	24,898
Oxford	470	16,500	N/A	14,399	N/A	N/A	-	-	N/A
Peterborough	571	7,386	346	7,717	264	2,350	4,049	428	14,808
Portsmouth	110	N/A	-	1,613	-	314	-	-	1,927
Ripon	703	3,304	N/A	3,847	727	2,812	-	479	7,865
Rochester	205	3,535	-	3,680	-	N/A	-	-	N/A
St Albans	426	12,071	43	10,993	86	3,430	12,599	105	27,213
St Edmundsbury	451	1,239	N/A	N/A	74	1,482	-	-	N/A
St Paul's	2,209	N/A	76,610	38,625	168,173	N/A	-	-	206,798
Salisbury	2,015	N/A	11,918	29,906	4,122	49,098	10,377	1,480	94,983
Sheffield	55	59	-	37	-	161	-	-	198
Southwell	235	3,544	23	4,444	22	1,438	-	158	6,062
Truro	291	24,622	-	9,992	-	2,441	6,985	984	20,402
Wakefield	10	250	-	615	-	207	-	82	904
Wells	1,600	40,674	-	18,948	-	15,015	17,511	-	51,472
Winchester	N/A	N/A	1,459	12,451	1,528	17,313	8,138	1,009	40,439
Worcester	385	N/A	-	N/A	-	N/A	1,396	-	N/A
York	1,785	63,944	31,960	48,539	32,585	40,878	-	5,536	127,538
Total	29,217	273,160	157,524	453,183	243,408	242,383	164,292	21,097	1,124,363
Number of Cathedrals	36	24	16	34	18	32	20	15	38

* Ely Cathedral earned an additional £3,295 in a shop in the High Street and £9,245 in the Almonry Café.

231

Table 11: Peak Season Visitor Expenditure per head

31 July to 13 August 1993

| Cathedral | Number per 100 visitors: | | | Value per visitor: | | | | | |
	guide books sold	all items sold	paid admissions	all items sold £	paid admissions £	donations £	catering £	other revenue £	Total gross revenue £
Birmingham	1	20	-	N/A	-	9p	-	-	N/A
Blackburn	7	96	-	N/A	-	N/A	-	-	N/A
Canterbury	5	N/A	7	47p	3p	19p	-	7p	76p
Carlisle	2	38	-	33p	-	42p	49p	-	1.24p
Chelmsford	8	17	-	30p	-	12p	-	-	42p
Chester	N/A	N/A	-	30p	-	8p	17p	-	56p
Chichester	2	59	6	63p	1p	27p	58p	2p	1.51p
Coventry	9	N/A	-	N/A	-	35p	N/A	N/A	N/A
Derby	2	N/A	N/A	10p	N/A	21p	-	-	N/A
Durham	9	57	16	74p	7p	15p	28p	2p	1.26p
Ely	7	98	50	1.29p	1.21p	11p	27p	2p	2.90p
Exeter	3	25	-	44p	-	30p	23p	0.02p	98p
Gloucester	3	19	7	27p	3p	16p	30p	-	77p
Guildford	1	N/A	-	N/A	-	30p	N/A	8p	N/A
Hereford	3	N/A	38	56p	39p	26p	35p	-	1.56p
Leicester	6	-	-	3p	-	N/A	-	-	N/A
Lichfield	3	N/A	-	81p	-	39p	26p	-	1.45p
Lincoln	2	39	2	48p	3p	54p	16p	-	1.20p
Liverpool	1	N/A	4	86p	6p	11p	79p	-	1.82p
Norwich	3	N/A	-	52p	-	18p	15p	-	84p
Oxford	2	70	N/A	61p	N/A	N/A	-	-	N/A
Peterborough	5	65	3	68p	2p	21p	36p	4p	1.31p
Portsmouth	4	N/A	-	65p	-	13p	-	-	78p
Ripon	8	35	N/A	41p	8p	30p	-	5p	84p
Rochester	2	28	-	29p	-	N/A	-	-	N/A
St Albans	2	50	0.02	46p	0.4p	14p	53p	0.4p	1.14p
St Paul's*	4	N/A	61	41p	1.32p	4p	-	-	1.77p
Salisbury	4	N/A	24	60p	8p	99p	21p	3p	1.91p
Sheffield	2	2	-	3p	-	N/A	-	N/A	N/A
Southwell	4	56	0.4	70p	0.3p	23p	-	2p	95p
Truro	1	74	-	30p	-	7p	21p	3p	62p
Wakefield	2	9	-	23p	-	8p	-	3p	34p
Wells	4	109	-	51p	-	40p	47p	-	1.38p
Winchester	N/A	N/A	4	36p	4p	50p	24p	2p	1.17p
Worcester	4	N/A	-	N/A	-	N/A	13p	N/A	N/A
York	1	36	18	27p	18p	23p	-	3p	71p
Average	3	50	18	46p	25p	26p	29p	4p	1.09p
Number of Cathedrals	34	21	15	31	16	30	19	15	26
Average in 1978	8	39	N/A	13p	N/A	4p	7p	N/A	22p
Number of Cathedrals in 1978	18	10	N/A	18	N/A	14	7	N/A	17

* Data relates to the period from 18 September to 1 October.

N/A = Not Available. This includes some cathedrals where there is an element of non-comparability of data.

Note: the number of visitors is based on the count between 9.00 am and 6.00 pm for the calculation of averages.

Table 12: Top Ten Cathedrals by Visitor Revenue Source

31 July to 13 August 1993

	Value of all items sold	£	Value of donations	£	Value of catering	£
1	Canterbury	58,111	Salisbury	49,098	Wells	17,511
2	York	48,539	York	40,878	Durham	13,830
3	St Paul's	38,625	Canterbury	23,321	Chichester	12,930
4	Durham	36,903	Lincoln	19,308	St Albans	12,599
5	Salisbury	29,906	Winchester	17,313	Liverpool	12,182
6	Ely	20,892	Wells	15,015	Chester	10,853
7	Chester	19,172	Exeter	10,319	Guildford	10,740
8	Wells	18,948	Durham	7,443	Salisbury	10,377
9	Lincoln	17,234	Chichester	5,926	Winchester	8,138
10	Norwich	15,229	Coventry	5,900	Exeter	7,985

	Value of paid admissions	£	Value of other sources	£	Total gross revenue	£
1	St Paul's	168,173	Canterbury	8,713	St Paul's	206,798
2	York	32,585	York	5,536	York	127,538
3	Ely	19,607	Salisbury	1,480	Salisbury	94,983
4	Hereford	5,343	Winchester	1,009	Canterbury	94,955
5	Salisbury	4,122	Truro	984	Durham	62,763
6	Canterbury	3,810	Durham	927	Wells	51,472
7	Durham	3,660	Ripon	479	Ely	47,061
8	Winchester	1,528	Chichester	465	Lincoln	43,277
9	Liverpool	998	Peterborough	428	Winchester	40,439
10	Lincoln	974	Ely	336	Chester	35,262

	Value of all items sold	£ per visitor	Value of donations	£ per visitor	Value of catering	£ per visitor
1	Ely	1.29	Salisbury	99p	Liverpool	79p
2	Liverpool	86p	Lincoln	54p	Chichester	58p
3	Lichfield	81p	Winchester	50p	St Albans	53p
4	Durham	74p	Carlisle	42p	Carlisle	49p
5	Southwell	70p	Wells	40p	Wells	47p
6	Peterborough	68p	Lichfield	39p	Peterborough	36p
7	Portsmouth	65p	Coventry	35p	Hereford	35p
8	Chichester	63p	Exeter	30p	Gloucester	30p
9	Oxford	61p	Guildford	30p	Durham	28p
10	Salisbury	60p	Ripon	30p	Ely	27p

	Value of paid admissions	£ per visitor	Value of other sources	£ per visitor	Total gross revenue	£ per visitor
1	St Paul's	1.32	Guildford	8p	Ely	2.90
2	Ely	1.21	Canterbury	7p	Salisbury	1.91
3	Hereford	39p	Ripon	5p	Liverpool	1.82
4	York	18p	Peterborough	4p	St Paul's	1.77
5	Canterbury	8p	Salisbury	3p	Hereford	1.56
6	Ripon	8p	Truro	3p	Chichester	1.51
7	Salisbury	8p	Wakefield	3p	Lichfield	1.45
8	Durham	7p	York	3p	Wells	1.38
9	Liverpool	6p	Chichester	2p	Peterborough	1.31
10	Winchester	4p	Durham	2p	Durham	1.26

Table 13: Paid Admissions at Cathedrals - Number and Value

31 July to 13 August 1993

Cathedral	Number of paid admissions	Value of paid admissions £	£ per visitor
St Paul's	76,610	168,173*	2.20
Crypt, York	10,796	6,151	57p
Chapter House Exhibition, Salisbury	10,761	2,964	28p
Chapter House, York	8,662	5,930	68p
Ely	8,052	19,607	2.44
Corona Tower, Canterbury	7,202	3,137	44p
Foundations, York	6,571	10,183	1.55
Tower, York	5,931	10,321	1.74
Tower, Durham	4,962	3,722	75p
Mappa Mundi Exhibition, Hereford	2,854	4,565	1.60
Chained Library, Hereford	2,242	778	35p
Treasury, Durham	2,104	1,750	83p
Exhibition, Gloucester	1,648	721	44p
Treasury, Chichester	1,590	159	10p
Gallery and Library, Winchester	1,459	1,529	1.05
Audio-visual, Canterbury	1,471	674	46p
Mosaic, Chichester	1,206	121	10p
Roof areas, Salisbury	1,157	1,157	1.00
Audio-visual, Durham	992	298	30p
Tower, Lincoln	747	974	1.30
Tower, Liverpool	514	857	1.67
Visitors' Centre, Peterborough	209	209	1.00
Tower, Hereford	200	156	78p
Embroidery, Liverpool	141	141	1.00
Treasury, Peterborough	137	55	40p
Treasury, Ripon	N/A	727	N/A
Treasury, St Edmundsbury	N/A	74	N/A

* Includes admission to galleries.

Table 14: Miscellaneous Revenue from Visitors to Cathedrals

31 July to 13 August 1993

	£		£
Charge made to commerical tour companies, York	5,535	Votive Candles, Peterborough	210
Guided Tours, Canterbury	4,893	Tower Tours, Winchester	170
Votive Candles and prayer card sales, Canterbury	1,656	Guided Tours, Winchester	166
Toilet admission charge, Canterbury	1,504	Votive Candles, Southwell	158
Votive Candles, Truro	984	Photography permits, Peterborough	141
Votive Candles, Salisbury	949	Audio telephones, Salisbury	130
Votive Candles, Durham	927	Pre-booked Tours, St Albans	105
Calligraphy, Winchester	673	Telescope in close, Salisbury	92
Groups booking fee, Canterbury	660	Votive Candles, Wakefield	82
Votive Candles, Ripon	479	Ceiling Lights, Peterborough	77
Votive Candles, Chichester	465	Pre-booked Tours, Exeter	70
Votive Candles, Ely	336	Toilet charge, Salisbury	63
Brass rubbing centre, Guildford	325	Brass rubbing, Salisbury	7
Mediaeval clock, Salisbury	239		

Finance

This appendix provides the more detailed analysis of the results of the survey of cathedral finances described in Chapter 13. Tables 1 to 6 break down the overall figures in Table 1 of Chapter 13 between the six categories of cathedral as defined in paragraph 3 of that chapter:

(a)   the dean and chapter cathedrals (D&CC), sub-divided as follows:

   (i)   Table 1 – the 4 largest D&CC (Canterbury, St Paul's, Salisbury and York);

   (ii)   Table 2 – the 9 next largest D&CC with income of around £1 million and more (Chichester, Durham, Ely, Gloucester, Hereford, Lincoln, Wells, Winchester and Worcester);

   (iii)   Table 3 – the 7 remaining D&CC which are of pre-19th century establishment in their present form (Carlisle, Chester, Exeter, Lichfield, Norwich, Peterborough and Rochester);

   (iv)   Table 4 – the 7 D&CC whose current dioceses are fundamentally of 19th and 20th century establishment (Bristol, Guildford, Liverpool, Manchester, Ripon, St Albans and Truro);

(b)   the parish church cathedrals (PCC), sub-divided as follows:

   (i)   Table 5 – the 5 PCC with tourist income of £10,000 or more (Birmingham, Coventry, St Edmundsbury, Southwark and Southwell);

   (ii)   Table 6 – the 9 PCC with tourist income of less than £10,000 (Blackburn, Bradford, Chelmsford, Derby, Leicester, Newcastle, Portsmouth, Sheffield and Wakefield).

Notes: 1.   Figures in the tables are subject to rounding errors.

        2.   The definitions used in the financial analysis (see Chapter 13) are given in the attachment to this appendix.

Table 1: Analysis of the Top 4 D&CC (by income)
(Canterbury, St Paul's, Salisbury, York)

All figures in £'000

Balance Sheet:

	Chapter		Trust Funds	
	Cost	Market Value	Cost	Market Value
Property Investments	15,092	60,061	539	610
Other Investments	7,828	10,754	14,532	14,862
Other Assets	4,552	4,552	4,179	4,179
	27,471	75,366	19,249	19,650
Liabilities	2,306	2,306	124	124
Net Assets	25,165	73,060	19,126	19,527
Maintenance Overhang	13,375	13,375		
Net Chapter Assets after Overhang	11,790	59,685		

Income Analysis:

	Chapter	Trust	Total	Percentage
Other Investment Income	763	1,633	2,395	19%
Investment Property Income	2,128	8	2,136	17%
Direct Tourist Income	3,865	0	3,865	30%
Net Shop, Refectory & Other Trading Income	583	0	583	5%
Church Commissioners' Stipends & Grants	459	0	459	4%
HBMC & Other Grants	232	0	232	2%
Diocesan Stipends & Grants	30	0	30	0%
Collections/Almsgiving	318	0	318	3%
Appeals	427	856	1,283	10%
Friends	230	0	230	2%
Legacies	267	260	527	4%
Transfers from Trusts	1,613	(1,613)	0	0%
Other Income	574	85	659	5%
Total Income	**11,487**	**1,229**	**12,716**	**100%**

Expenditure Analysis:

	Total	Percentage
Upkeep of Fabric	2,844	25%
Chapter Costs	884	8%
Administration Costs	1,517	13%
Services/Music/Choir School	1,337	12%
Vergers/Upkeep of Interior	1,009	9%
Upkeep of Precinct/Gardens	598	5%
Long-term Maintenance Charge	275	2%
Visitors/Tourists/Education	848	8%
Library/Archives	243	2%
Special Projects	579	5%
Outward Giving	160	1%
Payments to Diocese	26	0%
Other Expenditure	940	8%
Total Expenditure	**11,260**	**100%**

	Chapter	Trust	Total
Surplus/(Deficit)	**227**	**1,229**	**1,457**

Other Income

Library/Archives	29
Fees	146
Sundry Operating Income	67
Profit on Sale of Property/Investments	418
Other Non-Operating Income	0
Total	**659**

Other Expenditure

Insurance for Cathedral	203
Loss on Sale of Property/Investments	23
Interest Paid	17
Other Long-term Charges	0
Other Operating Expenditure	697
Total	**940**

		Sensitivity (% change in Income Type to Break Even)
Surplus/(Deficit) Excluding Profit/Loss on Sale of Property/Investments	1,062	369%
Surplus/(Deficit) Excluding Investment Income	(3,075)	32%
Surplus/(Deficit) Excluding Net Tourism	(1,560)	48%
Surplus/(Deficit) Excluding Church Commissioners' Grants & Stipends	998	318%
Surplus/(Deficit) Excluding All Grants & Stipends	736	202%
Surplus/(Deficit) Excluding Appeals & Legacies	(353)	80%
Net Tourist/Visitor/Pilgrim Profit Margin	3,017	78%
Total Return on Investments	5%	
Net Return on Investment Property	4%	
Net Return on Other Investments	9%	
Administration as a percentage of Income	12%	
Restoration Expenditure (in last 10 years)	20,170	5,043 per Cathedral

Balance Sheet Analysis:

Maintenance Overhang as percentage of Net Assets	14%
Expenditure Cover: Net Assets (Chapter)/Expenditure	6.5
Expenditure Cover: Net Assets (Total)/Expenditure	8.2
Years to Clear Overhang at Current Year's Expenditure Rate	4.7
Years to Clear Overhang at 10 Year Average Expenditure Rate	6.6

Projections: Surplus/(Deficit)

	Budget (no Restoration)	Restoration	Budget (after Restoration)
One Year Ahead	1,041	2,003	(962)
Two Years Ahead	573	1,831	(1,258)
Three Years Ahead	208	1,430	(1,222)
Four Years Ahead	163	1,055	(892)
Five Years Ahead	154	1,160	(1,006)
	2,139	**7,479**	**(5,340)**

Table 2: Analysis of the 9 next largest D&CC with income > £1 million
(Chichester, Durham, Ely, Gloucester, Hereford, Lincoln, Wells, Winchester, Worcester)

All figures in £'000

Balance Sheet:

	Chapter		Trust Funds	
	Cost	Market Value	Cost	Market Value
Property Investments	5,507	22,078	32	32
Other Investments	11,778	13,364	3,588	4,157
Other Assets	6,024	5,990	2,881	2,624
	23,309	41,433	6,501	6,812
Liabilities	1,974	1,974	57	57
Net Assets	21,335	39,459	6,444	6,756
Maintenance Overhang	13,880	13,880		
Net Chapter Assets after Overhang	7,455	25,579		

Income Analysis:

	Chapter	Trust	Total	Percentage
Other Investment Income	1,220	2,583	3,804	31%
Investment Property Income	1,798	0	1,798	15%
Direct Tourist Income	1,286	0	1,286	11%
Net Shop, Refectory & Other Trading Income	566	0	566	5%
Church Commissioners' Stipends & Grants	962	0	962	8%
HBMC & Other Grants	780	20	800	7%
Diocesan Stipends & Grants	197	0	197	2%
Collections/Almsgiving	517	0	517	4%
Appeals	56	720	776	6%
Friends	503	0	503	4%
Legacies	340	146	486	4%
Transfers from Trusts	2,440	(2,440)	0	0%
Other Income	484	14	498	4%
Total Income	**11,150**	**1,044**	**12,194**	**100%**

Expenditure Analysis:

	Total	Percentage
Upkeep of Fabric	4,021	35%
Chapter Costs	1,042	9%
Administration Costs	1,296	11%
Services/Music/Choir School	1,235	11%
Vergers/Upkeep of Interior	1,008	9%
Upkeep of Precinct/Gardens	918	8%
Long-term Maintenance Charge	535	5%
Visitors/Tourists/Education	187	2%
Library/Archives	123	1%
Special Projects	250	2%
Outward Giving	194	2%
Payments to Diocese	24	0%
Other Expenditure	523	5%
Total Expenditure	**11,357**	**100%**
Surplus/(Deficit)	**(207)**	**1,044**

Total Surplus/(Deficit): 837

Other Income

Library/Archives	41
Fees	94
Sundry Operating Income	69
Profit on Sale of Property/Investments	64
Other Non-Operating Income	229
Total	**498**

Other Expenditure

Insurance for Cathedral	225
Loss on Sale of Property/Investments	1
Interest Paid	35
Other Long-term Charges	30
Other Operating Expenditure	232
Total	**523**

238

		Sensitivity (% change in Income Type to Break Even)
Surplus/(Deficit) Excluding Profit/Loss on Sale of Property/Investments	774	1,324%
Surplus/(Deficit) Excluding Investment Income	(4,765)	15%
Surplus/(Deficit) Excluding Net Tourism	(262)	76%
Surplus/(Deficit) Excluding Church Commissioners' Grants & Stipends	(125)	87%
Surplus/(Deficit) Excluding All Grants & Stipends	(1,122)	43%
Surplus/(Deficit) Excluding Appeals & Legacies	(425)	66%
Net Tourist/Visitor/Pilgrim Profit Margin	1,099	85%
Total Return on Investments	14%	
Net Return on Investment Property	8%	
Net Return on Other Investments	22%	
Administration as a percentage of Income	11%	
Restoration Expenditure (in last 10 years)	21,140	2,349 per Cathedral

Balance Sheet Analysis:

Maintenance Overhang as percentage of Net Assets	30%
Expenditure Cover: Net Assets (Chapter)/Expenditure	3.5
Expenditure Cover: Net Assets (Total)/Expenditure	4.1
Years to Clear Overhang at Current Year's Expenditure Rate	3.5
Years to Clear Overhang at 10 Year Average Expenditure Rate	6.6

Projections: Surplus/(Deficit)

	Budget (no Restoration)	Restoration	Budget (after Restoration)
One Year Ahead	4,014	3,952	62
Two Years Ahead	3,733	3,837	(104)
Three Years Ahead	2,756	2,711	45
Four Years Ahead	2,391	2,390	1
Five Years Ahead	2,673	2,496	177
	15,567	15,386	181

239

Table 3: Analysis of the next 7 D&CC with income < £1 million
(Carlisle, Chester, Exeter, Lichfield, Norwich, Peterborough, Rochester)

All figures in £'000

Balance Sheet:

	Chapter		Trust Funds	
	Cost	Market Value	Cost	Market Value
Property Investments	16,097	23,494	0	0
Other Investments	1,788	2,660	3,760	4,211
Other Assets	11,094	11,094	1,493	1,493
	-28,979	36,801	5,253	5,704
Liabilities	2,182	2,182	81	81
Net Assets	26,797	34,619	5,172	5,623
Maintenance Overhang	5,380	5,380		
Net Chapter Assets after Overhang	21,417	29,239		

Income Analysis:

	Chapter	Trust	Total	Percentage
Other Investment Income	272	386	658	13%
Investment Property Income	1,264	0	1,264	25%
Direct Tourist Income	435	0	435	9%
Net Shop, Refectory & Other Trading Income	274	0	274	5%
Church Commissioners' Stipends & Grants	773	0	773	15%
HBMC & Other Grants	331	0	331	7%
Diocesan Stipends & Grants	148	0	148	3%
Collections/Almsgiving	342	0	342	7%
Appeals	87	343	430	9%
Friends	115	0	115	2%
Legacies	115	0	115	2%
Transfers from Trusts	1,132	(1,132)	0	0%
Other Income	140	0	140	3%
Total Income	**5,427**	**(404)**	**5,023**	**100%**

Other Income

Library/Archives	6
Fees	57
Sundry Operating Income	17
Profit on Sale of Property/Investments	27
Other Non-Operating Income	33
Total	**140**

Expenditure Analysis:

	Total	Percentage
Upkeep of Fabric	1,441	26%
Chapter Costs	702	13%
Administration Costs	640	12%
Services/Music/Choir School	817	15%
Vergers/Upkeep of Interior	564	10%
Upkeep of Precinct/Gardens	385	7%
Long-term Maintenance Charge	30	1%
Visitors/Tourists/Education	127	2%
Library/Archives	18	0%
Special Projects	157	3%
Outward Giving	106	2%
Payments to Diocese	7	0%
Other Expenditure	500	9%
Total Expenditure	**5,495**	**100%**

Other Expenditure

Insurance for Cathedral	165
Loss on Sale of Property/Investments	135
Interest Paid	18
Other Long-term Charges	0
Other Operating Expenditure	182
Total	**500**

	Chapter	Trust	Total
Surplus/(Deficit)	**(67)**	**(404)**	**(471)**

Sensitivity (% change in Income Type to Break Even)

			Sensitivity
Surplus/(Deficit) Excluding Profit/Loss on Sale of Property/Investments		(363)	435%
Surplus/(Deficit) Excluding Investment Income		(2,392)	-25%
Surplus/(Deficit) Excluding Net Tourism		(779)	-153%
Surplus/(Deficit) Excluding Church Commissioners' Grants & Stipends		(1,245)	-61%
Surplus/(Deficit) Excluding All Grants & Stipends		(1,723)	-38%
Surplus/(Deficit) Excluding Appeals & Legacies		(1,016)	-86%
Net Tourist/Visitor/Pilgrim Profit Margin	308	71%	
Total Return on Investments		6%	
Net Return on Investment Property		5%	
Net Return on Other Investments		10%	
Administration as a percentage of Income		13%	
Restoration Expenditure (in last 10 years)		8,378	1,197 per Cathedral

Balance Sheet Analysis:

Maintenance Overhang as percentage of Net Assets	13%
Expenditure Cover: Net Assets (Chapter)/Expenditure	6.3
Expenditure Cover: Net Assets (Total)/Expenditure	7.3
Years to Clear Overhang at Current Year's Expenditure Rate	3.7
Years to Clear Overhang at 10 Year Average Expenditure Rate	6.4

Projections: Surplus/(Deficit)

	Budget (no Restoration)	Restoration	Budget (after Restoration)
One Year Ahead	819	807	12
Two Years Ahead	530	734	(204)
Three Years Ahead	336	502	(166)
Four Years Ahead	125	471	(346)
Five Years Ahead	28	300	(272)
	1,838	**2,814**	**(976)**

Table 4: Analysis of the 19th and 20th century D&CC
(Bristol, Guildford, Liverpool, Manchester, Ripon, St Albans, Truro)

All figures in £'000

Balance Sheet:

	Chapter		Trust Funds	
	Cost	Market Value	Cost	Market Value
Property Investments	4,541	9,757	645	645
Other Investments	3,672	4,738	929	1,172
Other Assets	2,602	3,502	843	863
	10,815	17,997	2,417	2,680
Liabilities	968	968	89	89
Net Assets	9,847	17,029	2,328	2,591
Maintenance Overhang	1,470	1,470		
Net Chapter Assets after Overhang	8,377	15,559		

Income Analysis:

	Chapter	Trust	Total	Percentage
Other Investment Income	785	492	1,278	25%
Investment Property Income	299	34	333	7%
Direct Tourist Income	156	48	204	4%
Net Shop, Refectory & Other Trading Income	332	0	332	7%
Church Commissioners' Stipends & Grants	996	0	996	20%
HBMC & Other Grants	134	0	134	3%
Diocesan Stipends & Grants	137	1	139	3%
Collections/Almsgiving	428	0	428	8%
Appeals	0	354	354	7%
Friends	41	50	91	2%
Legacies	161	100	261	5%
Transfers from Trusts	598	(598)	0	0%
Other Income	425	68	492	10%
Total Income	**4,493**	**549**	**5,042**	**100%**

Expenditure Analysis:

	Total	Percentage
Upkeep of Fabric	1,183	22%
Chapter Costs	815	15%
Administration Costs	610	11%
Services/Music/Choir School	616	12%
Vergers/Upkeep of Interior	562	11%
Upkeep of Precinct/Gardens	44	1%
Long-term Maintenance Charge	210	4%
Visitors/Tourists/Education	96	2%
Library/Archives	12	0%
Special Projects	388	7%
Outward Giving	76	1%
Payments to Diocese	27	0%
Other Expenditure	708	13%
Total Expenditure	**5,348**	**100%**

Surplus/(Deficit)	**(855)**	**549**	**(306)**

Other Income

Library/Archives	6
Fees	76
Sundry Operating Income	74
Profit on Sale of Property/Investments	145
Other Non-Operating Income	192
Total	**492**

Other Expenditure

Insurance for Cathedral	144
Loss on Sale of Property/Investments	20
Interest Paid	12
Other Long-term Charges	346
Other Operating Expenditure	187
Total	**708**

Sensitivity (% change in Income Type to Break Even)

			Sensitivity (% change in Income Type to Break Even)
Surplus/(Deficit) Excluding Profit/Loss on Sale of Property/Investments		(431)	-244%
Surplus/(Deficit) Excluding Investment Income		(1,917)	-19%
Surplus/(Deficit) Excluding Net Tourism		(414)	-283%
Surplus/(Deficit) Excluding Church Commissioners' Grants & Stipends		(1,302)	-31%
Surplus/(Deficit) Excluding All Grants & Stipends		(1,575)	-24%
Surplus/(Deficit) Excluding Appeals & Legacies		(920)	-50%
Net Tourist/Visitor/Pilgrim Profit Margin	108	53%	
Total Return on Investments		10%	
Net Return on Investment Property		3%	
Net Return on Other Investments		22%	
Administration as a percentage of Income		12%	
Restoration Expenditure (in last 10 years)		3,157	451 per Cathedral

Balance Sheet Analysis:

Maintenance Overhang as percentage of Net Assets	7%
Expenditure Cover: Net Assets (Chapter)/Expenditure	3.2
Expenditure Cover: Net Assets (Total)/Expenditure	3.7
Years to Clear Overhang at Current Year's Expenditure Rate	1.2
Years to Clear Overhang at 10 Year Average Expenditure Rate	4.7

Projections: Surplus/(Deficit)

	Budget (no Restoration)	Restoration	Budget (after Restoration)
One Year Ahead	85	110	(25)
Two Years Ahead	139	204	(65)
Three Years Ahead	229	250	(21)
Four Years Ahead	105	110	(5)
Five Years Ahead	105	110	(5)
	663	784	(121)

Table 5: Analysis of the 5 PCC with tourist income > £10,000
(Birmingham, Coventry, St Edmundsbury, Southwark, Southwell)

All figures in £'000

Balance Sheet:

	Chapter Cost	Chapter Market Value	Trust Funds Cost	Trust Funds Market Value
Property Investments	2,089	5,890	14	14
Other Investments	3,263	4,399	232	320
Other Assets	1,955	1,955	219	219
	7,307	12,245	465	553
Liabilities	1,143	1,143	1	1
Net Assets	6,164	11,102	464	553
Maintenance Overhang	2,211	2,211		
Net Chapter Assets after Overhang	3,953	8,891		

Income Analysis:

	Chapter	Trust	Total	Percentage
Other Investment Income	386	74	460	13%
Investment Property Income	159	0	159	5%
Direct Tourist Income	185	0	185	5%
Net Shop, Refectory & Other Trading Income	52	0	52	2%
Church Commissioners' Stipends & Grants	761	0	761	22%
HBMC & Other Grants	35	0	35	1%
Diocesan Stipends & Grants	67	0	67	2%
Collections/Almsgiving	260	1	260	8%
Appeals	1,106	0	1,106	32%
Friends	28	0	28	1%
Legacies	100	0	100	3%
Transfers from Trusts	66	(66)	0	0%
Other Income	218	0	219	6%
Total Income	**3,423**	**9**	**3,432**	**100%**

Expenditure Analysis:

	Total	Percentage
Upkeep of Fabric	205	8%
Chapter Costs	410	16%
Administration Costs	450	18%
Services/Music/Choir School	299	12%
Vergers/Upkeep of Interior	399	16%
Upkeep of Precinct/Gardens	35	1%
Long-term Maintenance Charge	150	6%
Visitors/Tourists/Education	56	2%
Library/Archives	2	0%
Special Projects	236	9%
Outward Giving	29	1%
Payments to Diocese	43	2%
Other Expenditure	243	9%
Total Expenditure	**2,556**	**100%**

	Chapter	Trust	Total
Surplus/(Deficit)	**866**	**9**	**875**

Other Income

Library/Archives	22
Fees	40
Sundry Operating Income	53
Profit on Sale of Property/Investments	104
Other Non-Operating Income	0
Total	**219**

Other Expenditure

Insurance for Cathedral	80
Loss on Sale of Property/Investments	34
Interest Paid	49
Other Long-term Charges	1
Other Operating Expenditure	78
Total	**243**

		Sensitivity (% change in Income Type to Break Even)
Surplus/(Deficit) Excluding Profit/Loss on Sale of Property/Investments	806	1,267%
Surplus/(Deficit) Excluding Investment Income	256	141%
Surplus/(Deficit) Excluding Net Tourism	746	678%
Surplus/(Deficit) Excluding Church Commissioners' Grants & Stipends	115	115%
Surplus/(Deficit) Excluding All Grants & Stipends	13	102%
Surplus/(Deficit) Excluding Appeals & Legacies	(331)	73%
Net Tourist/Visitor/Pilgrim Profit Margin	129	70%
Total Return on Investments	6%	
Net Return on Investment Property	3%	
Net Return on Other Investments	10%	
Administration as a percentage of Income	13%	
Restoration Expenditure (in last 10 years)	1,989	398 per Cathedral

Balance Sheet Analysis:

Maintenance Overhang as percentage of Net Assets	19%
Expenditure Cover: Net Assets (Chapter)/Expenditure	4.3
Expenditure Cover: Net Assets (Total)/Expenditure	4.6
Years to Clear Overhang at Current Year's Expenditure Rate	10.8
Years to Clear Overhang at 10 Year Average Expenditure Rate	11.1

Projections: Surplus/(Deficit)

	Budget (no Restoration)	Restoration	Budget (after Restoration)
One Year Ahead	445	822	(377)
Two Years Ahead	276	677	(401)
Three Years Ahead	(104)	268	(372)
Four Years Ahead	67	218	(151)
Five Years Ahead	68	134	(66)
	752	**2,119**	**(1,367)**

245

Table 6: Analysis of the 9 PCC with tourist income < £10,000

(Blackburn, Bradford, Chelmsford, Derby, Leicester, Newcastle, Portsmouth, Sheffield, Wakefield)

All figures in £'000

Balance Sheet:

	Chapter		Trust Funds	
	Cost	Market Value	Cost	Market Value
Property Investments	968	2,819	95	95
Other Investments	2,504	3,060	321	338
Other Assets	1,700	2,317	473	473
	5,172	8,195	889	907
Liabilities	537	537	34	34
Net Assets	4,635	7,659	855	872
Maintenance Overhang	2,084	2,084		
Net Chapter Assets after Overhang	2,551	5,575		

Income Analysis:

	Chapter	Trust	Total	Percentage
Other Investment Income	341	74	414	11%
Investment Property Income	72	11	83	2%
Direct Tourist Income	16	0	16	0%
Net Shop, Refectory & Other Trading Income	34	0	34	1%
Church Commissioners' Stipends & Grants	1,472	0	1,472	38%
HBMC & Other Grants	450	115	565	15%
Diocesan Stipends & Grants	213	0	213	5%
Collections/Almsgiving	453	0	453	12%
Appeals	3	307	310	8%
Friends	53	4	57	1%
Legacies	76	0	76	2%
Transfers from Trusts	352	(352)	0	0%
Other Income	203	2	205	5%
Total Income	**3,736**	**161**	**3,897**	**100%**

Expenditure Analysis:

	Total	Percentage
Upkeep of Fabric	860	23%
Chapter Costs	916	24%
Administration Costs	435	12%
Services/Music/Choir School	302	8%
Vergers/Upkeep of Interior	357	10%
Upkeep of Precinct/Gardens	97	3%
Long-term Maintenance Charge	205	5%
Visitors/Tourists/Education	49	1%
Library/Archives	4	0%
Special Projects	120	3%
Outward Giving	74	2%
Payments to Diocese	164	4%
Other Expenditure	172	5%
Total Expenditure	**3,755**	**100%**

	Chapter	Trust	Total
Surplus/(Deficit)	**(19)**	**161**	**142**

Other Income

Library/Archives	4
Fees	59
Sundry Operating Income	44
Profit on Sale of Property/Investments	80
Other Non-Operating Income	18
Total	**205**

Other Expenditure

Insurance for Cathedral	95
Loss on Sale of Property/Investments	6
Interest Paid	1
Other Long-term Charges	0
Other Operating Expenditure	70
Total	**172**

		Sensitivity (% change in Income Type to Break Even)
Surplus/(Deficit) Excluding Profit/Loss on Sale of Property/Investments	68	192%
Surplus/(Deficit) Excluding Investment Income	(355)	29%
Surplus/(Deficit) Excluding Net Tourism	175	-426%
Surplus/(Deficit) Excluding Church Commissioners' Grants & Stipends	(1,330)	10%
Surplus/(Deficit) Excluding All Grants & Stipends	(2,109)	6%
Surplus/(Deficit) Excluding Appeals & Legacies	(244)	37%
Net Tourist/Visitor/Pilgrim Profit Margin	-215%	
Total Return on Investments	8%	
Net Return on Investment Property	3%	
Net Return on Other Investments	12%	
Administration as a percentage of Income	11%	
Restoration Expenditure (in last 10 years)	3,064	340 per Cathedral

(33)

Balance Sheet Analysis:

Maintenance Overhang as percentage of Net Assets	24%
Expenditure Cover: Net Assets (Chapter)/Expenditure	2.0
Expenditure Cover: Net Assets (Total)/Expenditure	2.3
Years to Clear Overhang at Current Year's Expenditure Rate	2.4
Years to Clear Overhang at 10 Year Average Expenditure Rate	6.8

Projections: Surplus/(Deficit)

	Budget (no Restoration)	Restoration	Budget (after Restoration)
One Year Ahead	205	266	(61)
Two Years Ahead	225	302	(77)
Three Years Ahead	98	188	(90)
Four Years Ahead	46	115	(69)
Five Years Ahead	(38)	90	(128)
	536	961	(425)

DEFINITIONS

Income

Collections/ Almsgiving:
Income received from congregational collections, covenants and any other donations (excluding those for specific appeals, from tourists/visitors and from trusts).

Appeals:
Amounts received from specific appeals.

Friends:
All amounts given by the cathedral's 'Friends' to the cathedral, including the amounts spent by Friends on the cathedral's behalf.

Legacies:
All legacies received.

Visitors/Tourists/ Education:
All income received from visitors/tourists to the cathedral via collection boxes, entrance charges, candles (net), etc. Also any income arising from the provision of tourist or school educational facilities (excluding any shop or refectory earnings).

Shop (net):
Net earnings from the provision of shop and other retail outlets.

Refectory (net):
Net earnings from the provision of refectory/restaurant/ café or other catering facilities.

Other Trading Income (net)
This includes any income received from other trading activities including work performed by the cathedral's staff, e.g. masons, stained glass artist, members of the works staff (such as gardeners), etc. for other bodies.

Library and Archives:
Income from library and archives.

Fees:
Income received from letting the cathedral to outside bodies and for holding special services and events.

Operating Grant Income:
Grant income received from bodies such as local authorities relating to cathedral operations e.g. a grant for floodlighting the cathedral.

Church Commissioners' Stipends:
Stipends and other associated costs (e.g. NIC) paid by the Church Commissioners for the dean or provost and two residentiary canons.

Diocesan Stipends and Grants:
Stipends and other associated costs (e.g. NIC) paid by the diocese for cathedral clergy (or receipts by the chapter from the diocese in lieu) and other moneys received from the diocese.

Church Commissioners' Grants:
Any income received under section 31 of the Cathedrals Measure 1963 or as a repair or any other sort of grant from the Church Commissioners.

| Profits on Sale of Property/Investments: | Any book profits made on the sale of property or investments. |
| Sundry Operating Income: | Other operating income which cannot be included under the above headings (e.g. concert ticket sales). |

Expenditure

Chapter Costs:	All costs directly associated with the chapter e.g. clergy and staff costs and benefits, including housing upkeep, payroll costs and other expenses.
Outward Giving:	Donations and subscriptions of an outward giving nature, including outward almsgiving.
Services:	Costs of holding services e.g. sanctuary supplies, vestments, printing service cards, etc. It does not include the cost of providing the music.
Vergers:	All costs directly associated with the vergers, including salaries, payroll costs, benefits including housing upkeep, and other expenses.
Music:	Costs of the music staff and choir, visiting choirs, choir tours, vestments, sheet music, commissions, organ repairs and tuning, etc. It does not include choir school costs, except for school fees paid for choristers.
Library and Archives:	Library and archives staff and administration costs, cost of books and equipment.
Visitors/Tourists/ Education:	Costs of welcomers, printing, utilities, equipment, hospitality and other staff and administration costs associated with visitors and tourists. Also includes staff, administration and/or equipment costs of any educational facilities for tourists or visiting schools.
Administration:	Central administration costs including the salaries, payroll costs and training of administrative staff, their equipment costs and other general office costs.
Diocese:	Amounts paid to the diocese.
Choir School (net):	The amount of any deficit funding of the choir school met by the cathedral (if applicable) excluding the cost of school fees paid for choristers (included under 'Music').
Insurance – Cathedral:	Insurance of the cathedral fabric and contents and against any public liability.
Special Projects:	All costs associated with one-off projects such as building alterations (as opposed to upkeep) which do not fall under the headings below.

Upkeep of Fabric:	Costs of repairing and maintaining and of major restoration work to the fabric, including professional fees, materials, etc.
Upkeep of Precinct and Gardens:	Costs of maintaining houses and other property in the precinct and close and the costs of gardeners, precinct cleaners, security officers and their equipment (excluding that already included under 'Chapter Costs' or other headings). This should also include other associated costs such as lighting walkways, signs, notices, trees, etc.
Upkeep of Interior:	Costs of upkeep of the interior of the cathedral. These costs include cleaning, equipment and furniture purchases, maintaining alarms, repairing the interior of the cathedral, rates and heating.
Losses on Sale of Property Investments:	Any book losses made on the sale of property or investments.
Other Operating Expenditure:	Other costs associated with the running of the cathedral which cannot be included under the above headings.
Interest Paid:	All interest paid on loans, bank overdrafts and other borrowings.
Long-term Maintenance Charge:	An estimate in round terms of what further sum above the maintenance expenditure already included under 'Upkeep' should be spent on a year-on-year basis to prevent a maintenance backlog (or overhang) building up in the future. This figure does not include the amount needed to clear any existing backlog/overhang.
Other Long-term Charges:	Other charges not included under other headings which the cathedral is incurring or will have to face in the future as a result of current activities e.g. amortisation of leases of property.

Assets and Liabilities

Property and Other Investments:	At cost and market value (where known) but, if not, using the insurance value of the property as an approximate current market value.
Maintenance/ Restoration Overhang:	The best estimate (in round terms) of the cost of work to clear the maintenance/restoration backlog (or 'overhang')(i.e. the cost of bringing the cathedral and close up to a reasonable standard of maintenance). This figure includes an allowance for professional fees and VAT, but net of known grants.

250

Examples of Good Practice

We found a variety of good practice during our programme of cathedral visits and, although not every example may be appropriate or applicable to every cathedral, we hope that the examples set out below will be of interest.

A.   The Cathedral's Role and Relationships

I.   IN THE DIOCESE AND THE PARISHES

(1)   A regular (or rolling) programme of visits by parishes or deaneries to the cathedral.

(2)   Visits by chapter members and staff to parishes e.g. to accept preaching invitations or to give advice.

(3)   Visits by the cathedral choir to parishes and vice versa.

(4)   A link scheme and lay liaison officer for each parish.

(5)   Attendance by the dean/provost or other member of the chapter at all institutions.

(6)   Prayer cards signed by the dean/provost and sent to parishes.

(7)   Prayer cards, intercessions board and Christian Enquiry Agency cards available in the cathedral.

(8)   Evening pilgrimages by parishes and deaneries.

(9)   A follow-up cathedral service for all confirmation candidates six months afterwards.

(10)   Cathedral clergy used as confessors or spiritual directors for the parochial clergy.

(11)   Contact with other Christian churches and encouragement of ecumenical services.

(12)   Links with other dioceses and provinces worldwide.

(13)   Shared facilities with the diocesan office.

(14)   Special services held for diocesan staff.

II.   IN THE WIDER COMMUNITY

(1)   The dean/provost acts as ambassador to the local authority and business community.

(2)   A cathedral chaplaincy to city businesses.

(3)   Close involvement with industry and the local planning bodies.

(4)   Regular breakfast meetings with local business and professional people.

(5)   Links with local radio and television.

(6)   Participation in a city 'Open Day'.

(7)   The provision and distribution of food for the homeless and unemployed.

III.   IN EDUCATION AND THE ARTS

(1)   The provision of teachers' and students' guide packs and material linked to the National Curriculum.

(2)   An education centre and workshop days for school visits.

(3)   Cathedral lectures and theological seminars.

(4)   Involvement with the local university and teacher training college.

(5)   Joint chapter/university theological posts.

(6)   The provision of facilities for academic research in the cathedral library/archives and an 'Adopt a Book' scheme.

(7)   An annual/triennial festival of music.

(8)   The patronage of contemporary arts.

(9)   The making of its own cathedral vestments.

IV.   IN TOURISM

(1)   The provision of a visitors' or exhibition centre and heritage trail.

(2)   A ministry of welcome with guides and chaplain for both casual visitors and school parties.

(3)   The provision of leaflets in several languages and the use of multi-media presentations.

(4)   Tours of the cathedral which explain its use as well as its history.

(5)   A bookshop which can also supply the parishes.

(6)   A bookshop which includes the treasury.

(7)   Designation of an area for private prayer.

B.   The Cathedral's Management

I.   MUSIC/CHOIR SCHOOL

(1)   A choir school gives teaching opportunities to the organist and assistant organist.

(2)   Recruitment of choristers from local schools.

(3)   Continued musical training of choristers after their voices have broken.

(4)   The holding of organ and choir 'surgeries' for other churches.

(5)   The organist as a member of the Diocesan Liturgical Committee.

II.   FABRIC

(1)   Cathedral workshops which employ trainees and retain craft skills, with material resources being shared with the diocese.

(2)   The provision of facilities for the disabled e.g. an access ramp, a loop system, braille materials.

(3)   The importance of good signs throughout the cathedral and precinct.

(4)   A separate Development Trust or Preservation Council to raise funds for repairs.

(5)   Use of the European Regional Development Fund for the provision of new facilities.

(6)   Use of the FAC for advice on all fabric matters whichever body (CFCE or FAC) is the ultimate approving body.

III.   STAFF

(1)   A cathedral directory explaining 'Who we are and what we do'.

(2)   Regular staff meetings and 'awaydays', and an annual retreat.

(3)   A training video for all staff.

(4)   The use of two-way radios by the vergers and canon 'in residence'.

(5)   Appointment of a medical officer, visitor officer and monuments conservator.

IV.   VOLUNTEERS/LAY INVOLVEMENT/CATHEDRAL FRIENDS

(1)   Parish volunteers help in the cathedral refectory and shop.

(2)   Cathedral Friends provide a team of lecturers and an information desk in the cathedral, and take display boards to the parishes.

(3)   The Friends have a 'young age' group, and also a representative in each parish.

(4)   The publication of a booklet for all volunteers containing instructions and emergency procedures.

Index

The index references are to page numbers